IMAGES
of America

LAKE OSWEGO

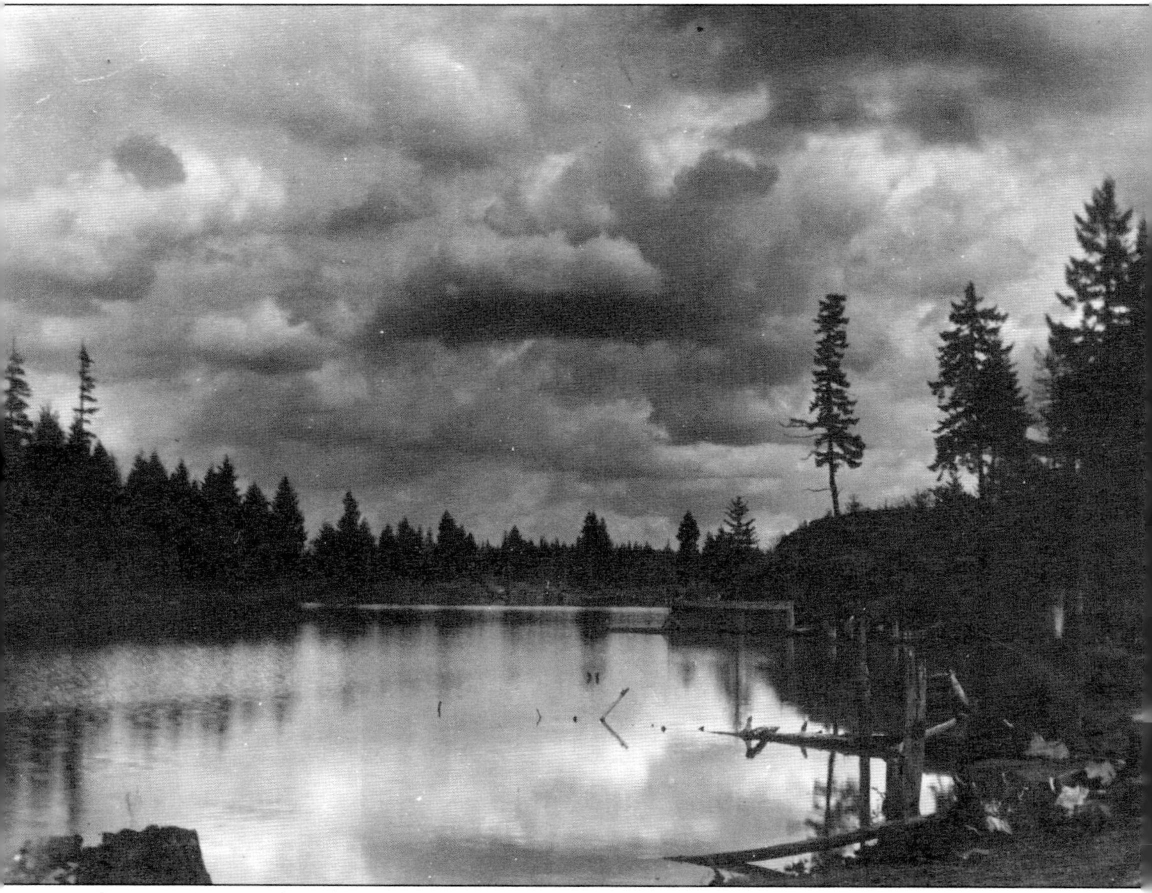

OSWEGO LAKE. This photograph shows the lakeshore in the years just prior to its development into residential neighborhoods. (Courtesy of Lake Oswego Public Library.)

ON THE COVER: Lillian Bickner sits in a covered canoe on Oswego Lake c. 1910 as plans to develop the lakeshore and surrounding land into an elegant residential district were underway. (Courtesy of Alex Blendl Studio.)

IMAGES
of America

LAKE OSWEGO

Laura O. Foster

ARCADIA
PUBLISHING

ISBN 978-0-7385-7085-3

Published by Arcadia Publishing
Charleston, South Carolina

Printed in the United States of America

Library of Congress Control Number: 2009924709

For all general information contact Arcadia Publishing at:
Telephone 843-853-2070
Fax 843-853-0044
E-mail sales@arcadiapublishing.com
For customer service and orders:
Toll-Free 1-888-313-2665

Visit us on the Internet at www.arcadiapublishing.com

To the historians, both past and present, of Lake Oswego whose curiosity and passion have helped make their town's history accessible to all.

Contents

ACKNOWLEDGMENTS

Thank you to the wonderful staff at the Lake Oswego Public Library, especially Claire Kellogg. The library is small enough to be free of the more rigid strictures of a larger institution and large enough to have a fabulous local history collection. Thank you also to Susanna Campbell Kuo, who generously shared her deep and broad knowledge of Lake Oswego with me. The Oswego Heritage Council's exhibits, support, and encouragement have been much appreciated. Thank you also to Sarah Higginbotham of Arcadia Publishing, whose gentle nudging, good organization, and enthusiastic encouragement provided three other elements needed to produce the book.

All historic images in this book are courtesy of the Lake Oswego Public Library.

INTRODUCTION

Beautiful Lake Oswego, a city of 36,000 residents, has a reputation within Oregon for expensive real estate and privileged schools. Many Portlanders know little more about Lake Oswego than it is an exclusive enclave that counts wealthy professionals, media people, and NBA players among its residents. It is that indeed, to an extent, but this city has a unique and decidedly gritty backstory that is nearly as well hidden as its now-private eponymous lake. Through the years, this mill village has evolved from a company town of heavy industry, to a quiet suburb of middle-class families who enjoyed their lakeside setting, to an upscale city, one of Oregon's wealthiest.

Throughout this book, which covers the years from 1850 to 1960, the town is referred to as Oswego. It was not until 1960, when Oswego merged with Lake Grove, a community at the west end of the lake, that it took the name Lake Oswego to honor both communities. The lake, once commonly called Sucker Lake, occasionally called Lake Tualatin, and sometimes called Lake Oswego, is more correctly called Oswego Lake. The creek that drains Oswego Lake was once known as Sucker Creek. Both the old and new names for the lake and creek are used interchangeably in this book.

A map of Oswego from the late 1920s on pages 98 and 99 is helpful to consult when various sites are discussed. On the map, "Oswego" is known today as Old Town. "1st Addition" on the map was once called New Town, though no longer. "South Oswego" on the map was once called South Town. "Lake View Villas" is the area now called Lake Grove. All these names are used in this book.

The Oswego story begins with the lake, a former channel of the Tualatin River that was scoured deeper by some of the millions of tons of debris carried into Oregon by the Missoula floods of the last ice age. When the floods retreated, a lake was formed, cradled between high bluffs. The lake's outlet was a small stream that ran for less than a mile before joining the Willamette River. For millennia, salmon thrived in this creek. In 1900, it was common for fishermen to haul 1 ton per day from the creek at the start of the yearly salmon run.

With the Donation Land Claim Act of 1850, settlers moved into the area, first claiming land with Willamette River frontage and then land west of the lake, which was rich in sediments deposited by the floods. High land surrounding the lake that is today coveted for its Cascade Mountain and Oswego Lake views was worth little to early settlers. Instead, they stayed low, next to waterways and fertile soils. Water-powered industry along the creek began Oswego's commercial story, with civic life centered in what is now called Old Town. West of the lake, in today's Lake Grove area, were farms. Oswego was a small mill community like many others across the country.

Early on, though, it was clear that the hills surrounding the lake held a secret not possessed by other basalt buttes and ridges in western Oregon. They hid deposits of iron ore, hematite formed millions of years ago when plant material was compressed between basalt flows; this type of ore is sometimes called bog hematite. In 1861, a miner's pick and horseshoe nails were displayed in a Portland wagon shop, made from ore mined in South Oswego. Soon after, some of Portland's early entrepreneurs, among them William S. Ladd (founder of Portland's first bank, the Ladd and Tilton Bank) and Henry D. Green (who, as co-owner of the Portland Water Company, was looking for a local source of water pipe), decided that a corporation formed to mine and refine this ore would round out their already rich portfolios. They formed the Oregon Iron Company and in 1867 and built a furnace at the mouth of Sucker Creek. Today the 40-foot-tall furnace stack from the smelter and slag dumped into the Willamette River are all that remain of that venture. The beautiful furnace stack, hand carved of basalt quarried from the shores of the lake, looks like a medieval relic. It is the centerpiece of George Rogers Park, a park named after a man who early on worked to maintain the old furnace site as part of the city's heritage. The furnace stack and artifacts from long-gone buildings at the park site are, some historians say, Oregon's most significant industrial archeological site.

Ore mining and smelting gave new shape to the young town. Oregon Iron and Steel, the successor company to Oregon Iron, built a larger, more modern iron furnace beginning in 1883, a half-mile downriver from the first furnace at today's Foothills Park area, and a pipe foundry adjacent to it in 1888. Neighborhoods such as First Addition and South Oswego were platted out to house workers recruited from Ohio, Pennsylvania, New York, and other areas to work in booming Oswego. In the 1880s and early 1890s, pig iron from Oswego was shaped into railcar wheels, pipe for Portland's water system, and structural and decorative elements used to construct many of Portland's cast-iron buildings. (Today downtown Portland has the nation's second largest collection of cast-iron-fronted buildings, second only to New York City's Soho district.)

Ore was not the only natural resource being extracted in Oswego. The town's hillsides were logged of their Douglas fir, Western red cedar, Oregon white oak, and red alder to produce the charcoal required by the smelting process. A swamp adjacent to the lake was mined for clay used to make molds at the pipe foundry. The lake itself was used as a source of power, and like the town, the lake's dimensions grew as its outfall was dammed with increasingly higher wooden dams, and its inflow was increased by a canal that connected the lake to the nearby Tualatin River. With the expansion in industry and population, the city's social and civic life also grew, with new schools, churches, and fraternal organizations. In 1890, the still-new furnace reached the peak of its production.

The era of heavy industry did not last. The furnace blew out for the last time in 1894, a victim of national recession and cheaper sources of pig iron. Three hundred people lost their jobs, and many left town. The pipe foundry, the only industry remaining, operated only intermittently. The city fell into a funk, and those who stayed faced hard times with little prospects. Oregon Iron and Steel owned 13,000 acres of barren hillsides in and around Oswego and was at a loss as to what to do with its near-worthless real estate. Elsewhere in the Portland area, after timber had been logged from hillsides, land was often abandoned by the landowner, as it was worth less than the taxes owed on it. But around 1900, the lake was "discovered." Oswego children had always gone swimming and boating in it, despite its less than scenic, stump-rimmed shoreline. One resident remembered, "My girl companions and I would lash two canoes together and paddle up the lake half way, bed down for the night and drift." Her private paradise was soon to be discovered by the masses. In an era when exercise in the great outdoors was becoming more fashionable, in the early 1900s Portlanders began taking the train to Oswego for a day's outing, increasingly seeking to borrow the boats of Oswego residents. One local family, the Nelsons, capitalized on the demand and established a boat-rental business with the permission of the lake's owner, Oregon Iron and Steel.

It did not take long before Oregon Iron and Steel saw an opportunity to repurpose its land. With Oswego's daily train service to Portland, it seemed feasible that Portlanders could be induced to move out of the city and into a suburban setting that offered a more relaxed lifestyle. In 1905, the company raised the lake level with a new wooden dam to submerge more stumps and create more high-value lakefront. It then sold large tracts to developers who platted the land into residential lots. One of those developers, Paul Murphy, bought 3,000 acres. He had just recently developed Portland's Laurelhurst, a "residential park" neighborhood of winding streets and parklike vistas. His advertising slogan, "Live Where You Play," defined the lifestyle promised by Oswego. Murphy would remain active in Oswego real estate for three more decades, earning the moniker "Mr. Oswego."

In 1909, against the wishes of Oregon Iron and Steel, which did not want to see its landholdings taxed or its operations come under government scrutiny, Oswego incorporated. The move was made to create a tax base that could fund the development of a safe and reliable municipal water supply; and so ended Oswego's days as a company town.

In 1912, Oregon Iron and Steel successfully petitioned the U.S. Geographic Board to change the name of its lake from Sucker Lake to Oswego Lake to erase any image problems the former name might present to potential home buyers. Despite initial development forays at the lake's west end, however, buyers were reluctant to commit to living in what was then an area remote from good roads. So in 1913, a system of scenic boulevards was laid out in what was called the Country Club District, a residential park neighborhood with restrictions on house costs, styles of architecture, and uses of property. This district surrounded the Lake Oswego Country Club, which was established in the 1920s. Architects designed homes in picturesque styles such as Arts and Crafts and English Tudor, and roads curved with the land's topography, creating parklike settings. A country club golf course was built atop the old iron ore mine, and Oregon Iron and Steel donated land for a hunt club, complete with polo grounds and easements that created miles of bridle paths, to further entice potential buyers.

With increasingly better roads and such inducements, demand picked up. By the 1920s, lots were selling so well in the upscale Country Club District that the Ladd Estate Company, which took control of Oregon Iron and Steel land after the company had defaulted on loans, found a way to create more lakefront. It dug a channel between a swampy duck pond that lay east of the lake in order to connect it with the main lake. The swamp, once so mucky that local cows had to sometimes be rescued from its muddy clutches, was flooded and given an elegant new name, Lakewood Bay. The newly platted land around it was called the Lakewood Addition. "Addition" was the term then used for what would now be called a subdivision.

Meanwhile, Oswego was still home to industry. The old pipe foundry closed in the 1920s, but in its place came a cement plant, also located east of State Street in the industrial area along the Willamette River.

By the 1930s, the lake's perimeter was bejeweled with more and more homes—"stockbroker Tudors" some called them—and public access to the lake was being shut off. To address this, the Oswego Municipal Swim Park was built by relief funds in 1936 during the depths of the Depression. While Oswego, which was increasingly wealthy, suffered less than other Oregon towns during the Depression, development in those years was geared to less costly neighborhoods. In 1936, for example, architect Richard Sundeleaf designed cabana-like homes, floating above Lakewood Bay on stilts; each cabana rented for $25 per month. Architect John Yeon produced inexpensive homes in the Lakewood Addition using a new material, exterior plywood, in the modern Northwest Regional style. These homes sold for just $4,500.

In 1941, the last vestiges of Oregon Iron and Steel disappeared as the Lake Oswego Corporation (also called the Lake Corp) was formed to control the lake and protect the interests of lakefront property owners. The Lake Corp was charged with cleaning the lake, patrolling it, and maintaining its water level so that property owners did not have to deal with the lake's natural fluctuation in elevation. The Lake Corp owns both the canal and its headgate at the Tualatin River and water rights to that river, both for irrigation and power generation. It owns the dam at the lake's outfall, which is used not only to control the lake's elevation but also for generation of electricity. The Lake Corp also owns the lake bottom and perimeter, a unique situation for a large body of water in the middle of an incorporated city. Lake Oswego Corporation shareholders are the lakefront property owners and residents whose properties come with easements allowing them access to the lake at various private swim and boat parks. Other residents of the town are restricted to two public water parks, one at the lake's east end, and one at the west end. Nonresidents are not allowed on the lake, except as a guest of a shareholder or other Oswego resident.

In the 1940s, water sports began to define the town as it cemented its reputation as a fine place to raise a family. Swimming and canoeing had been popular since the early 1900s, and by the 1930s, with new technology, waterskiing began to draw crowds. Annual water festivals promoted the sport, and local businesses such as Jantzen Swimwear supported water ski and water ballet teams. By 1950, three hundred motorboats roamed the lake, and Willa Worthington, daughter of a marina owner, had put Oswego on the water-sports map as the U.S. National Women's Water Ski Champion. The city's reputation as a wholesome place to live and play, just as Paul Murphy promised it was, had come to fruition.

One

Water Powers Oswego's Beginnings 1850–1865

In 1847, New Yorkers Albert and Miranda Durham ended their cross-country trek at Oregon City, the landing site for many Oregon pioneers. Albert soon left to prospect in the California goldfields and returned to Oregon in 1850 a wealthy man. He and Miranda moved to 640 acres they claimed on the west bank of the Willamette River, land that included a lake, a creek, and Willamette River frontage.

At the lake's outfall, Durham built a dam and water-powered sawmill and used the lake as a log pond, i.e., a holding tank for timber felled from the lakeshore. Both the creek and the lake were called "Sucker" for the fish abundant there. The milled lumber was hauled to the mouth of the creek at Oswego Landing (today's George Rogers Park) and loaded onto Durham's three ships for export to California and international markets. Durham's riverfront site was ideal for industry: in those pre-rail days, rivers were de facto highways. Transit alternatives such as paths and trails were mud-bound much of the year, making them unsuitable for shipping goods.

Durham laid out a small town on his claim, naming it after Oswego, New York. At a time when most settlers lived in log cabins, he built a large board home on a bluff overlooking the Willamette River at today's Furnace and Church Streets, but by the mid-1850s, further prosperity eluded Oswego. In 1863, however, Oswego's prospects brightened: ore from its hills had been smelted into pig iron and forged into tools. John Trullinger, who had emigrated from Iowa in 1848, bought an interest in Durham's mill, modernizing it with a waterwheel of his own invention. In 1865, Trullinger bought the town site and officially registered the plat. He had high hopes for Oswego, with its location at the end of a water-based route he hoped would capture the rich agricultural trade of the nearby Tualatin River valley. Also in that year, Portland financiers began their plans to transform Oswego into what they hoped would be a Pittsburgh of the West.

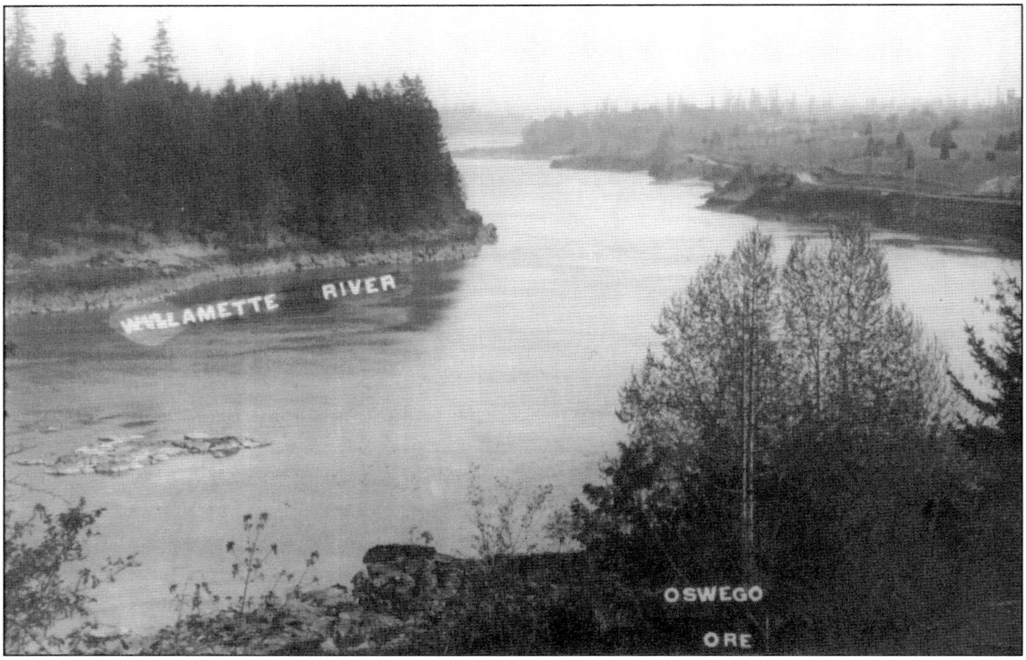

WILLAMETTE RIVER. This view looks upriver from Old Town Oswego. When Oswego was settled, the Willamette and other rivers were highways for people and their goods. Oswego, located at the confluence of Oswego Creek and the Willamette, was an auspicious spot for mill-owners, who could use both the creek's waterpower and the river's transport options.

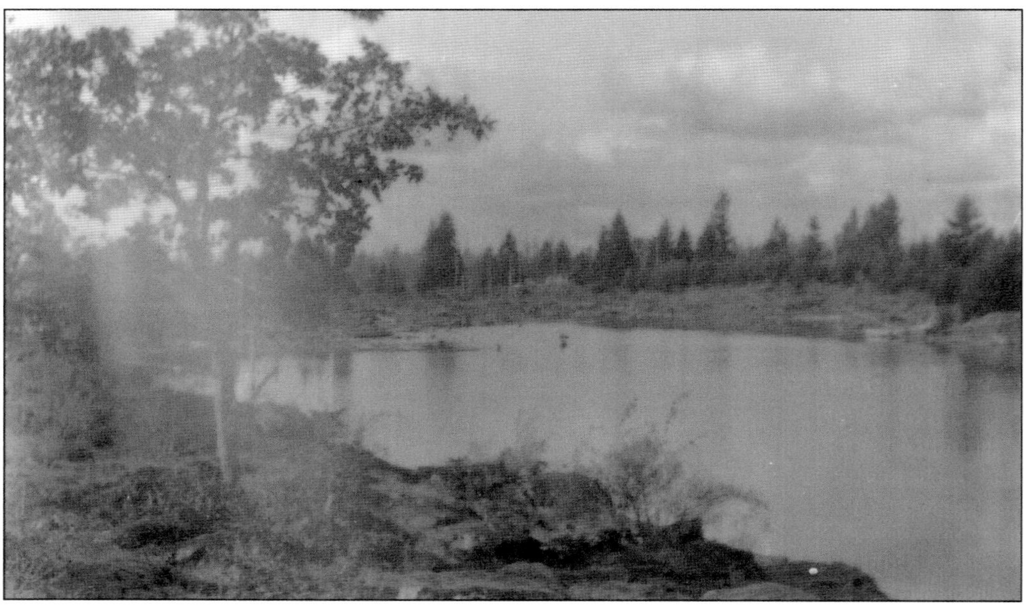

OSWEGO LAKE. Oswego Lake is a natural lake, its size enhanced by a dam and canal. Its orientation, northeast to southwest, is a result of the Missoula floods roaring into the area from the northeast and scouring an old river channel. Though the lake has been dammed since the 1850s by a series of increasingly higher wooden dams, this image shows it before a concrete dam raised the water to its current level. Stumps of trees logged for steamboat fuel, charcoal, or firewood were drowned by increasing levels of water.

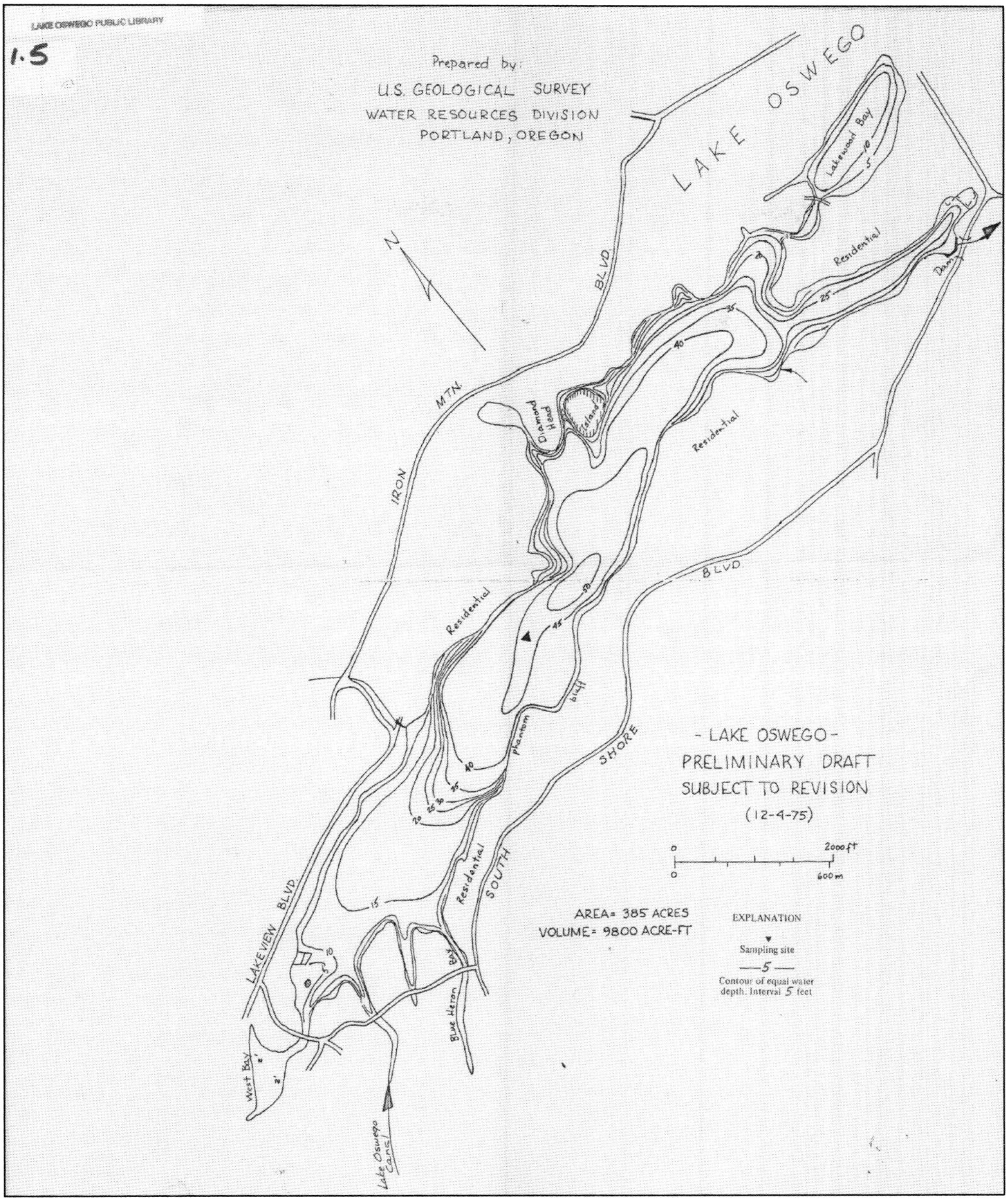

LAKE DEPTHS. At its deepest, Oswego Lake is 50 feet. This map gives an idea of the limits of the native lake and of the dam and canal-caused expansion into areas where depths are as shallow as 2 feet. Lakewood Bay, on the lake's northeast corner, was created by digging a channel from the lake to flood a swampy area. The dam is at the lake's easternmost edge. The canal from the Tualatin River enters the lake in its far southwest corner. The surface area of the lake is 415 acres; its watershed is about 7 square miles with only two significant creeks flowing into it from the surrounding hills—Springbrook on the north and Lost Dog on the southeast. With the opening of the canal in 1872, water (and later pollutants) from the 711-square-mile Tualatin River watershed began to enter the lake. This watershed roughly approximates the boundaries of Washington County, one of Oregon's most populous counties.

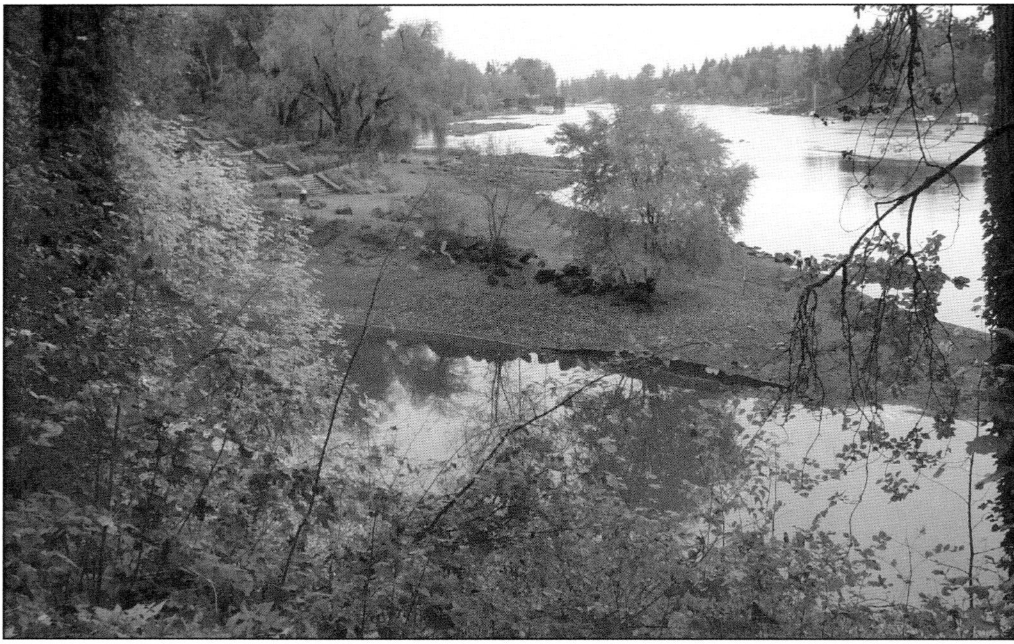

Mouth of Oswego Creek at the Willamette River. This is the site called Oswego Landing, a place where, from the 1850s until the 1920s, riverboats would take travelers to Portland or Oregon City and beyond. Here, at low water in early fall, the sandy beach is evident. See page 120 for another view of this river beach. On the left, stairs and a ramp lead up to George Rogers Park, site of Oswego's first heavy industry. (Author's collection.)

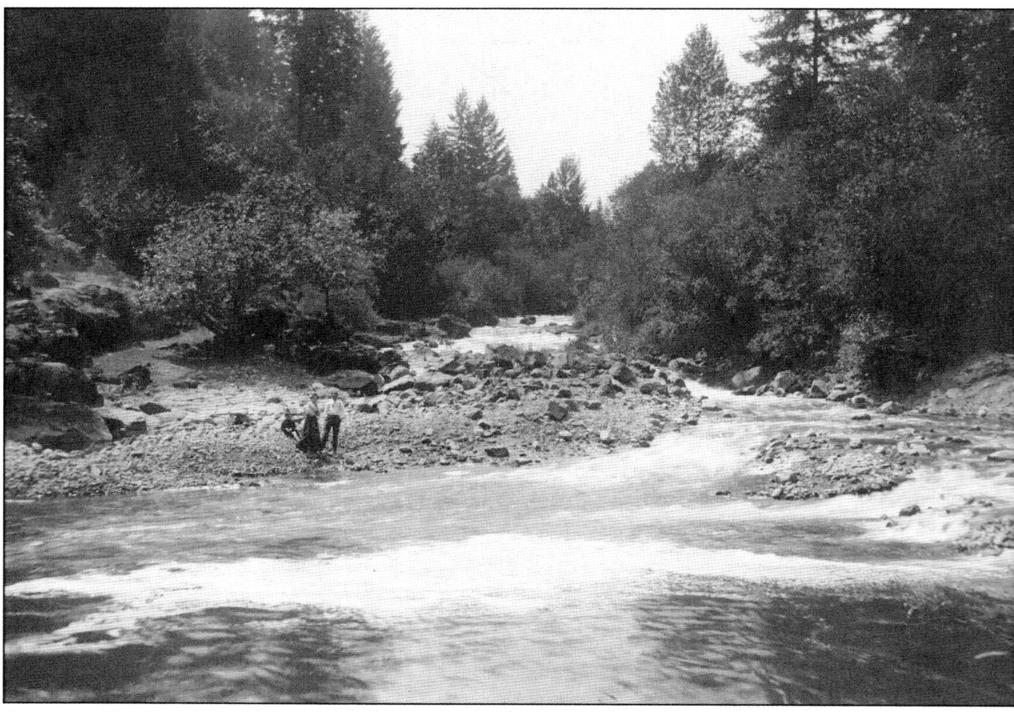

Oswego Creek. A mother and father contemplate the rapids on Oswego Creek while their son appears ready to engage in some timeless rock-throwing behavior, c. 1900.

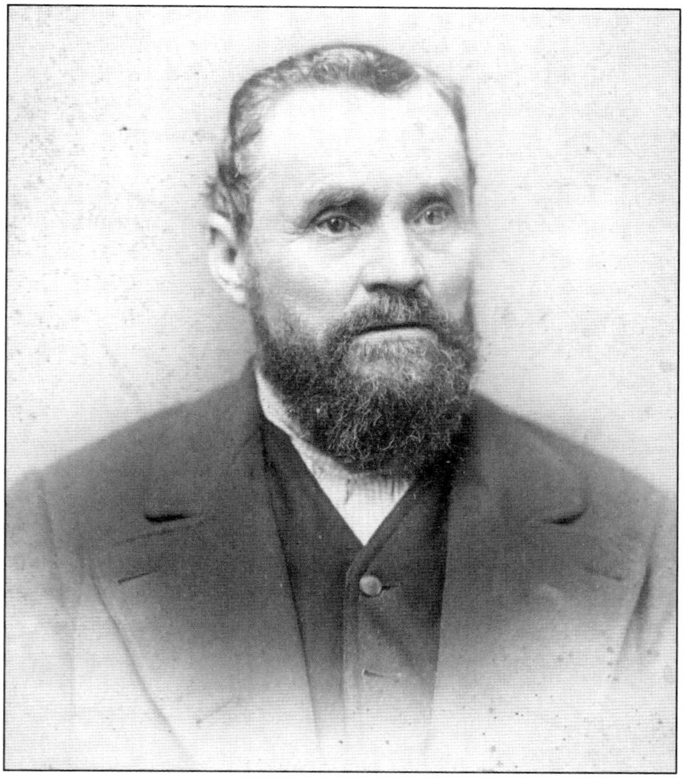

Oswego Founder Albert Alonzo Durham. After leaving Oswego in 1866, he moved west to the Tualatin River, to an area known today as Durham, where he built saw and flour mills on Fanno Creek at the site of today's Durham City Park. The location was near the Boones Ferry Road, a market road that would bring goods into Portland markets. The ferry, just downstream of Durham's mills, was on the Tualatin River.

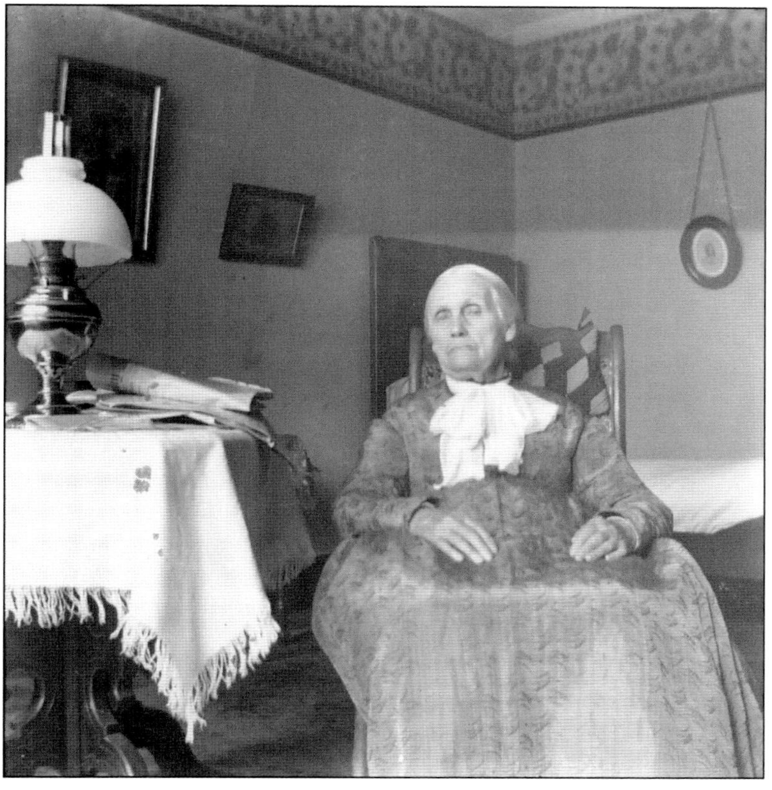

Miranda Durham. Hard-working pioneer Miranda Durham sits in her bedroom in her later years, probably around 1890. Note the austere single bed, the oil lamp, and the pile of reading material on her table, very likely in her home on Fanno Creek.

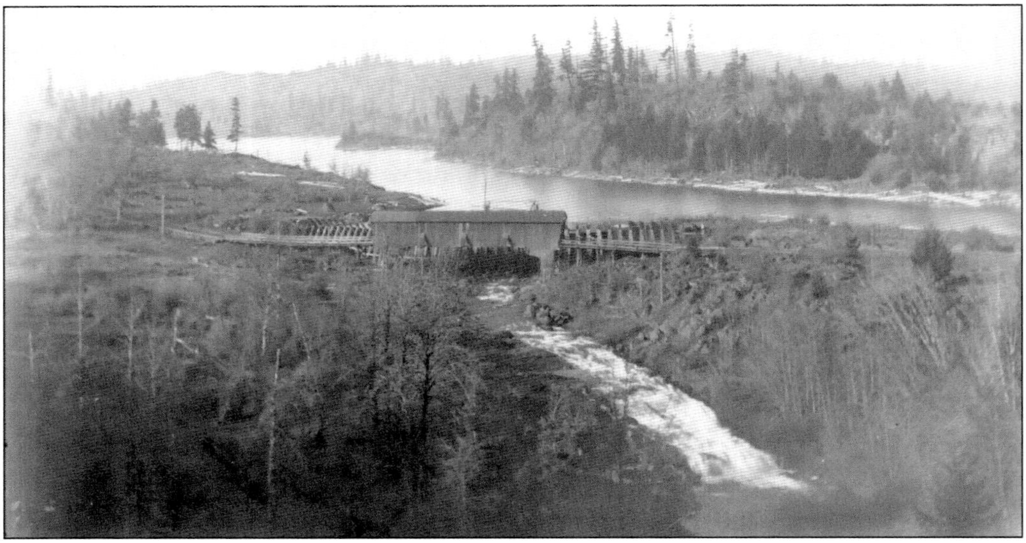

Oswego Creek, Covered Bridge, Wooden Dam, and Lake. This is the view looking west from Oswego Creek. The dam, then wooden, is visible, and beyond it is the undeveloped lake. At the dam is the covered bridge over what is today called McVey Avenue. That road continues southwest, as Stafford Road, a market road that led from Stafford, Oregon, to Oswego Landing via this bridge.

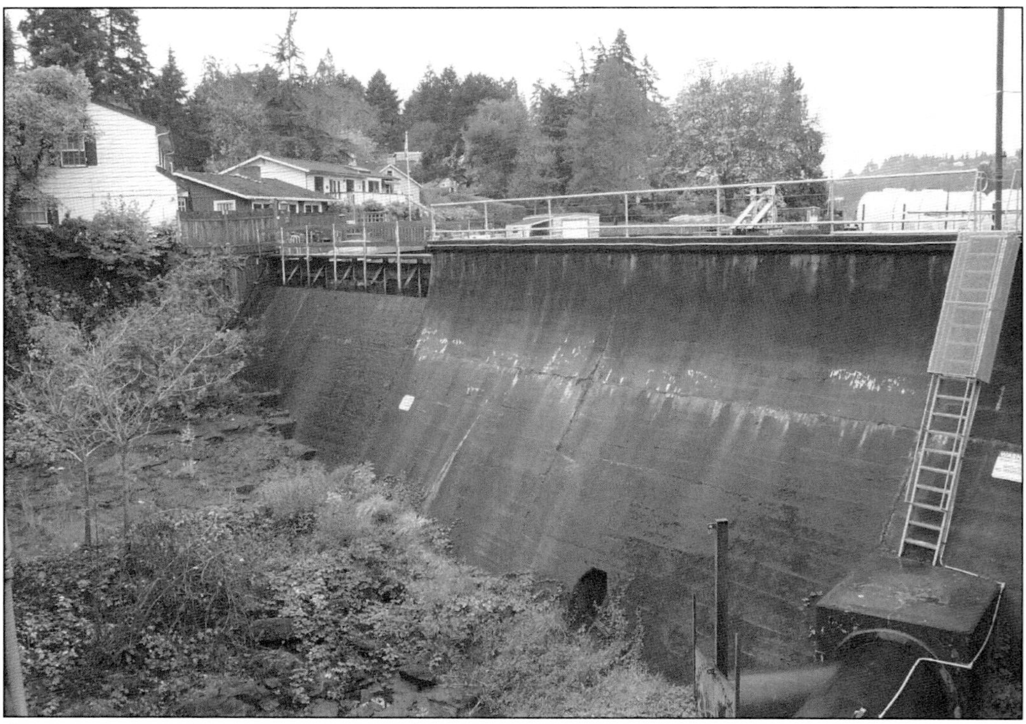

Concrete Dam, Oswego Lake. This dam is owned by the Lake Oswego Corporation (also called the Lake Corp). Earlier wooden dams were owned by mill owners and later dams by Oregon Iron and Steel. The Lake Corp also owns the headgate on the canal that controls inflow into the lake from the Tualatin River. Through the dam and canal, it maintains the lake's height at a uniform level throughout the year. (Author's collection.)

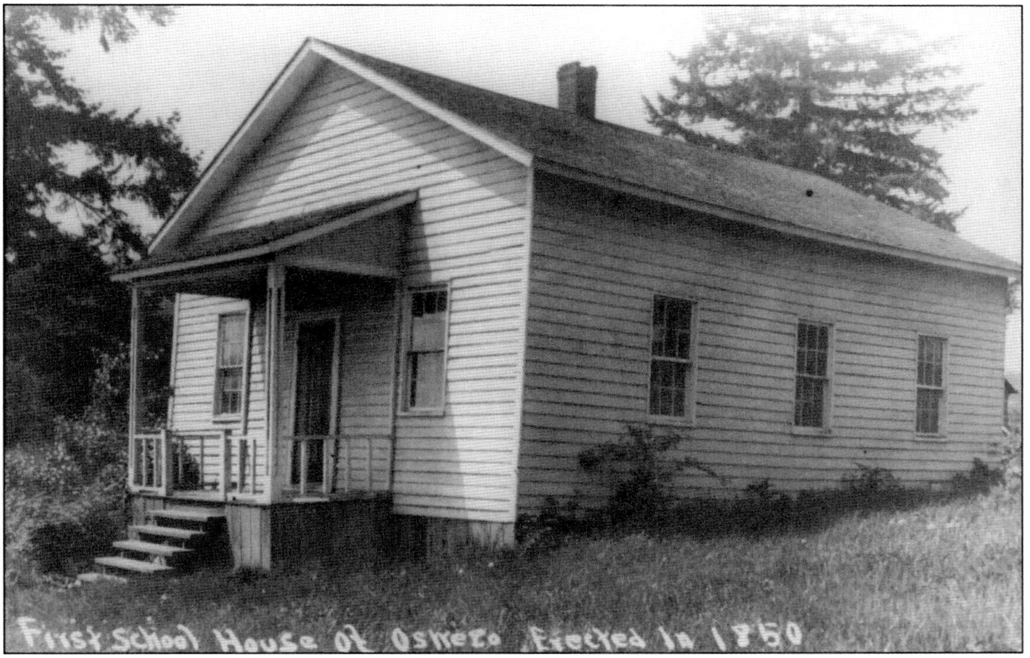

FIRST SCHOOL. This building was erected in 1850 at Furnace and Ladd Streets in Oswego. It was succeeded by the Grange Hall School, seen on page 18.

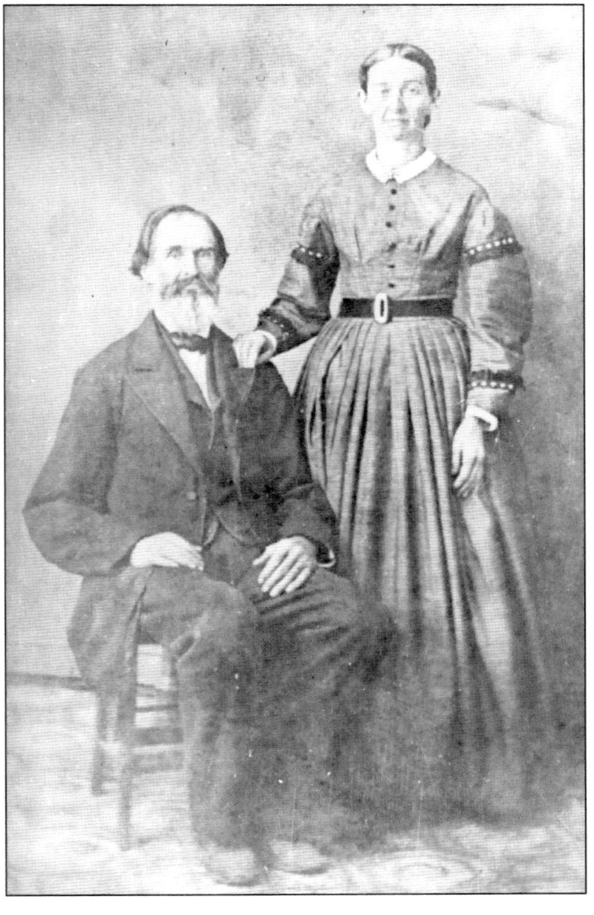

FIRST COUPLE TO WED IN OSWEGO. Waters and Lucretia Carman are seen in 1869 when he was 58 years old. Their marriage, the first in the new settlement of Oswego, took place in September 1853. They built a home in the 1850s at what is now 3811 Carman Drive. It was one of the first homes in the area to have running water, which was piped in from a spring on their property.

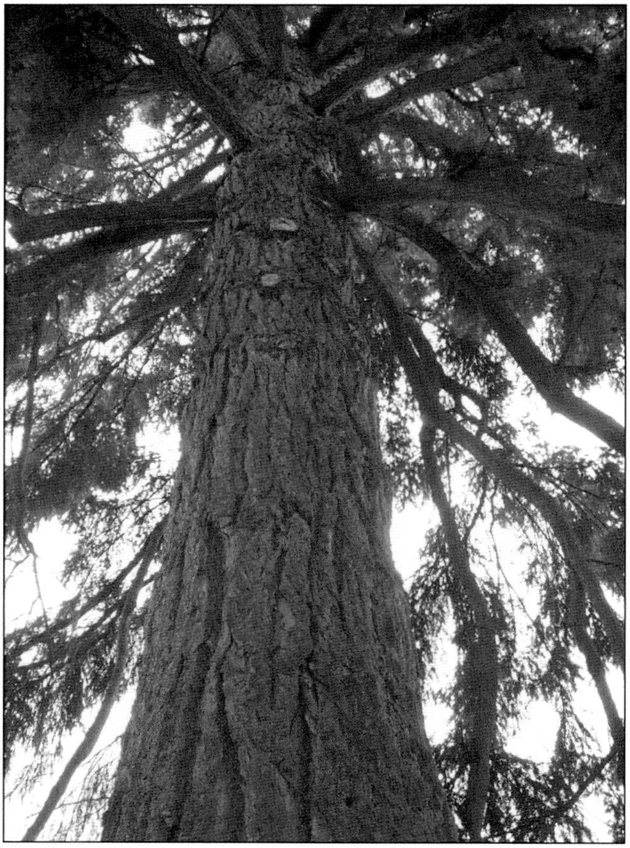

The Peg Tree. Under this Douglas fir in the 1850s, children attended Sunday school and meetings were held until proper buildings could be erected. A peg was drive into the tree, and a lantern hung from it to light nighttime meetings. The tree still stands on Leonard Street in Old Town, having survived an 1890s felling of similarly sized trees that lined the way to the old furnace. (Author's collection.)

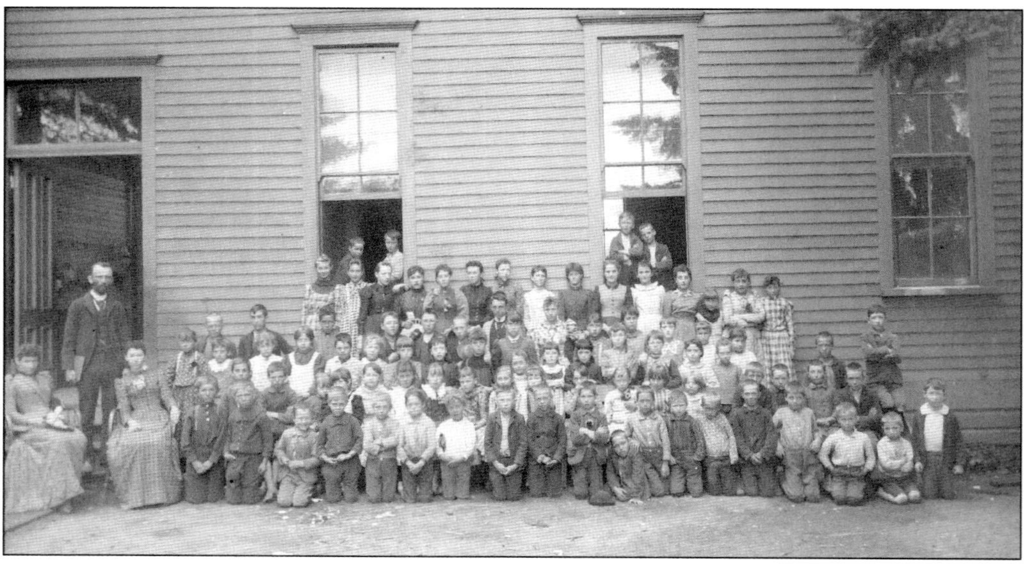

Grange Hall School. Many of the diary entries made in 1883 by 14-year-old Will Pomeroy note that he was "late for school." He walked 3.5 miles to get there after milking the cow at his home atop Iron Mountain. Second from left in the top row of this *c.* 1890 photograph is Lucia Bethke (later Bliss), who became Oswego's first librarian, from 1933 to 1947. The school was at the northwest corner of Furnace and Leonard Streets.

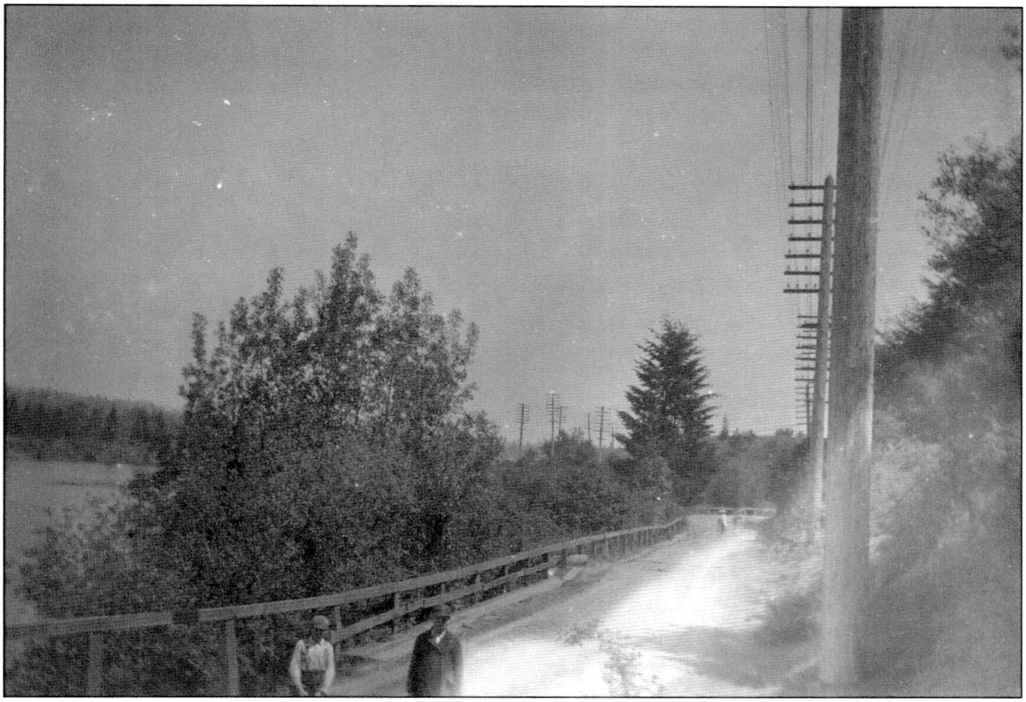

THE RIVER ROAD TO WEST LINN AND OREGON CITY. A former path used by native peoples, the River Road connected Oswego to West Linn and Oregon City. The first power lines on it were erected in 1889 by Willamette Falls Electric (forerunner of Portland General Electric), harnessing the power of Willamette Falls and carrying it to Portland in the first long distance transmission of electricity in the United States. Today the road is a multiuse, paved path.

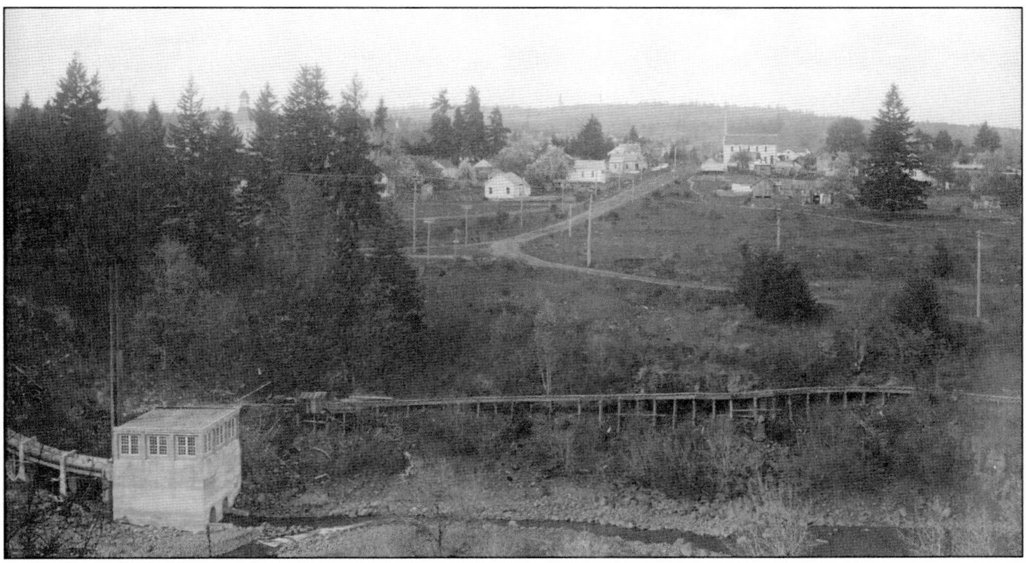

OLD TOWN OSWEGO. This c. 1910 view looks north from Oswego Creek. Odd Fellows Hall, which still exists, is the two-story building at center. The structure in the creek is an electric power plant, built in 1910. A crude rail track runs along the creek bank. Green Street approximates the alignment of a former portage between the lake and the Willamette and runs east-west above the creek.

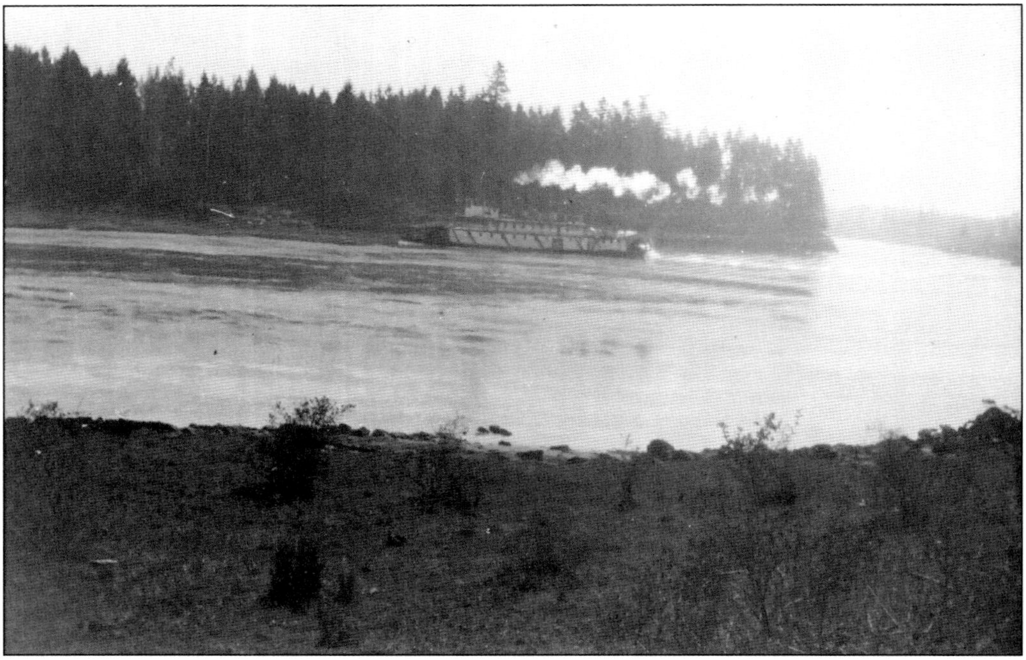

Willamette River Steamboat. Herbert Nelson talked of steamboats at Oswego Landing in a 1973 oral history: "I remember going down there and holding up my hand to a big steamboat coming up the river. They would put down the gangplank, I would walk up on deck to where the purser was standing and hand him a quarter, the price for a ride to Oregon City."

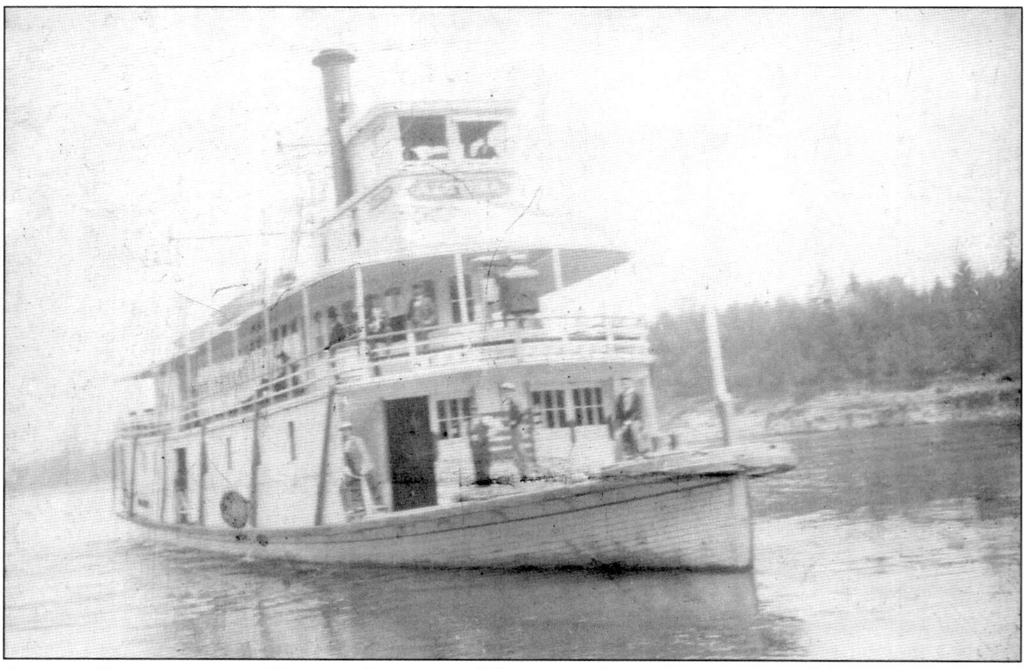

Altona Pulling in to Oswego Landing. The steamship *Altona* operated from 1890 to 1907 on the Willamette and then was transferred to Alaska, as rail lines in the Willamette Valley had supplanted much of the river's traffic. The ship was built in Portland for the Graham steamboat line; all its steamers had names that ended in "ona" such as the *Pomona*, *Latona*, and *Ramona*.

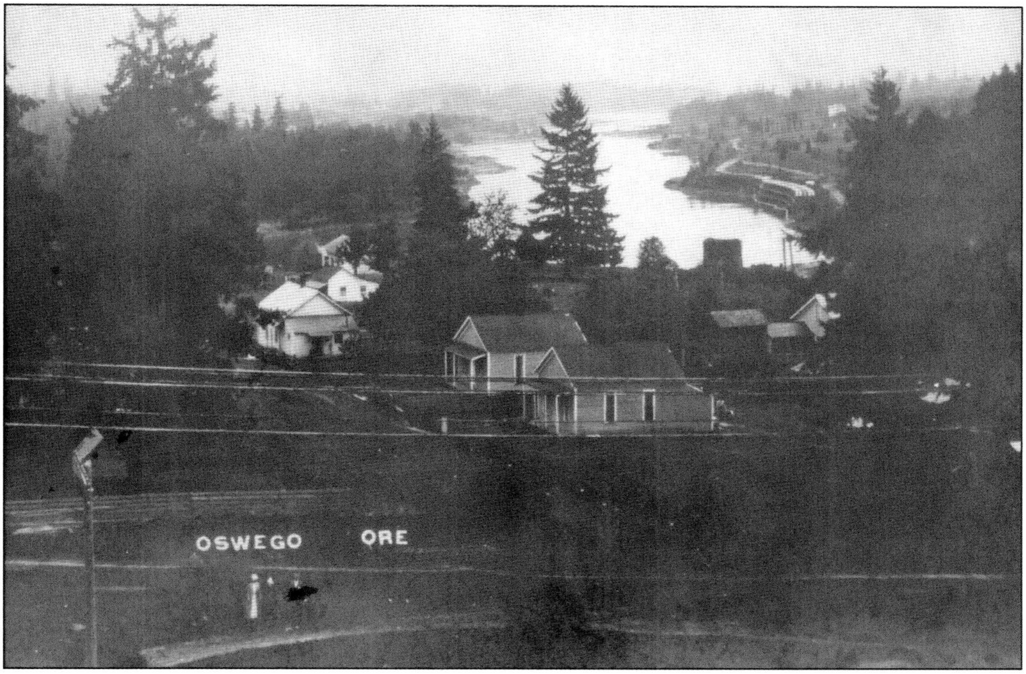

Old Town Oswego. This photograph was probably taken from the public school on State Street, looking upriver, after 1893. River Road is visible as are two workman's cottages built by Oregon Iron and Steel around 1880; the right cottage is extant.

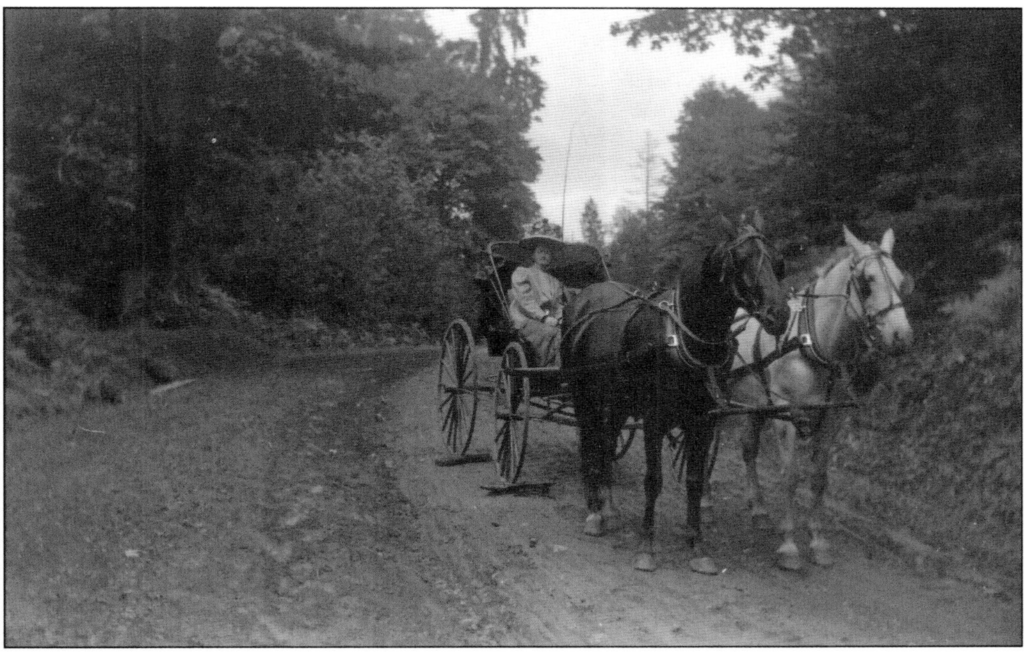

An Oswego Road and Driver. This photograph shows a fine ride on a dry day around 1910. Until the introduction of macadamized roads, western Oregon roads such as this one were quagmires of mud for much of the year and ribbons of dust during the dry season. The first modern paved road in Oregon is today's Southwest Macadam Road, a toll road from the 1870s that ran from Portland 6 miles, ending at the Milwaukie Ferry.

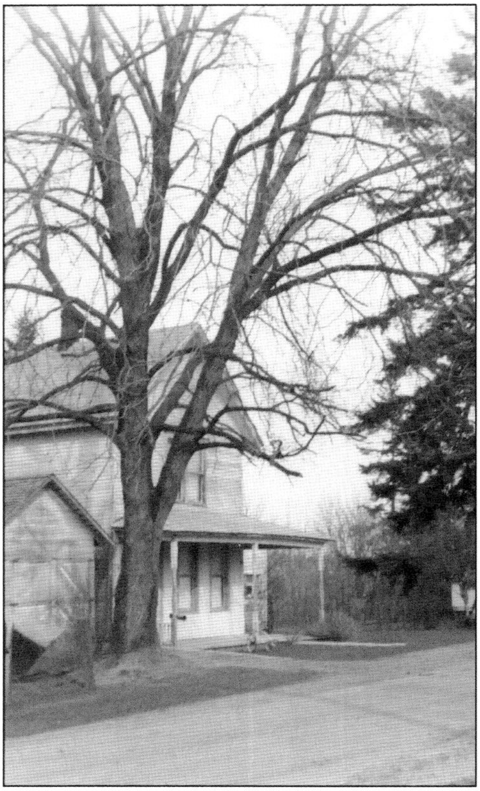

THE TRULLINGER HOME, OLD TOWN OSWEGO. In the 1860s, John Corse Trullinger founded a company to transport goods in a multi-segmented journey from Hillsboro to Oswego: farm produce was loaded onto steamers traveling the shallow and winding Tualatin River, then onto a horse-drawn railway that followed the alignment of the not-yet-built canal, then onto a scow running the length of the lake, and finally portaged to Oswego Landing. There it would be loaded onto riverboats.

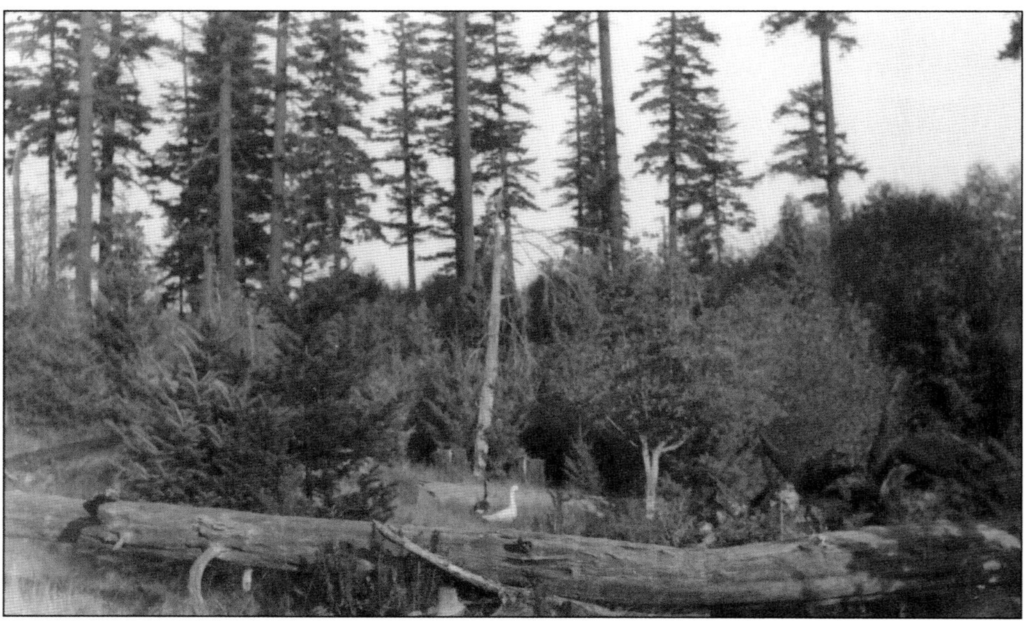

LIFE AT THE LAKE'S WEST END. Life was less focused on industry and more on agriculture at the lake's west end, today's Lake Grove area. These woods were on the Kruse property, settled by Otto and Frances Kruse in 1863. In 1973, family members Herbert and Harold Kruse remembered cutting timber from their woods; they would haul it to a narrow-gauge track at Bryant and load it up.

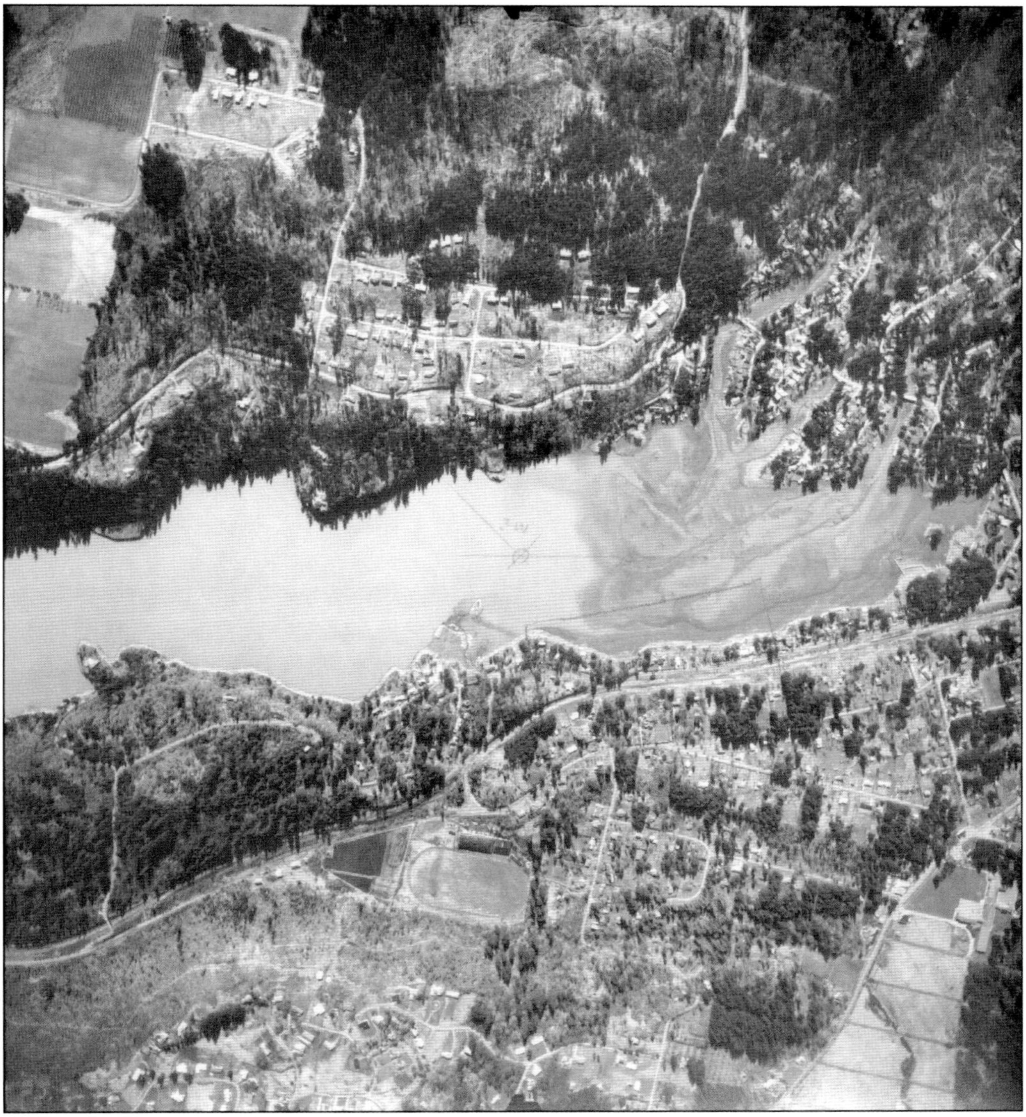

AERIAL VIEW, WEST END OF LAKE. This view from the 1950s shows the lake during a draw down. The westernmost tip of the lake (except for West Bay, which is not visible) is on the right. The canal connecting Oswego Lake to the Tualatin River is the inlet to the left of the tip. Note the deposition of sediments at its mouth, visible in the exposed, muddy lake bottom. This photograph gives an idea of the lake's natural size. The Lake Oswego Hunt Club is on the north shore, seen as the large oval at the bottom of the photograph. The lands south of the lake are rural at that point in time; today the farmed fields seen here are the Palisades neighborhood. The lake is drawn down periodically so lakeside property owners can build or repair docks, foundations, and seawalls.

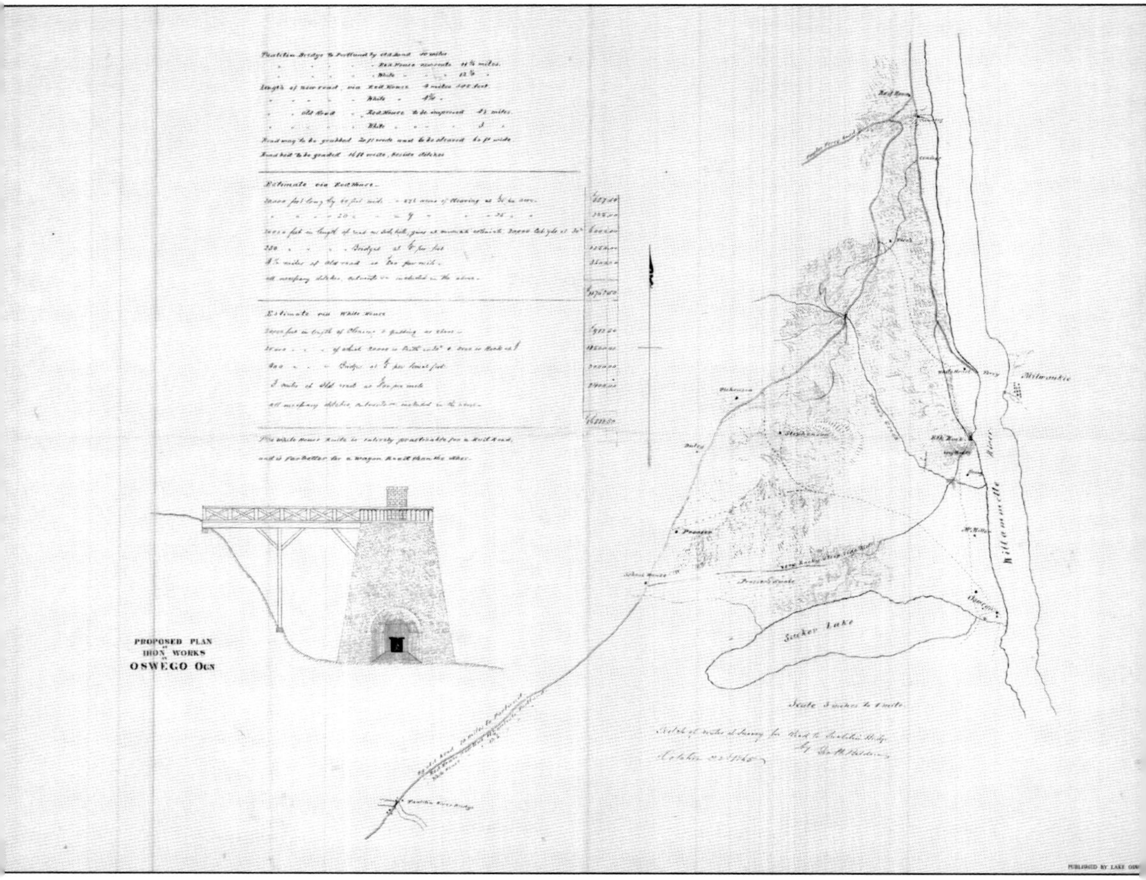

IRONWORKS AT OSWEGO, 1865. Handwritten notes on this "Proposed Plan for Iron Works at Oswego, Oregon" by an engineer describe the two alternative routes to Portland to transport pig iron produced by the furnace, and the costs to improve each by such work as "roadway to be grubbed 20 feet wide and to be cleared 60 feet wide." He concludes that the better road to Portland is the White House Road (today's Macadam Avenue) noting, "The White House Road is entirely practicable for a Rail Road and is far better for a wagon road than the other." The other road is shown as a dotted line heading northwest from Oswego and meeting the solid line that is Boones Ferry Road, which on this map he refers to as the Red House Road. This map shows the smaller size of Sucker Lake, although even then it was dammed to a small extent.

Two

Timber and Ore Fuel an Industrial Boom 1865–1894

The discovery of iron ore in the hills south of Oswego Lake jump-started the quiet mill town of Oswego. In 1865, Portland entrepreneurs William S. Ladd, Henry Failing, Henry Green, H. C. Leonard, and Addison Starr formed the Oregon Iron Company to smelt the ore into railcars, building materials, water pipe, tools, and other elements of urban infrastructure for a growing Portland. OIC's furnace was built at Oswego Landing, at the mouth of Sucker Creek, so that the pig iron it produced could be easily loaded onto steamboats. In 1868, the first cast iron stove made in Oregon was delivered to Portland's Ladd and Tilton Bank. The furnace had sporadic successes but in 1877 was sold at auction, its works already considered primitive. It operated as Oswego Iron Company for a few more years, until 1881, when it closed.

The idea to smelt iron still had merit, as the West Coast was booming, rail lines were sewing their seams all over the West, and the demand for iron was high. A new company was formed—Oregon Iron and Steel—aiming higher with a more sophisticated furnace and a multipronged approach that also included a pipe foundry. The venture was beset with problems, but in 1888 the furnace and pipe foundry went into operation. In 1890, the furnace's peak year, 12,304 tons of pig iron were produced, but production dropped steeply, and by 1894, with the country in a national recession and much of the rail-building era over, Oregon Iron and Steel produced its last pig iron. Three hundred workers lost their jobs, and the company town of Oswego entered a quiet spell for a few decades before its assets would again be tapped in an entirely different kind of venture.

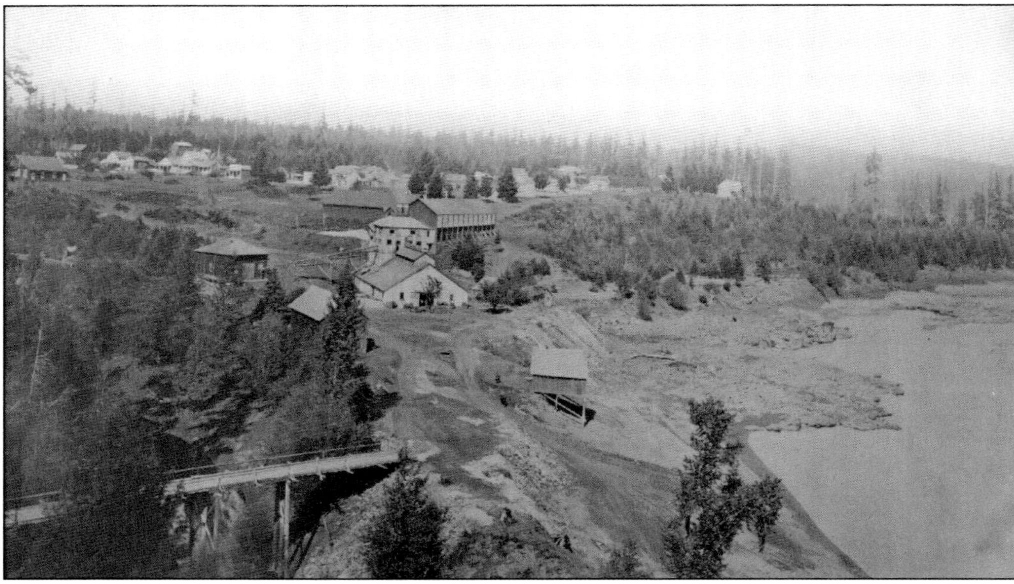

Oswego's Iron Furnace Works. In these images of the Oregon Iron Company works at Sucker Creek, note the early wooden bridges. The cruder bridge in the photograph above suggests an earlier date, *c.* 1870, when the furnace was operational. The furnace stack is in the wooden structure at center left; a trestle leads to it and smoke is pouring from its chimney. Behind it are charcoal sheds and an ore house. On the far right is the Portland Hotel (see page 30), built in the 1870s for employees at the furnace works. It is the building on the bluff with a second-story porch. In the photograph below, electrical lines indicate a later date, *c.* 1890, after the furnace had been replaced by another furnace a half-mile downriver. Note the absence of the brick chimney that had been atop the furnace; the bricks had probably been reused by nearby homeowners.

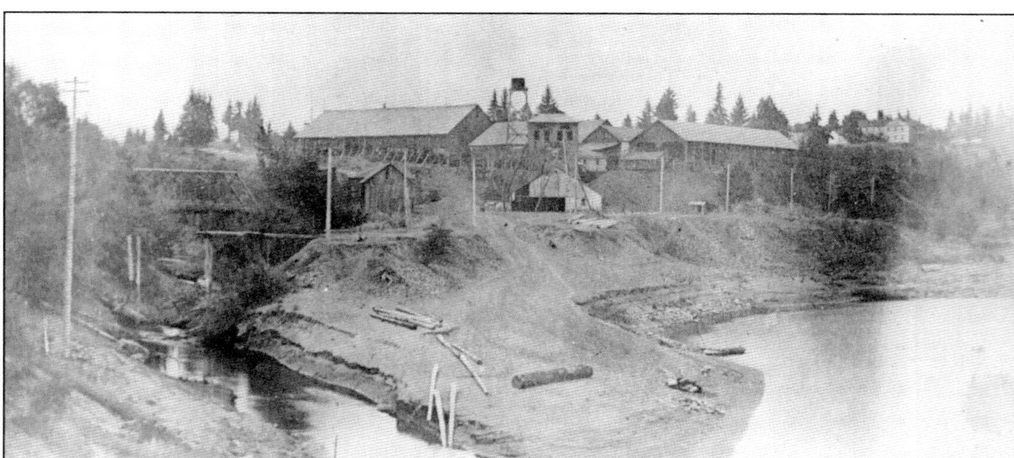

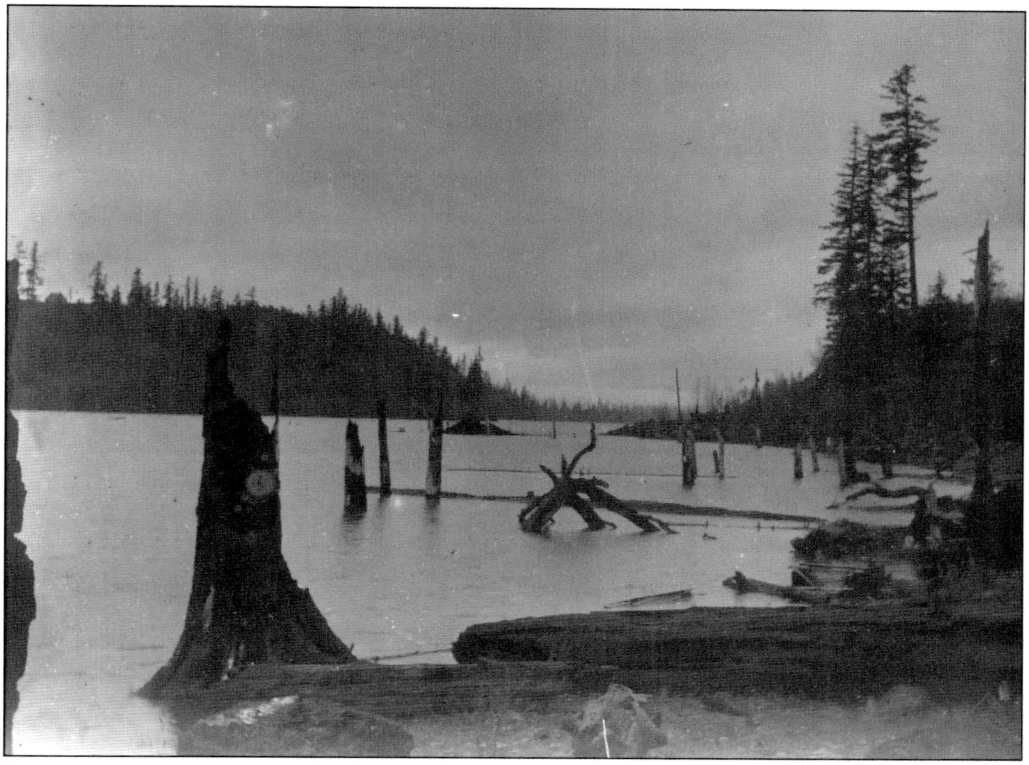

Stumps at Oswego Lake. As ore smelting began, trees were felled to make charcoal, a key ingredient in the process. Cut wood was stacked in nearby forests by colliers (charcoal burners or coal miners) who set the stacks afire and tended them as the wood smoldered down into charcoal. Furnaces back East used cheaper coke (baked coal) instead of charcoal. Charcoal making was Oregon Iron's biggest expense, putting it at a disadvantage to East Coast pig iron producers.

Kilns for Charcoal Making. Charcoal was produced in the crude way described above at Oswego's first furnace; at the new furnace, it was produced in these kilns. Behind them is the trestle that carried ore cars from the mine to the new furnace, which first went into blast in 1888. The furnace's smokestack was lined with 9 inches of firebrick.

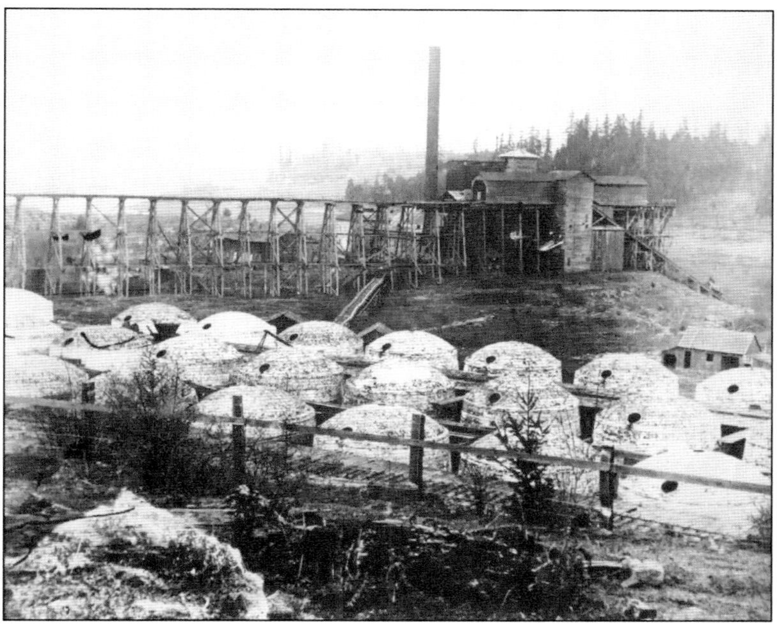

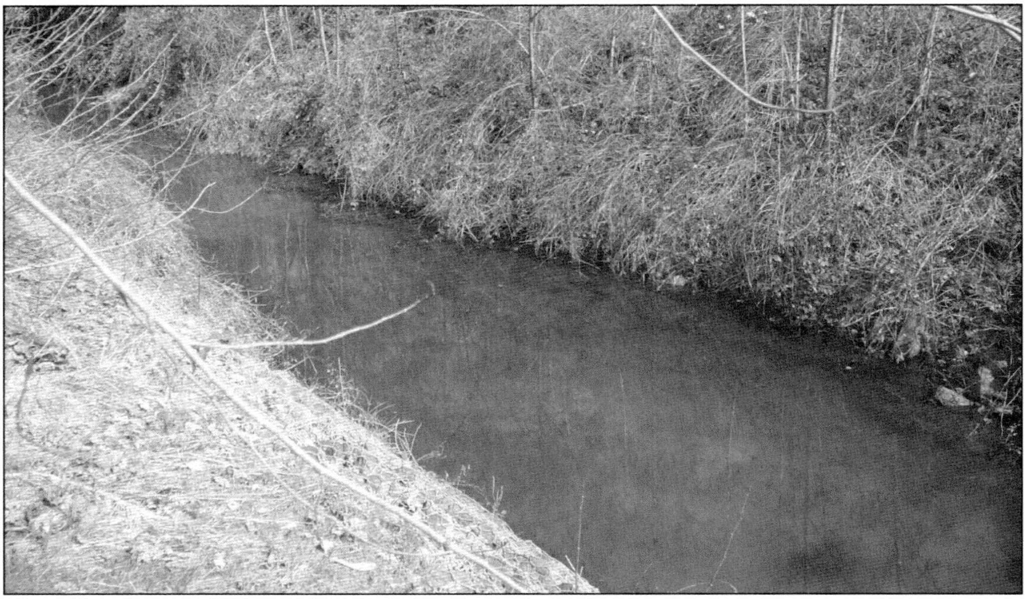

THE TUALATIN CANAL. The canal was dug in 1871 by the Tualatin River Canal Company between Colfax Landing on the Tualatin and the west end of Oswego Lake. The goal was shipment of goods entirely via water from the Tualatin Valley to Oswego Landing on the Willamette. The canal is narrow and wooded near the Tualatin, and larger and lined with homes closer to the lake. Rail lines into the valley brought the end of the canal's viability as a shipping route. (Author's collection.)

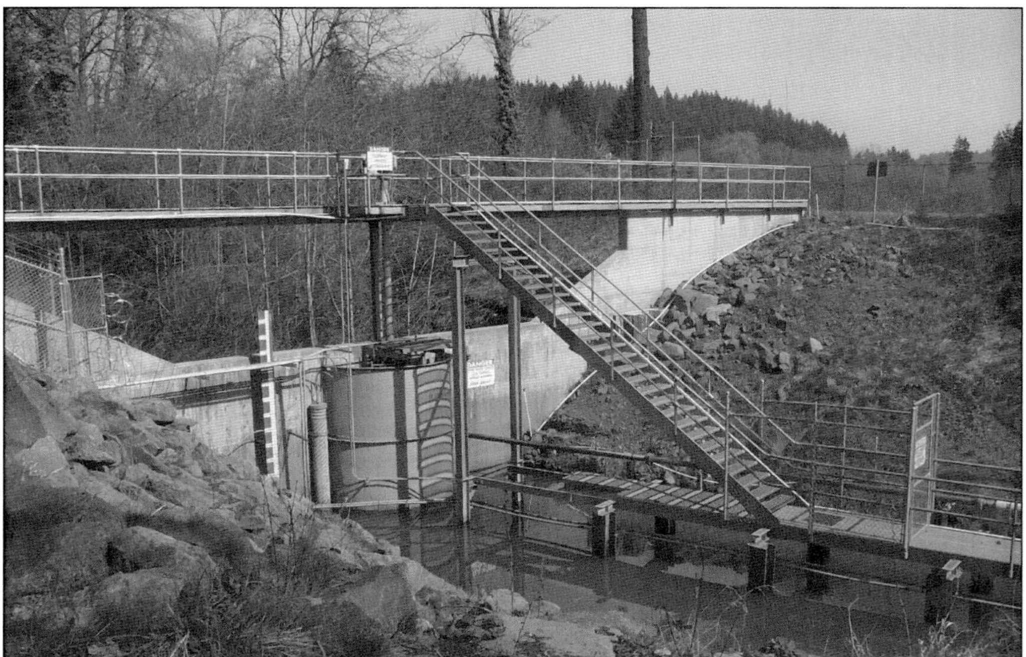

CANAL HEADGATE. The gate is owned and operated by the Lake Oswego Corporation. This gate regulates the inflow of water from the Tualatin in order to keep the lake's level consistent as well as for power generation and irrigation purposes. (Author's collection.)

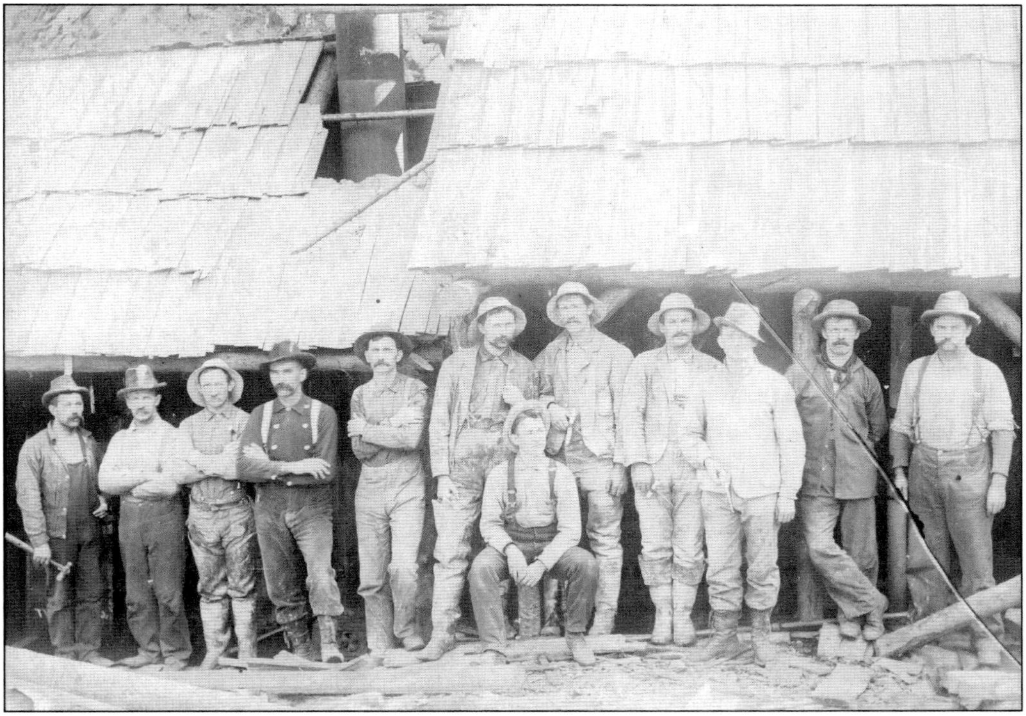

Miners at Mine Entrance. Ore was dug at the Patton Mine in South Oswego; in early days, it was strip-mined. A larger mine was the Prosser Mine on Iron Mountain (in the Country Club District). The mines were muddy and wet; in this photograph, some miners wear thigh-high boots and all wear hats. No other protective gear is seen. Miners' candles are held by the third, fourth, and fifth men from the right. The candle had a metal handle, ending in a point, which could be stuck in a rock crack to provide light while the man worked.

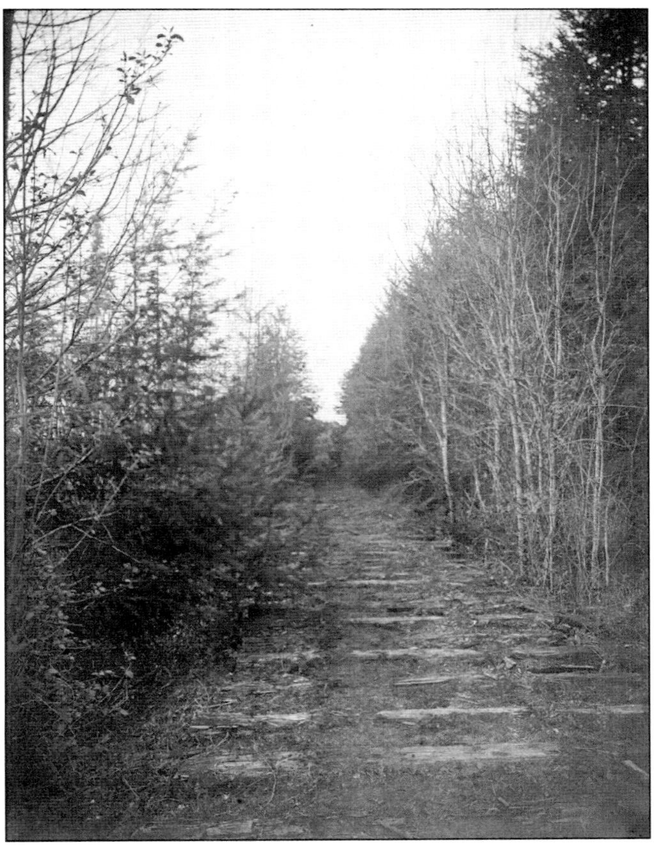

An Abandoned Mine Railway. This abandoned narrow-gauge ghost of a track is perhaps on Iron Mountain; the emerging growth of trees shows the land is healing itself from the intense logging it had experienced.

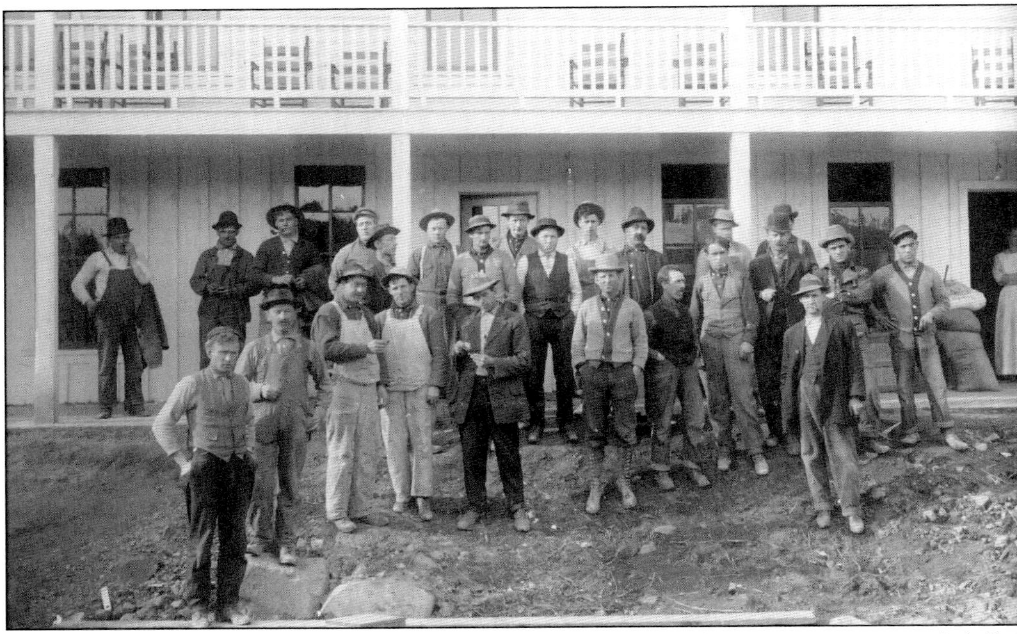

Men at Oswego's Portland Hotel. Nationally distributed advertisements recruited skilled charcoal makers, miners, and furnace workers to Oswego. Often single, the men would live in hotels such as this one. This photograph was taken after the iron smelters closed. The electric lights on the first-floor porch indicate it was after 1908 when Oswego was electrified. These men likely worked at the pipe foundry or the cement plant, which opened later.

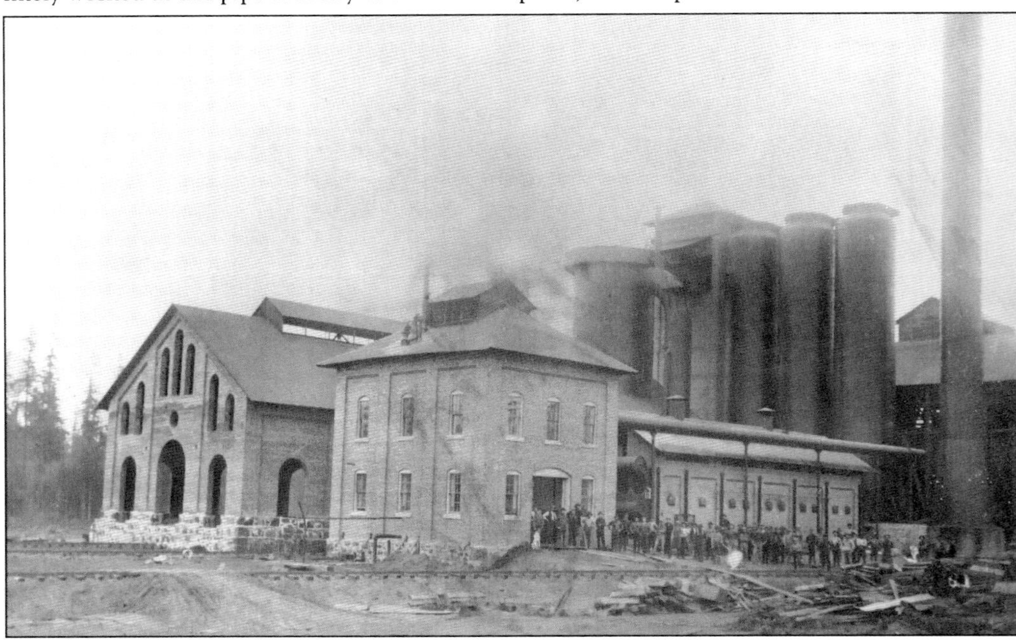

Oswego's Second Iron Furnace. This furnace operated from 1888 to 1894, producing pig iron that was recast as water pipe at the adjacent foundry, and pig iron recast elsewhere as ornamental and structural cast iron for Portland buildings. The three cylindrical buildings are blast stoves, the round building to their left is the blast furnace, and the Gothic-style building on the left is the casting house, where the molten iron was poured into pigs.

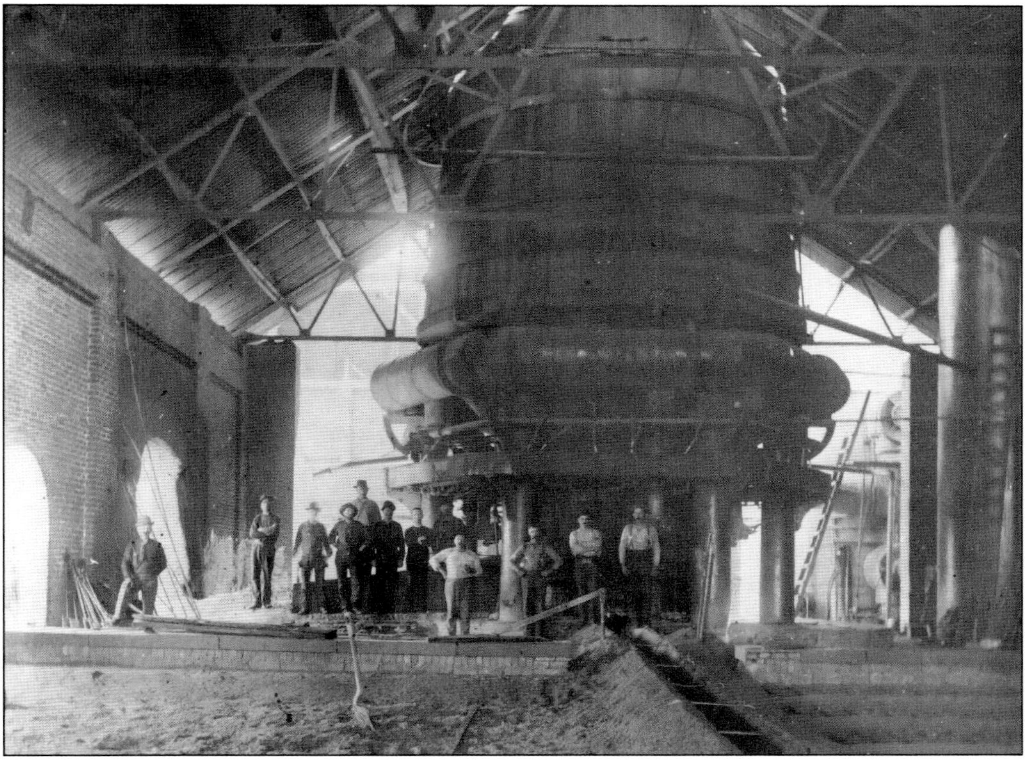

Casting Floor, Iron Furnace. In the casting house of the furnace, a central channel (seen above) would be carved into the sand-covered floor. The sand on either side of the central channel would be raked into "sow" channels branching off from it, with still smaller channels ("pigs") branching from the sows. The molten iron would flow out of the furnace into the central channel, then into the sow channels, and finally into the pig channels. The resulting "pig iron" was broken off the sows with sledgehammers. It was the final product.

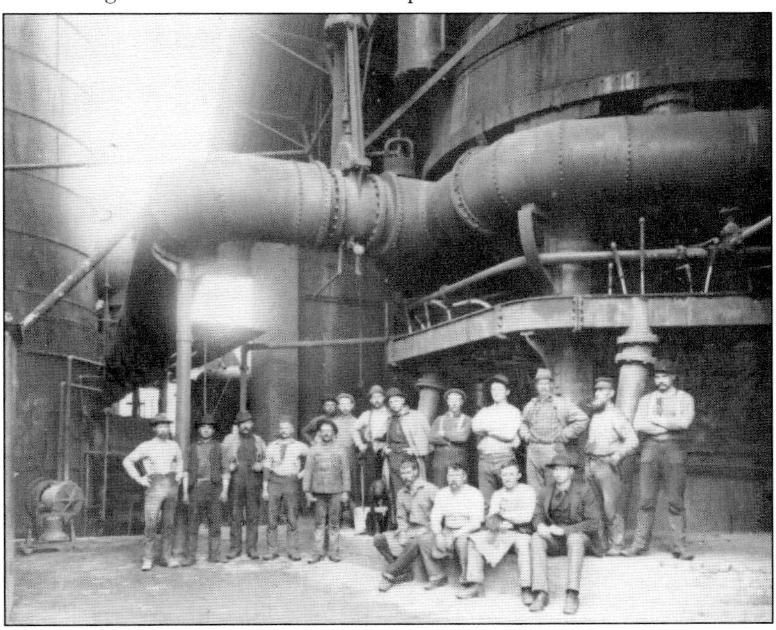

Furnace Workers with Dog. Tired-looking workers are seen in the casting house, with a dog, c. 1890. The man in the cape with his hands in his front pockets appears to be management. The second furnace buildings were dismantled in the late 1920s.

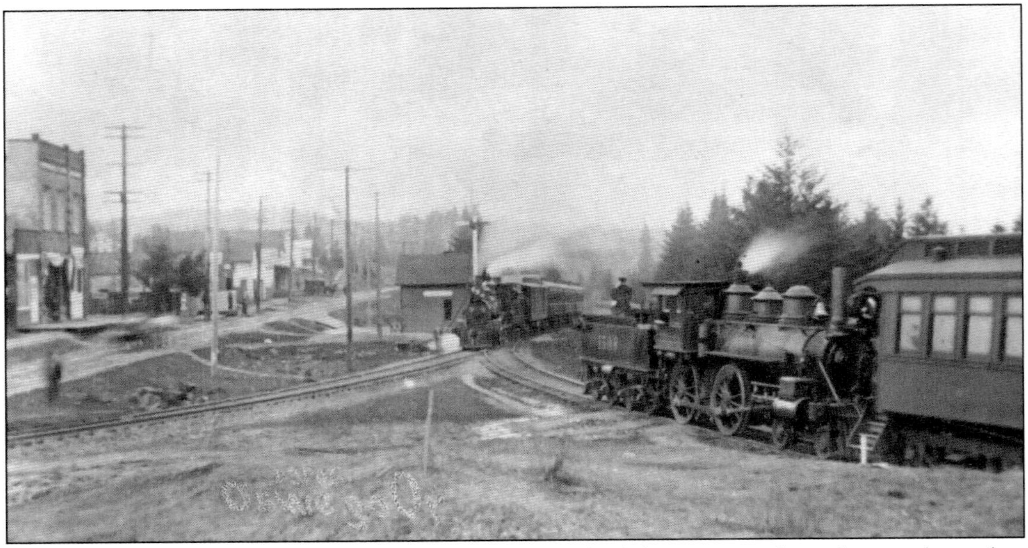

Oswego Depot and Steam Engine. The engine on the left is coming from the spur lines that lead to the iron furnace and pipe foundry. The depot is at A Avenue and Front Street (now State Street). The new industrial site and the depot's location added to First Addition's emergence as the center of the town.

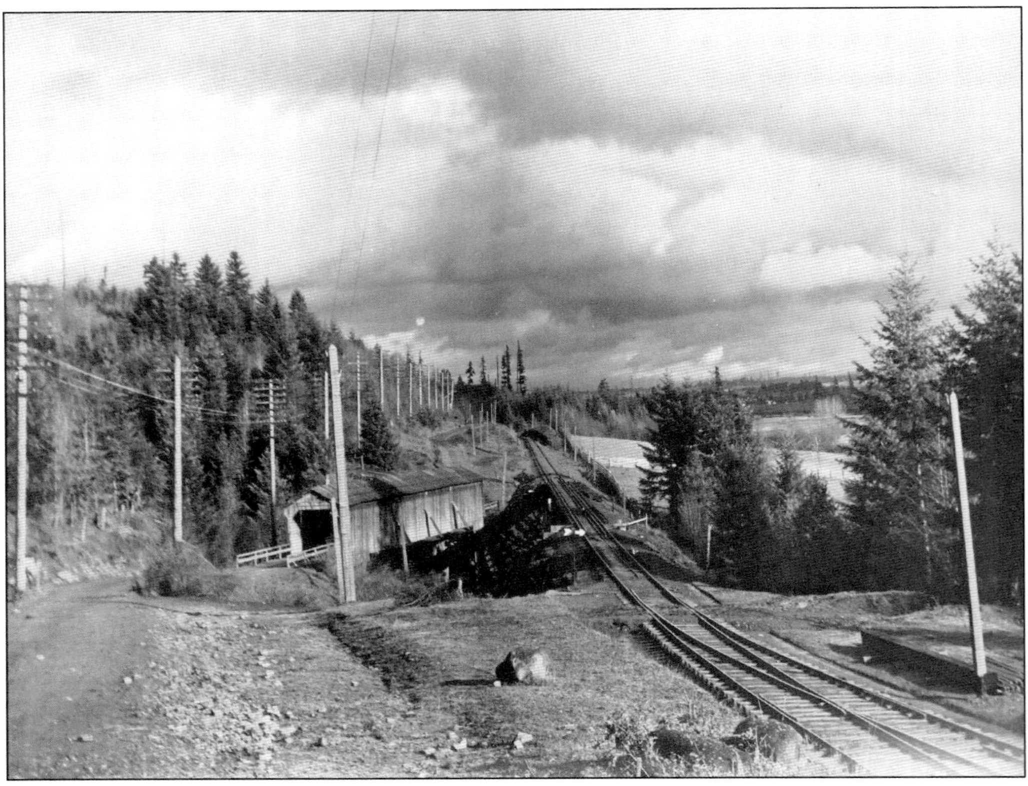

A Rail Link to Portland. A narrow-gauge rail line to Portland opened in 1887. This photograph shows the tracks running north over Tryon Creek and heading toward Elk Rock. In the rail line's early years, the track ended at Elk Rock and people and goods were loaded onto steamships for the remainder of the trip to Portland. In 1890, the Elk Rock Trestle was built. (See page 44.)

Cast-Iron Fronts in Portland. The rail line brought Oswego's ore to Portland. Along Portland's Front Avenue (now Naito Parkway) and First and Second Avenues (today's Old Town District) are 22 intact cast-iron fronted buildings, many of which are made from Oswego ore. They are the last surviving structures of 200 such buildings constructed during the cast iron era, which ended in the 1880s. (Author's collection.)

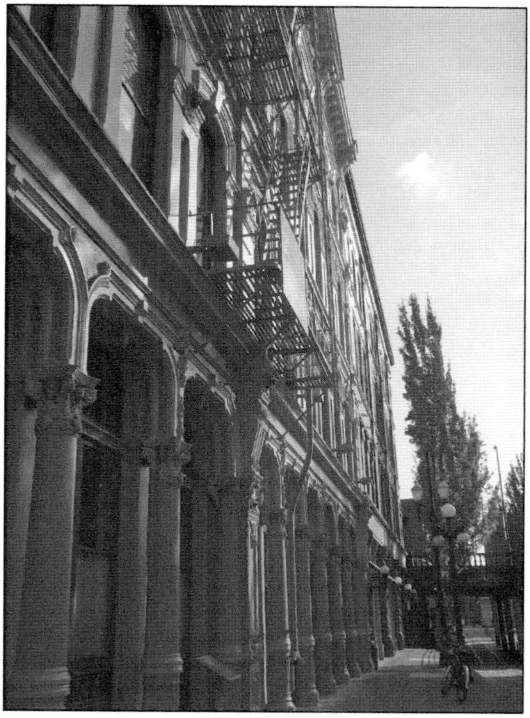

Slag. Slag is a by-product of iron smelting. As the raw rock is refined by extremely high temperatures, impurities within the ore separate out, floating to the surface as the ore liquefies. Slag can be found at Oswego's first furnace site along the river beach. It is not wasted, being used as a base for roads or railroad track ballast, among other uses. See page 125 for a modern example of recycling this material. (Author's collection.)

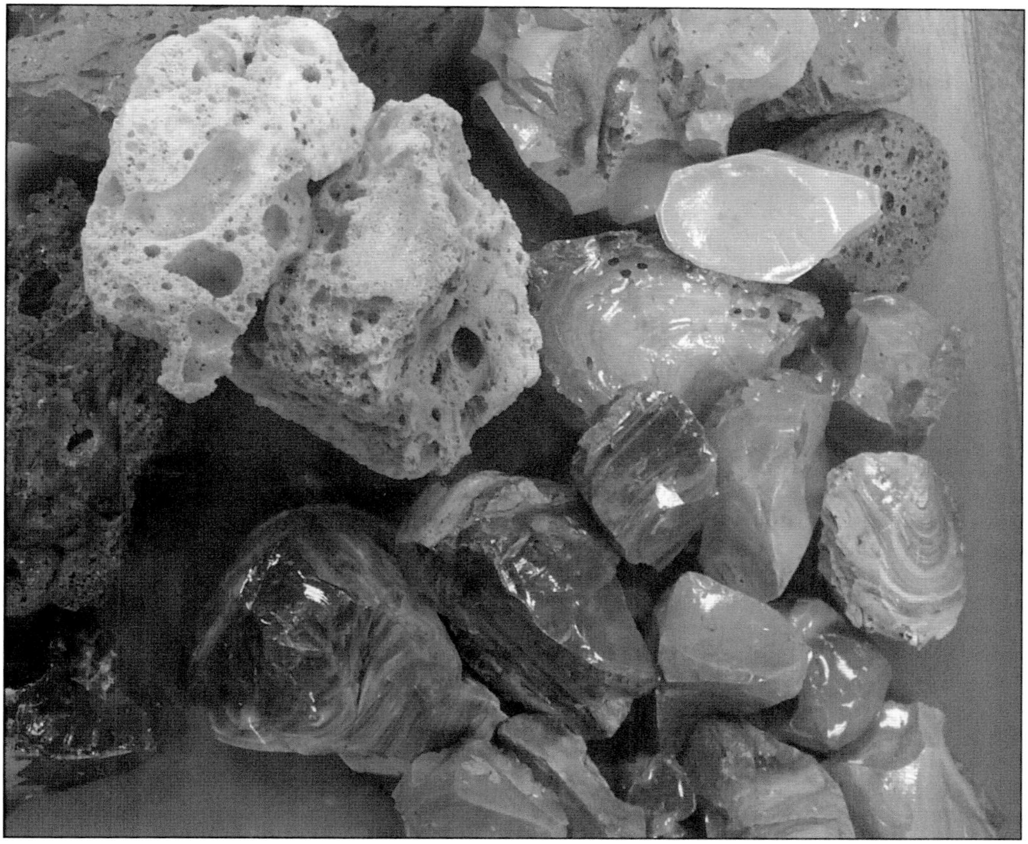

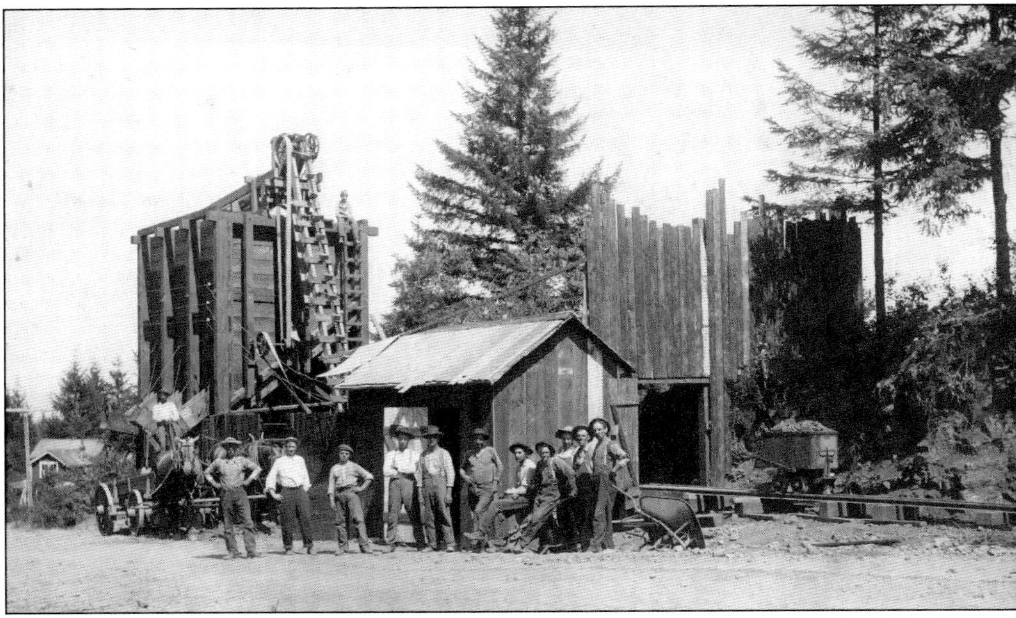

Rock Crusher and Crew. Rock crushers provided rock for railroad ballast and road building. A cart filled with large chunks of basalt is on the tracks at the right. The rocks enter the crusher, are pulverized, and the smaller pieces pour out of the crusher via two chutes, seen on the left, into waiting carts. Some very large draft horses wait patiently for their next load.

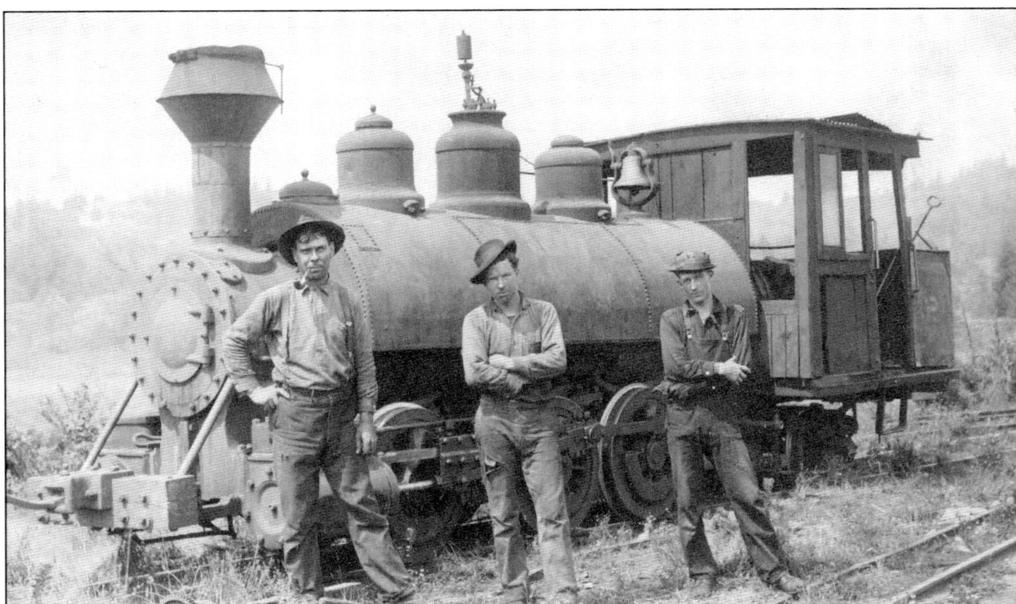

Steam Engine at Pipe Foundry. This *c.* 1890 photograph shows an engine used on the spur lines serving Oregon Iron and Steel's pipe foundry, adjacent to the iron smelter. These spur lines today are known as the Kincaid Curlicue Corridor, a walking path in Foothills Park.

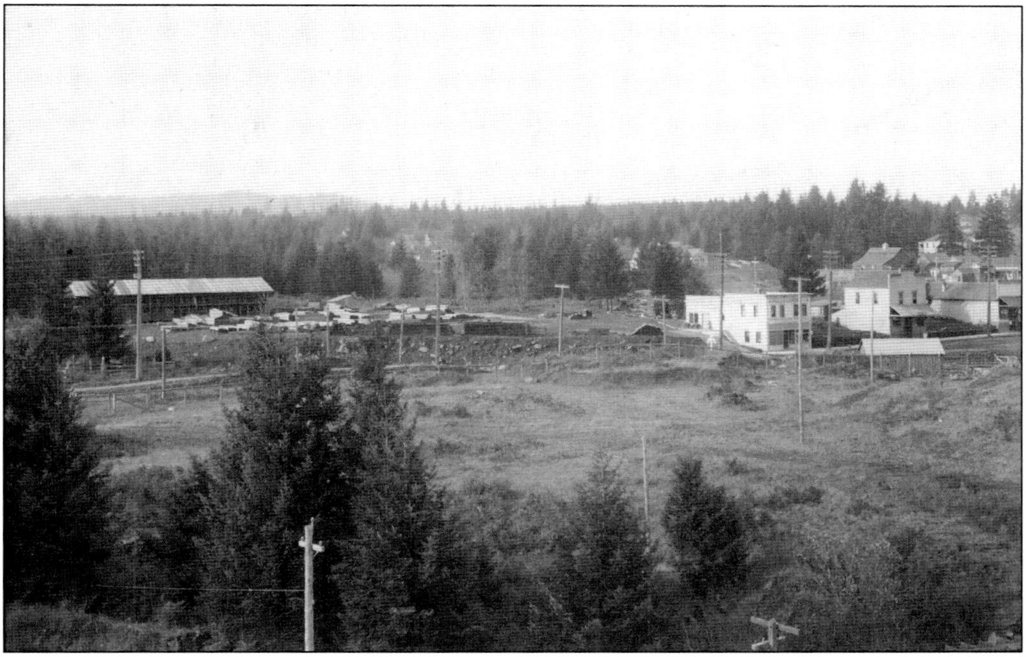

State Street Looking West. In 1913, Oswego Lumber Company is the white building on the right; left of it is its large lumberyard along State Street. By this point, State Street was Oswego's established business district. It was paved in 1920.

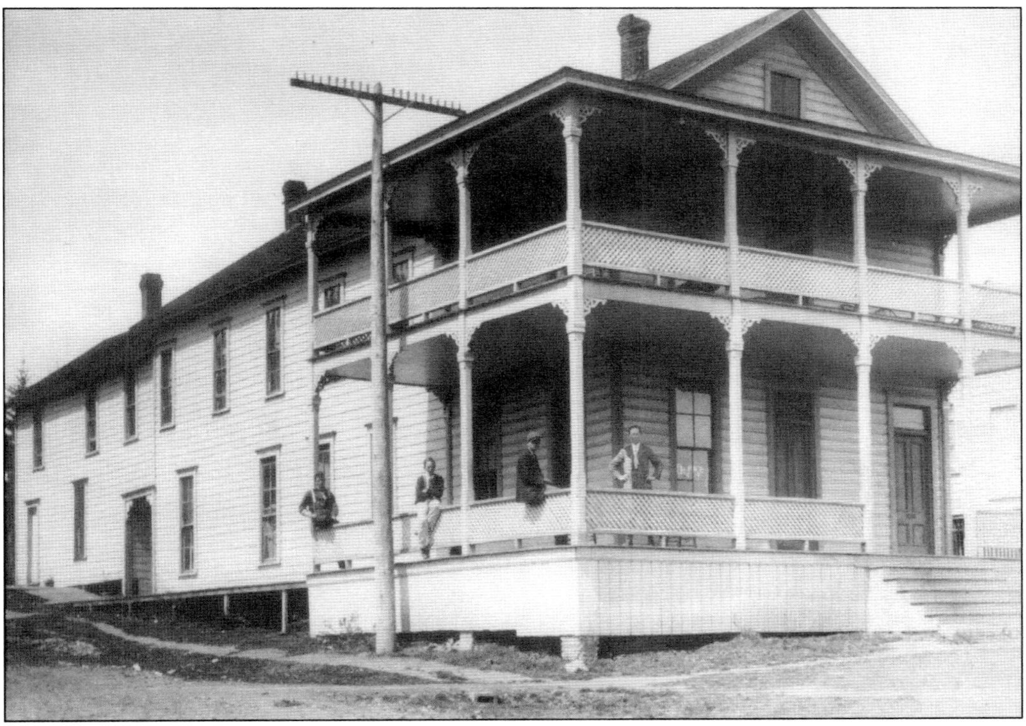

Johnson Hotel. Like the Portland Hotel in Old Town, the Johnson Hotel was home to workers at Oregon Iron and Steel's plants. It stood at the corner of First Street and B Avenue in New Town. It is also seen on the next page.

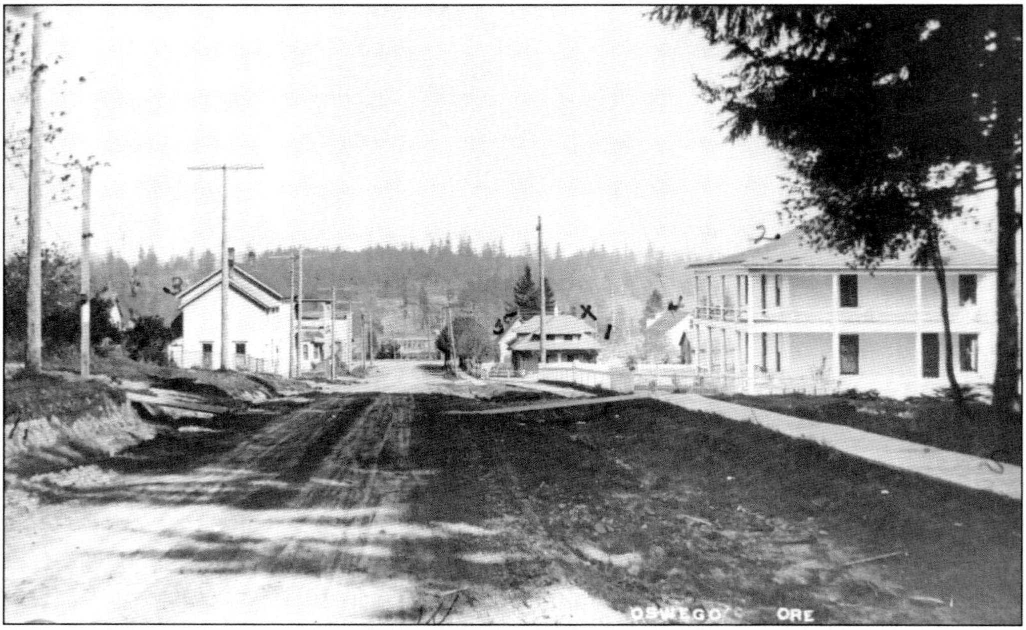

New Town. This view of New Town shows B Avenue, looking east toward the river, in 1908. The photographer numbered notable buildings. No. 2 is the Henry Koehler home, built in 1907. It had a large second-floor hall used for community dances. In 1909, when the city incorporated, it became the first city hall. No. 3 is the Johnson Hotel. No. 1 is the William J. and Edna Bickner home; the Bickner store is at No. 5.

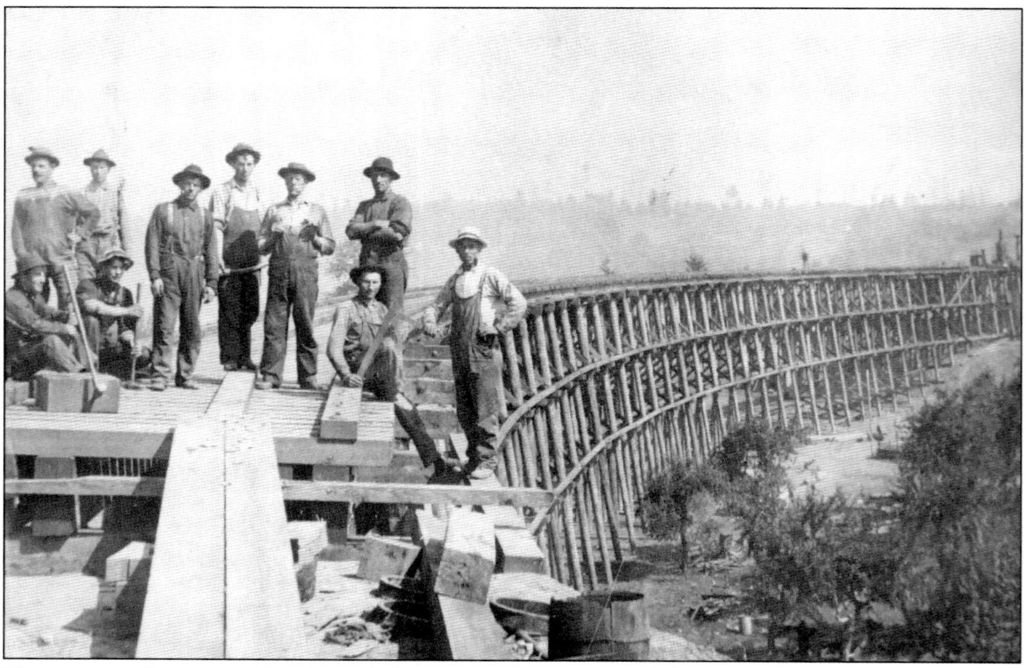

Trestle to Smelter. A 2.75-mile-long narrow-gauge track ran from the central mine adit (entrance) on Iron Mountain to the second iron furnace; it ran on grade parallel and to the south of A Avenue in New Town. East of State Street, the track ran on this trestle to its endpoint at the furnace. The trestle was torn down in 1910.

Worker Housing in Old Town. Oregon Iron and Steel built this house around 1880 when Oswego was a company-owned town. Nearby Ladd Street was still the primary business district but would eventually be supplanted by Front Avenue (State Street). (Author's collection.)

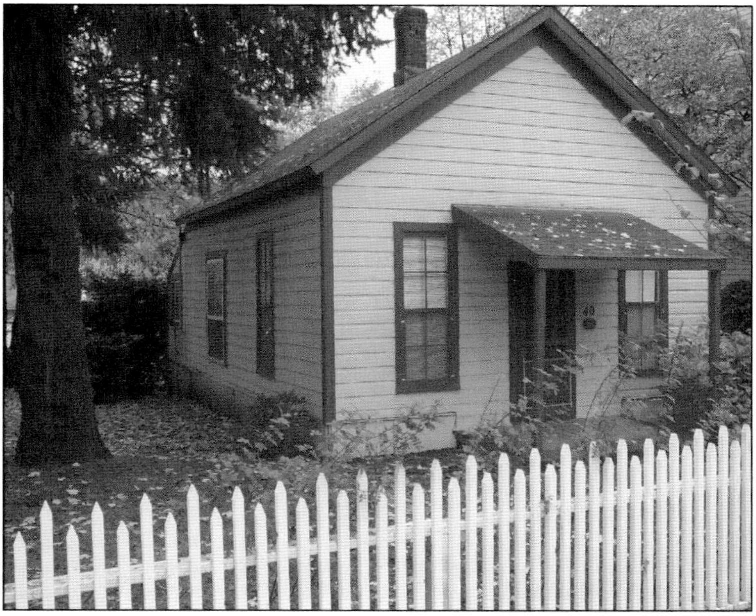

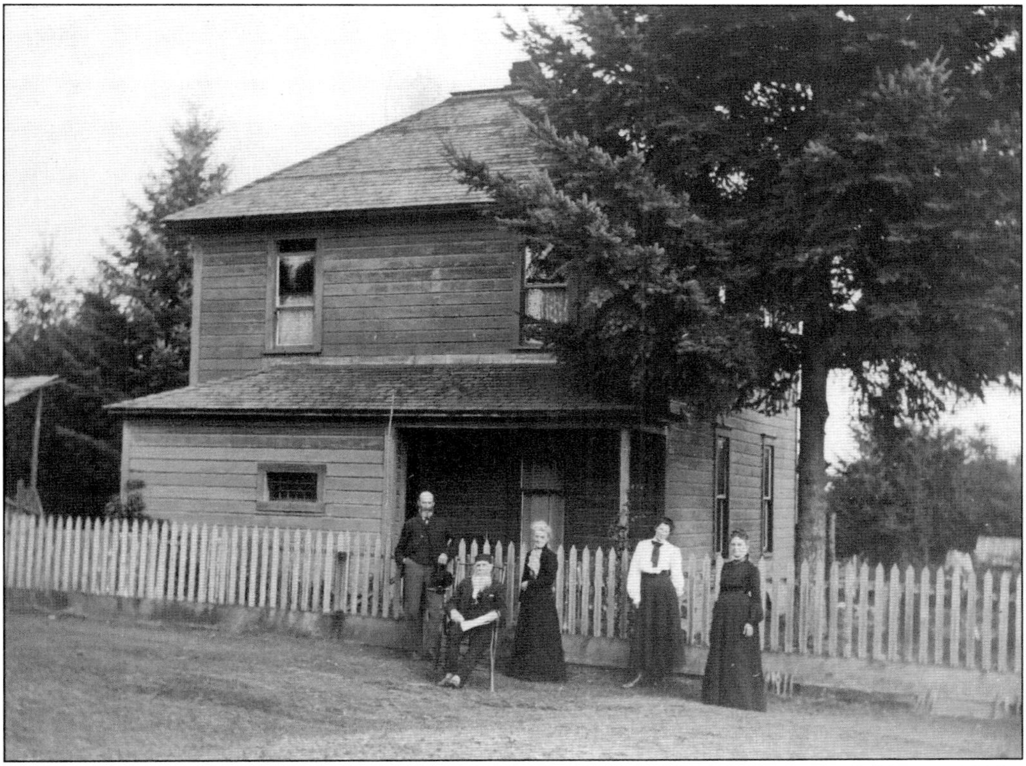

A New Town Home. Pictured is a home at B Avenue and Fifth Street in First Addition, 1890s. This neighborhood was platted in 1888 by Oregon Iron and Steel for its workers to build their homes. The second iron smelter was just a few blocks east of this home, an easy walk. Note the dirt road, absence of sidewalks, and fenced yard, probably for the family cow.

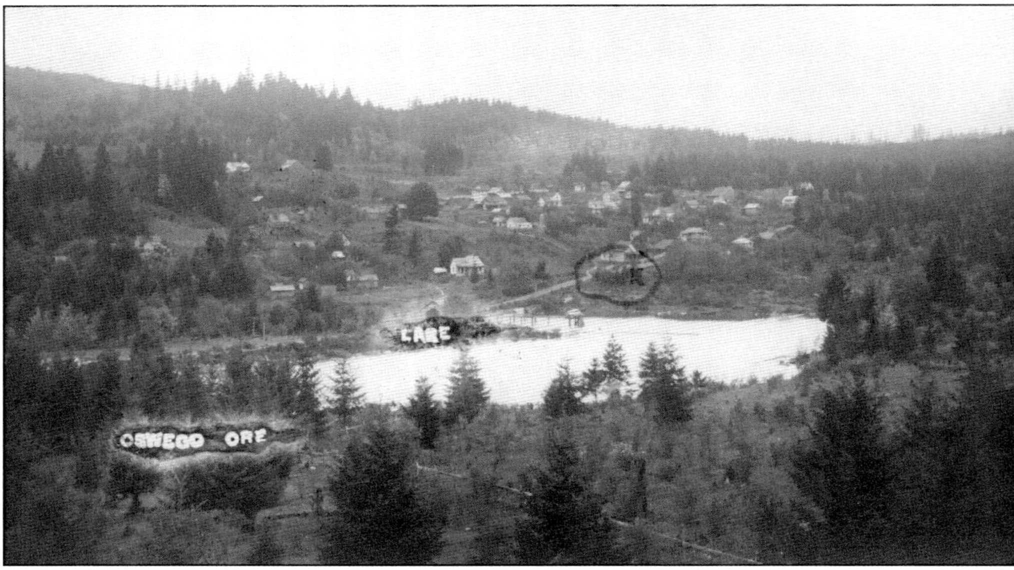

SOUTH OSWEGO. This 1913 photograph shows the south shore of the lake. The Bickner's first store, at McVey Avenue and Erickson Street, is circled. The covered bridge is on the left. A few years before this photograph was taken, residents of this area had rejected joining the newly incorporated town of Oswego; efforts to incorporate had been led by residents and merchants of New Town. Some South Oswego residents felt as though they had lost status to the "upstart" New Town area.

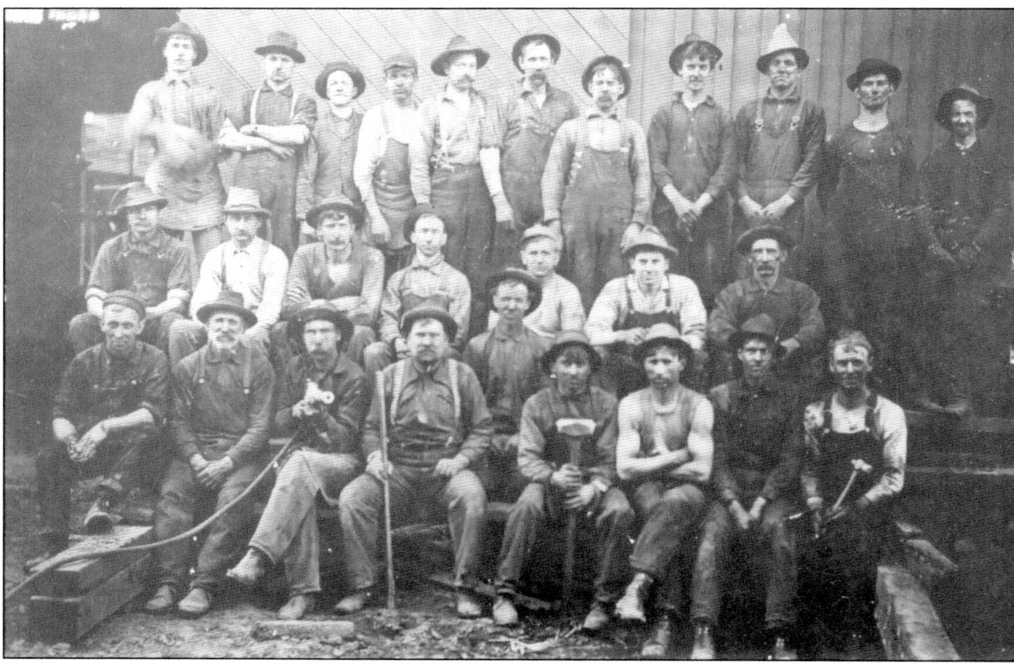

FOUNDRY WORKERS IN PIPE PLANT. These men lived in the neighborhoods seen on the preceding pages. The pipe foundry operated from 1888 to the 1920s. Faces are grimy at the end of a workday; men in the front row hold their tools. The man third from right in the first row has an extremely impressive set of biceps, perhaps from beating the clay cores out of the finished pipes. (See page 67.)

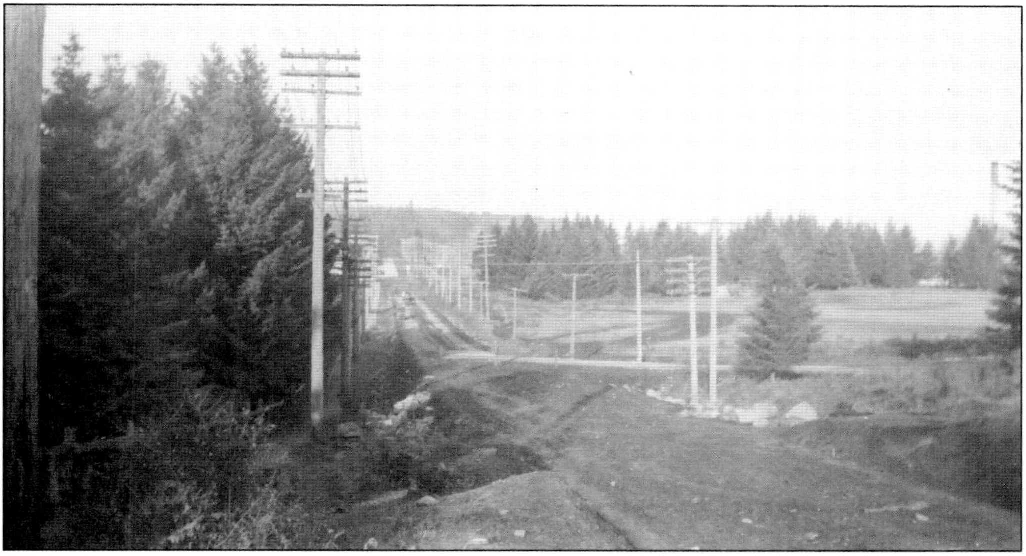

State Street Looking North. This view of State Street, before it was paved in 1920, looks north from about the site of today's Village Shopping Center at North Shore Road.

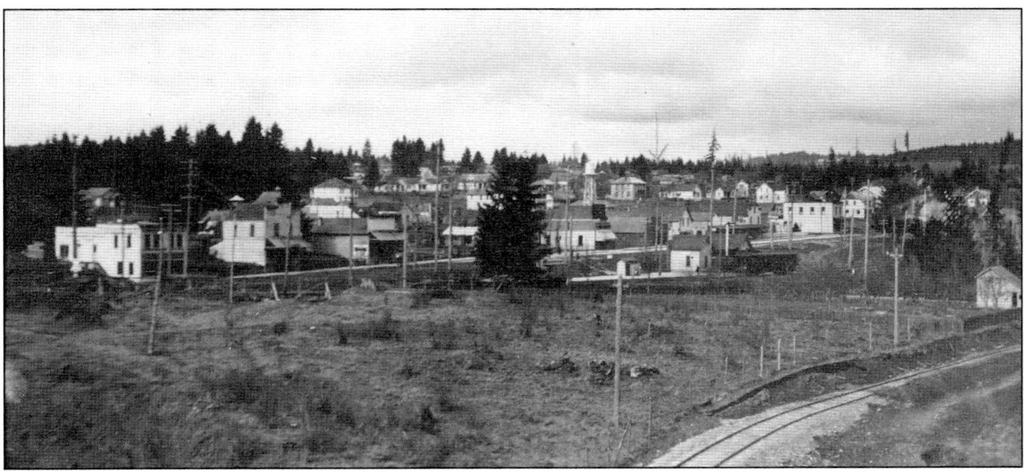

New Town Looking Northwest. This photograph was taken "from the rock crusher," the photographer notes. He has indicated his First Addition home with an arrow. State Street is in the middle distance, and a spur line to the industrial area is in the foreground.

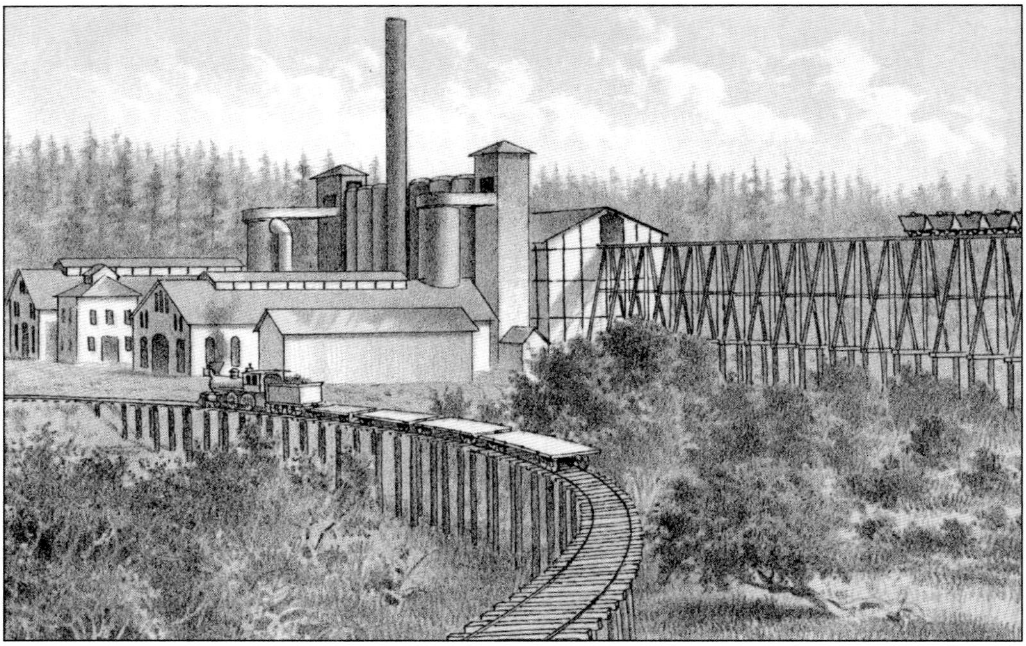

OREGON IRON AND STEEL'S FURNACE. Three hundred twenty-five men were employed to construct the furnace, its ancillary buildings, and the 160-foot-high chimney stack. Pig iron was taken from the furnace, loaded onto railcars, and transported to the pipe foundry where it was molded into pipe. On the upper right are ore cars on the high trestle, coming from the mine 2.75 miles away.

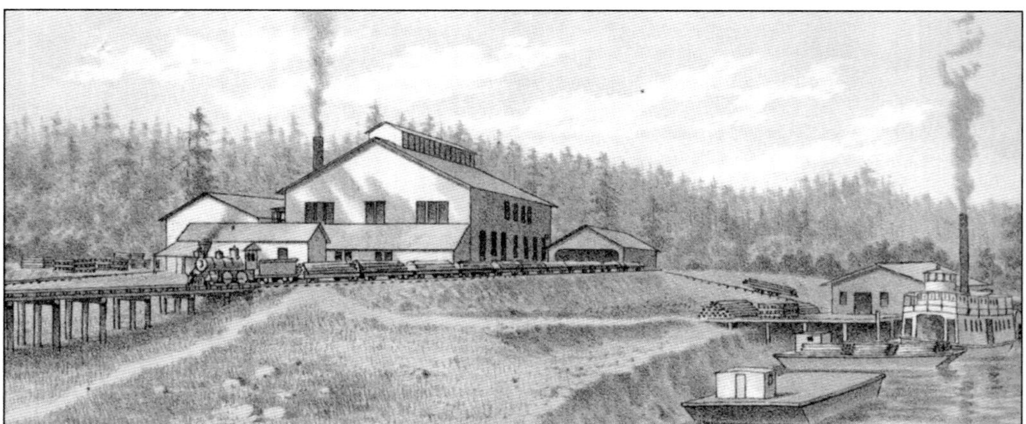

OREGON IRON AND STEEL'S PIPE FOUNDRY. The pipe foundry had a pit for casting pipe vertically. After the furnace closed in 1894, the foundry's raw material was either scrap iron or pig iron from Belgium brought over as ballast on ships.

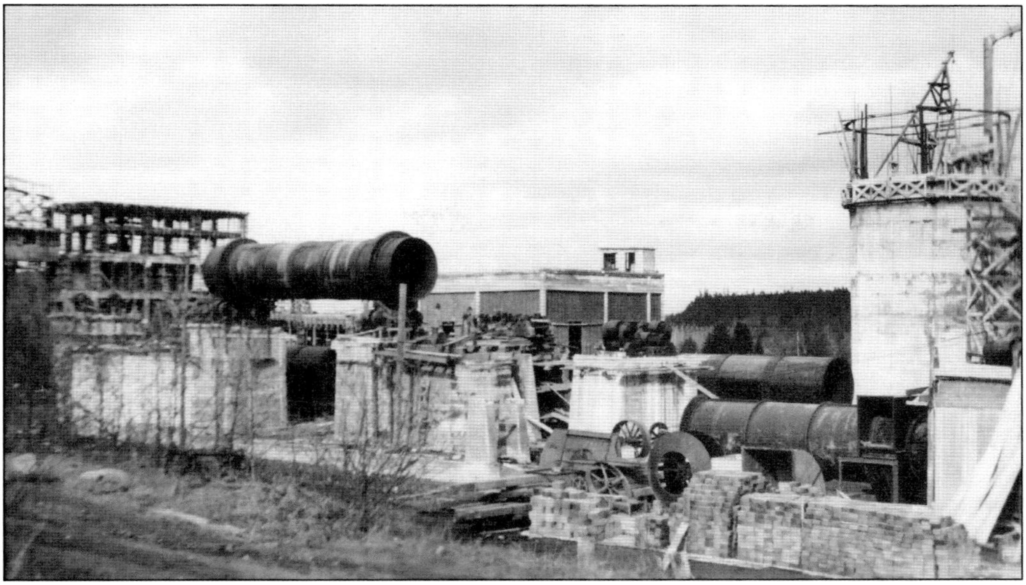

Large Pipe at Foundry. Forty-five-inch pipe was made here for Portland and Seattle's water supply systems. The pipe cores were made from hay ropes and clay mined from the duck pond. Coremakers specialized in handling the clay; if it was not dry enough when the molten iron was poured around it, the iron would fly like molten sparks. One worker remembered what the coremakers would do when this happened: "It would run out off their shirts. It wouldn't burn them but would just fall off of their shirts."

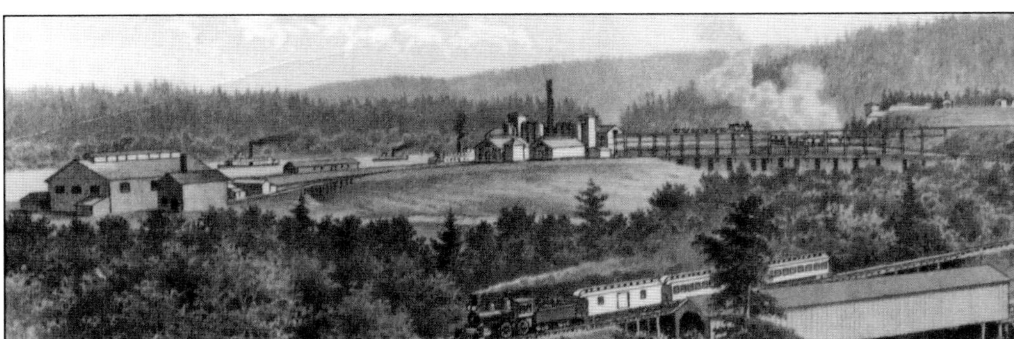

Panorama, Oregon Iron and Steel's Operations. The furnace is to the right, and the pipe foundry on the left, almost to the bank of Tryon Creek, which the train is crossing on a trestle.

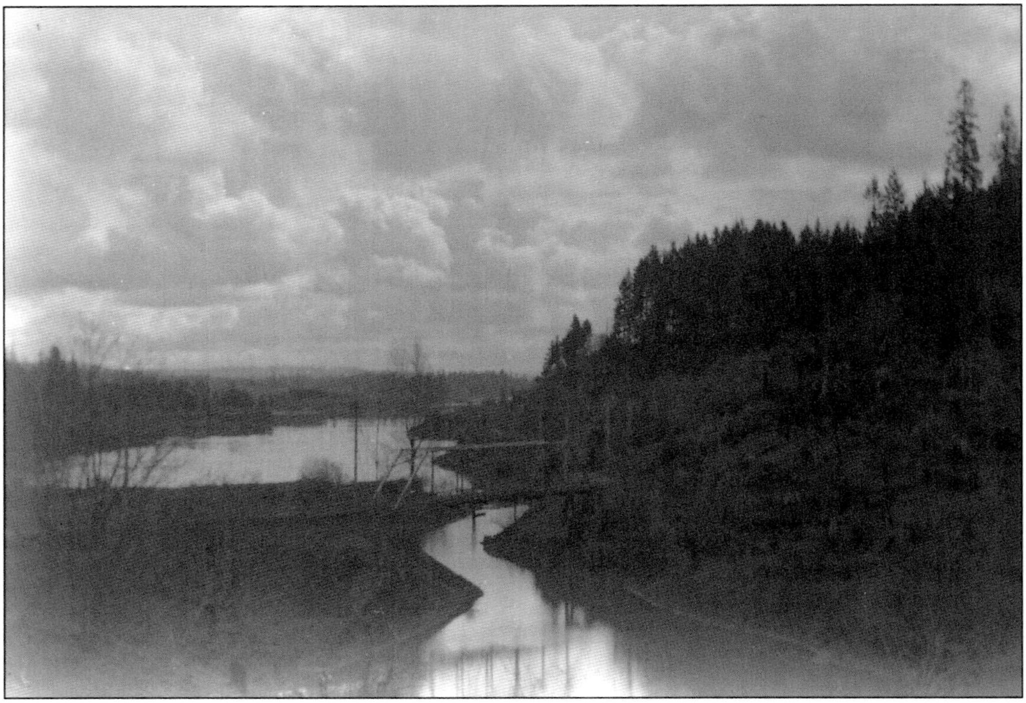

EARLY WOODEN BRIDGE. This wooden bridge across Oswego Creek was not covered. An even simpler bridge than this is seen on page 26. Bridges in Oregon began to be covered as early as the 1850s; perhaps frequent washouts prevented such an investment here. Bridges are covered to keep the trusses dry; in the days before treated lumber, a covered bridge could last 80 years, an uncovered span about nine years. This photograph was taken around 1890 based on the early electricity poles lining River Road.

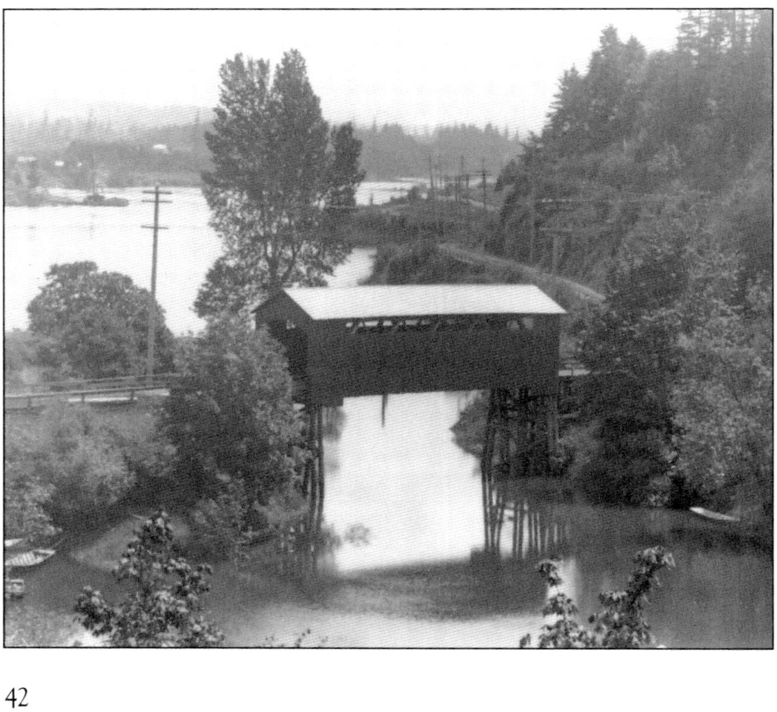

COVERED BRIDGE, OSWEGO CREEK. This image, from about 1913, shows a well-protected bridge along River Road. Photographs from the 1920s show it still standing, even after the Pacific Highway Bridge (now Highway 43) was built just upstream. The Pacific Highway supplanted River Road.

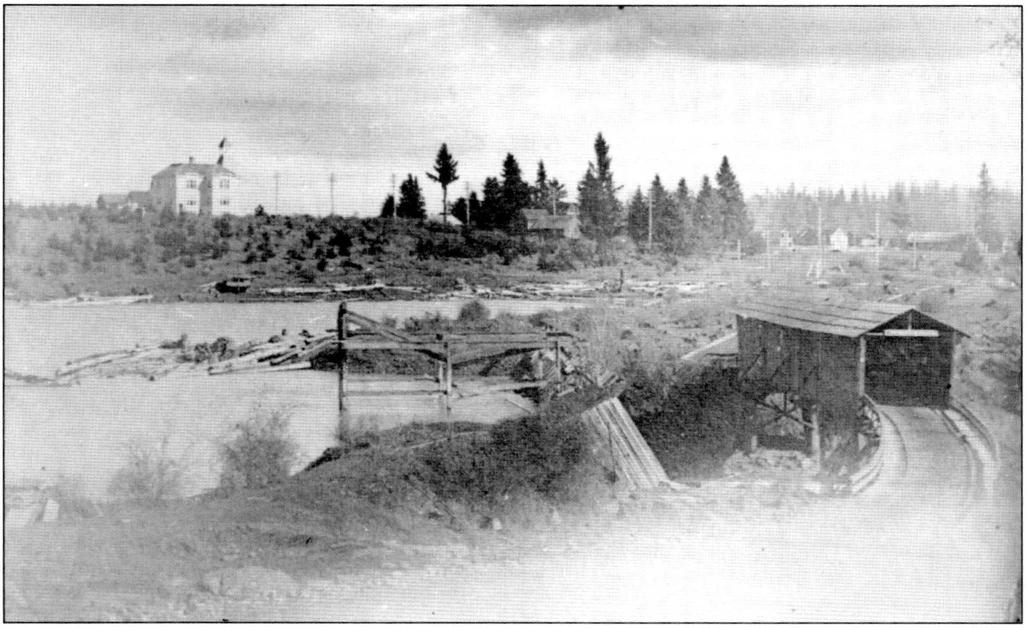

Early Covered Bridge, McVey Avenue. McVey Avenue, seen here, was named well after the date of this image for Arthur McVey, who worked at the Oregon Iron and Steel pipe foundry and as janitor at Oswego Public School from 1912 to 1947. He lived in Old Town at 144 Leonard Street, since demolished. This photograph dates from approximately 1893, the year the Oswego Public School (seen in the distant left) was built on State Street.

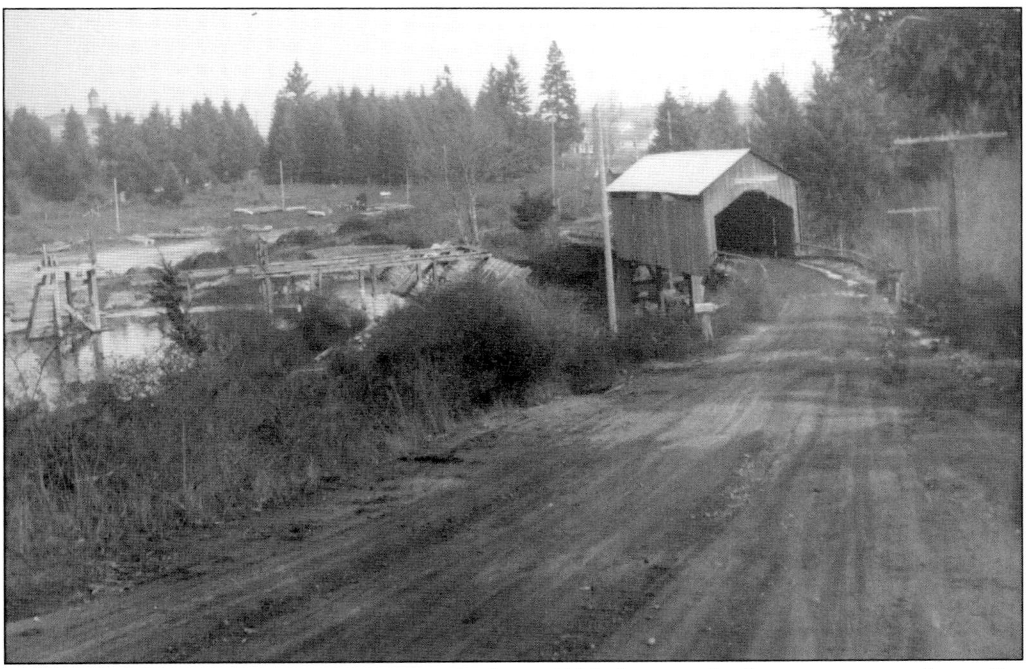

Later Covered Bridge, McVey Avenue. In this *c.* 1905 photograph, the same trees in the earlier image have grown up and the land does not look so raw. A new structure covers the bridge over the creek, and the wooden dam is visible in both images. In this picture, canoes litter the shore at the emerging Nelson boating concession.

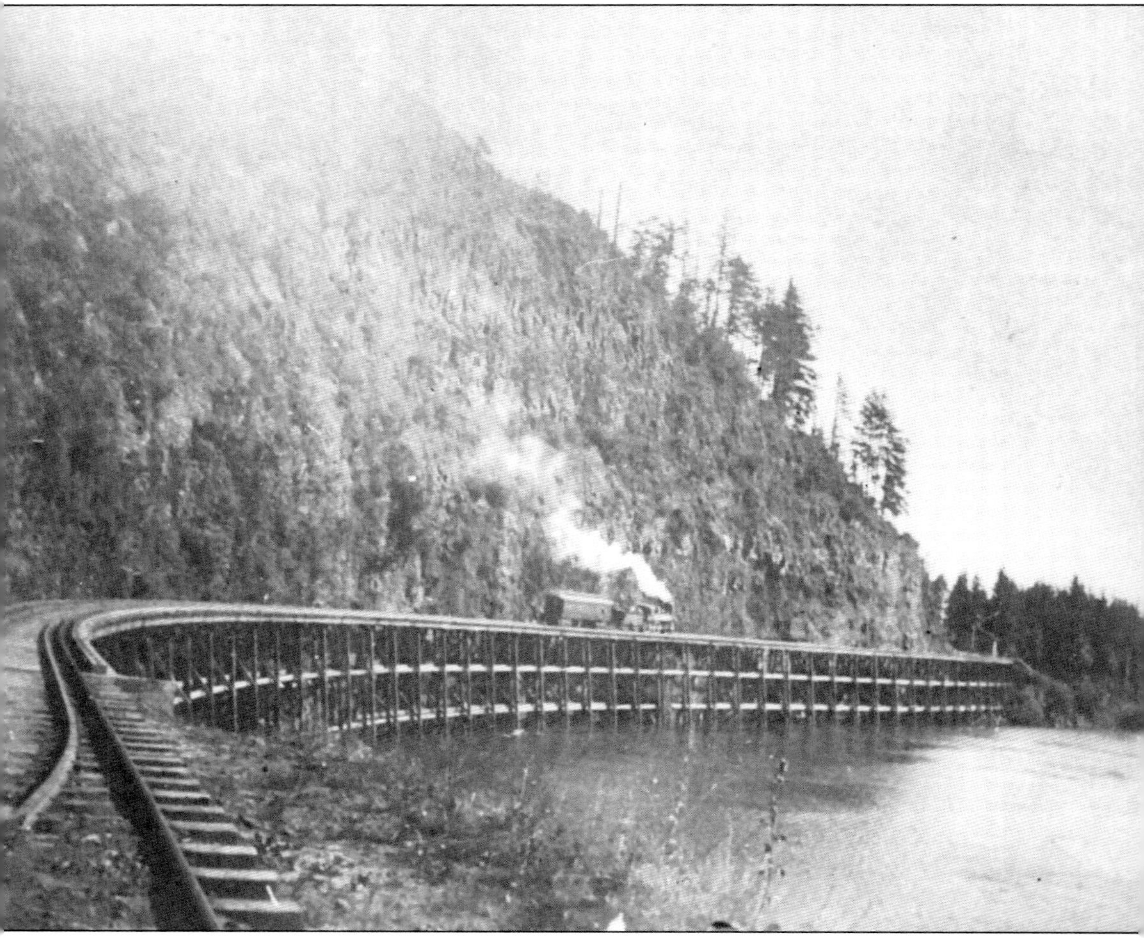

Elk Rock Train Trestle. Elk Rock is a solid basalt obstacle that early road and rail builders had to contend with. While the rail line from Oswego was built in 1887, in the first few years, a trestle had not been built to circumvent Elk Rock, so passengers got off and finished their trip into Portland via riverboat. By 1890, this trestle had been built. In 1973, two women recalled the trestle's thrills, as the train hugged the cliff so tightly passengers could practically reach out and touch the cliff. "[We] always took seats on the river side because it was a little more scary." Before each train could cross the trestle, it stopped and someone got out and walked the tracks to remove any rocks that had fallen off the cliff since the last run. In 1921, a tunnel was bored 1,396 feet through Elk Rock.

Three

Town and Country Live on through Boom and Bust 1865–1910

Oswego's first business district, along Ladd Street, clung close to Durham's first mill site. Furnace Street, with its river views, was where wealthy families lived, even into the early 1910s. This area was later called Old Town, after construction of the New Town addition in 1888.

South Town was platted in the area just south of the lake's east end in 1883; early residents were skilled ironworkers recruited by Oregon Iron and Steel from Ohio. Its only business was Gans' store, which became Bickner's Feed and Grocery and operated here until around 1914.

New Town, today called First Addition, was platted by Oregon Iron and Steel in 1888 as a neighborhood close to the new smelter. With the rail line to Portland complete by 1887, and a depot at A Avenue and Front Street (now State Street), New Town gradually usurped Old Town as Oswego's business district.

Old Town held its own, despite the northward shift in population and industry. A new school was built in 1893 at State and Wilbur Streets (at the site of today's Lakewood Center for the Arts). The Grange (on Leonard Street—now gone) and Odd Fellows on Durham Street (extant) remained thriving community halls.

By 1906, Oswego's prospects were brightening as a new railroad bridge was planned, with accompanying hopes of new businesses. In 1910, the Oregon Portland Cement Company planned a cement manufacturing plant, and Oswego Power and Light lit up the town. From the 1890s, some town leaders had promoted incorporating Oswego as a means to raise taxes that could provide infrastructure and services to residents. Oregon Iron and Steel, as the town's largest landowner, fought incorporation for years. The tide turned in 1909; populist sentiment against wealthy landowners and concern about lack of a municipal water supply meant that incorporation was voted in by New Town residents. Oswego was no longer a company town. South Town and Old Town remained separate until their 1922 annexation.

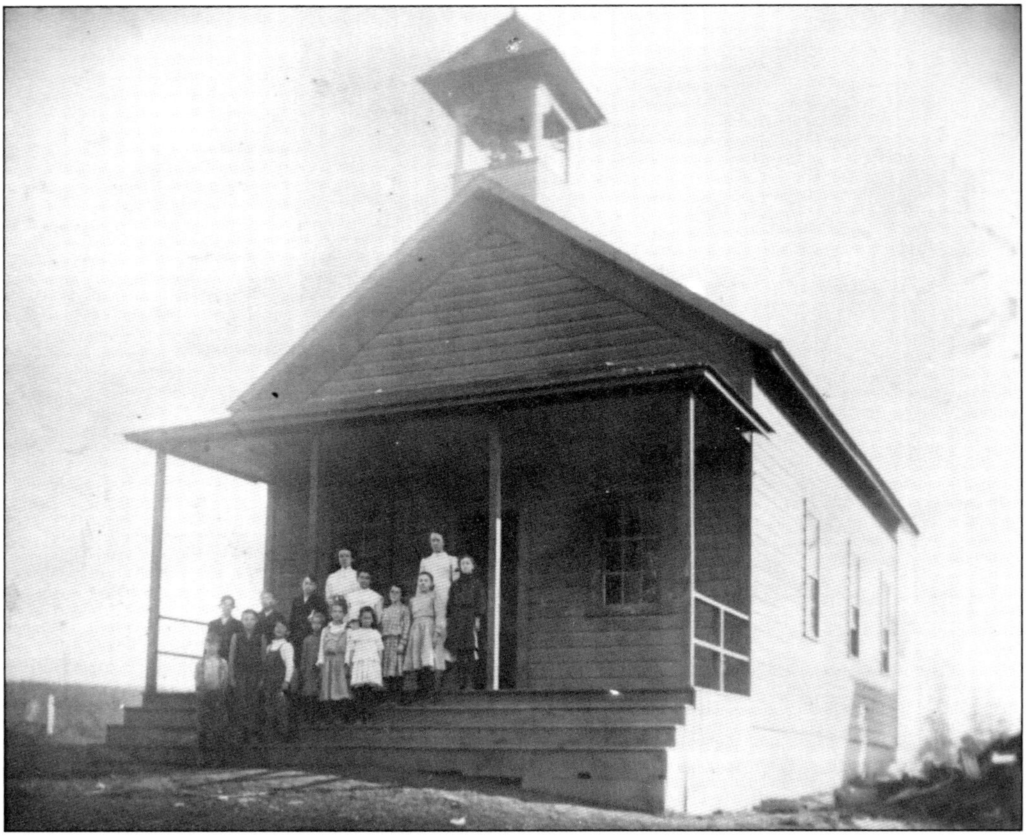

HAZELIA SCHOOL. Hazelia was named for the filbert groves (hazelnuts) common there. The Hazelia area, south of Oswego Lake, is now known as the Stafford Basin. This one-room school went up in 1884. The porch and belfry were added in 1905. A Grange Hall was built on the site in 1916.

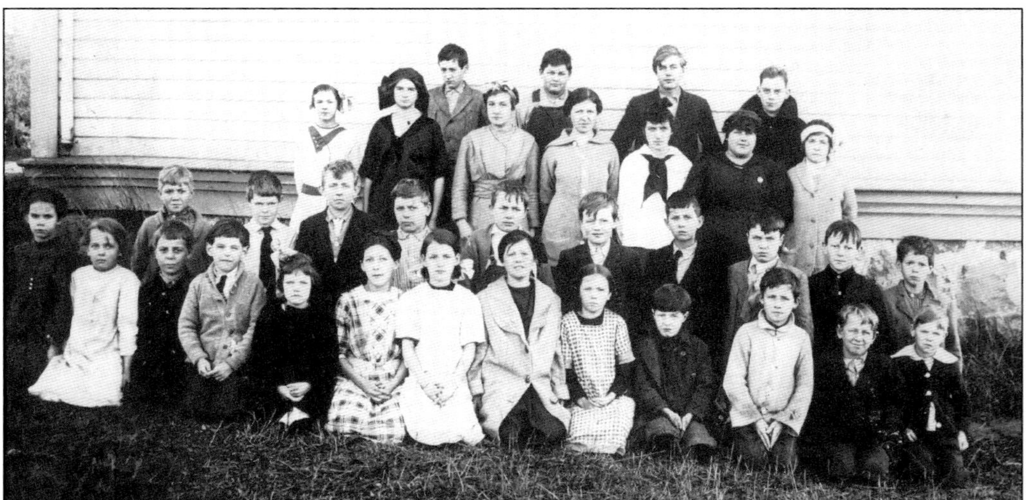

SPRINGBROOK SCHOOL STUDENTS. Springbrook School was named for the creek that flows into the lake's north side. The school was located on Boones Ferry Road; students came from the north and west sides of the lake. This photograph is from 1915.

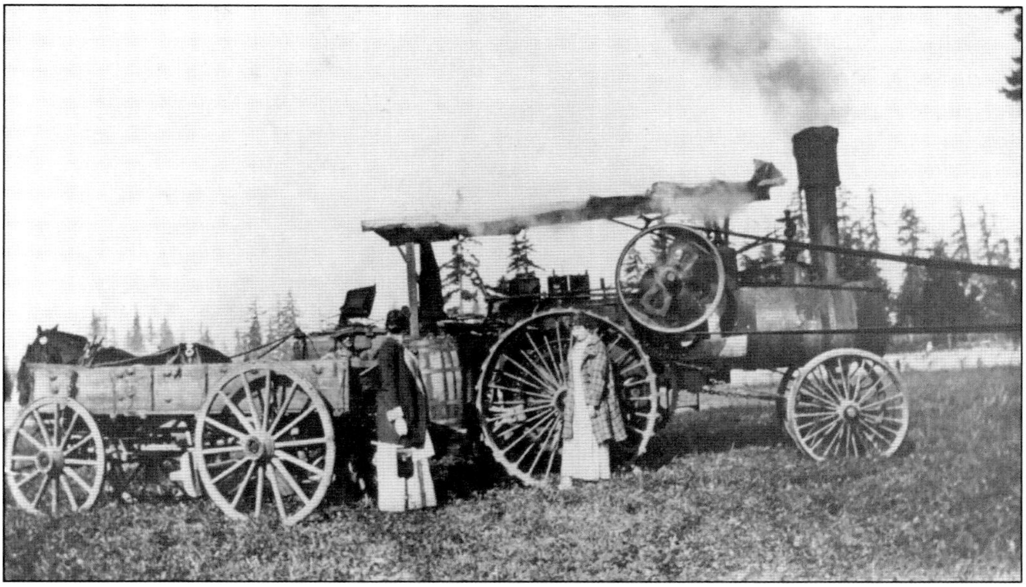

Steam Engine on Farm. This scene of farm life, *c.* 1910, is from the Kruse farm and shows a portable steam engine, a modern technology that was steered by horses, an ageless one. Such engines were used for threshing.

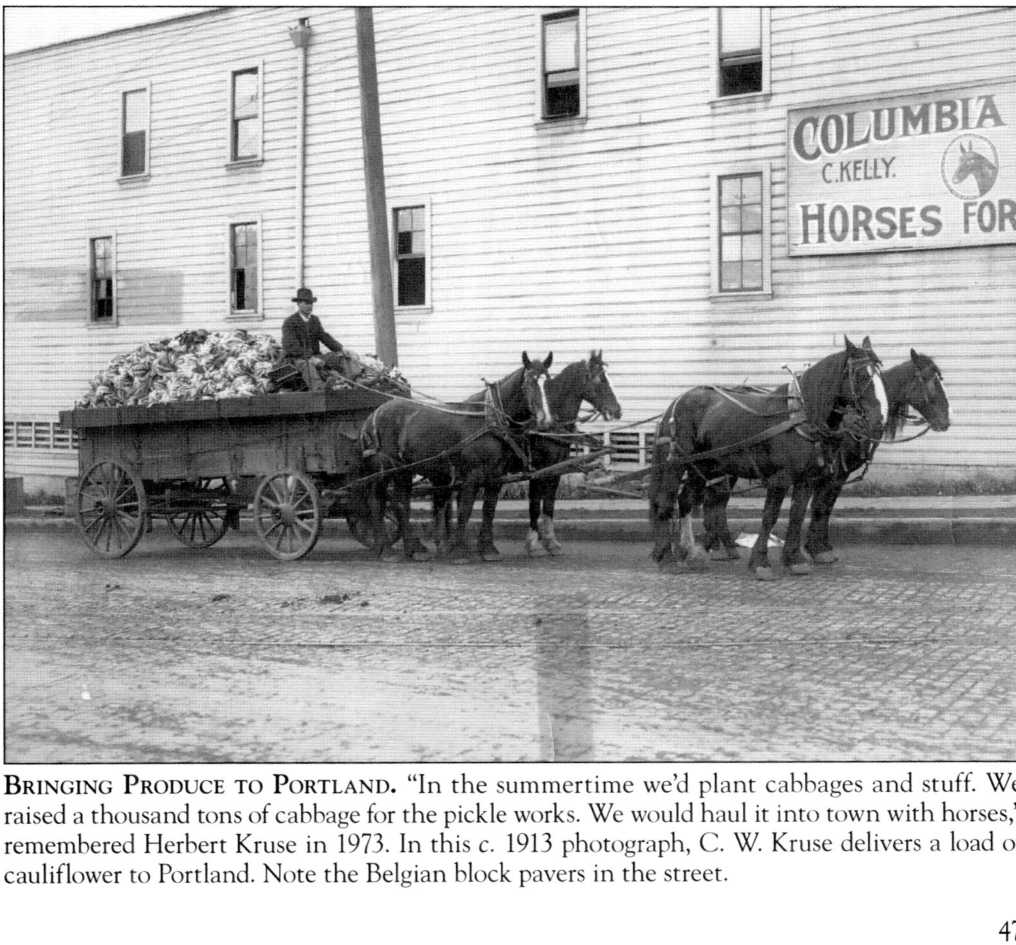

Bringing Produce to Portland. "In the summertime we'd plant cabbages and stuff. We raised a thousand tons of cabbage for the pickle works. We would haul it into town with horses," remembered Herbert Kruse in 1973. In this *c.* 1913 photograph, C. W. Kruse delivers a load of cauliflower to Portland. Note the Belgian block pavers in the street.

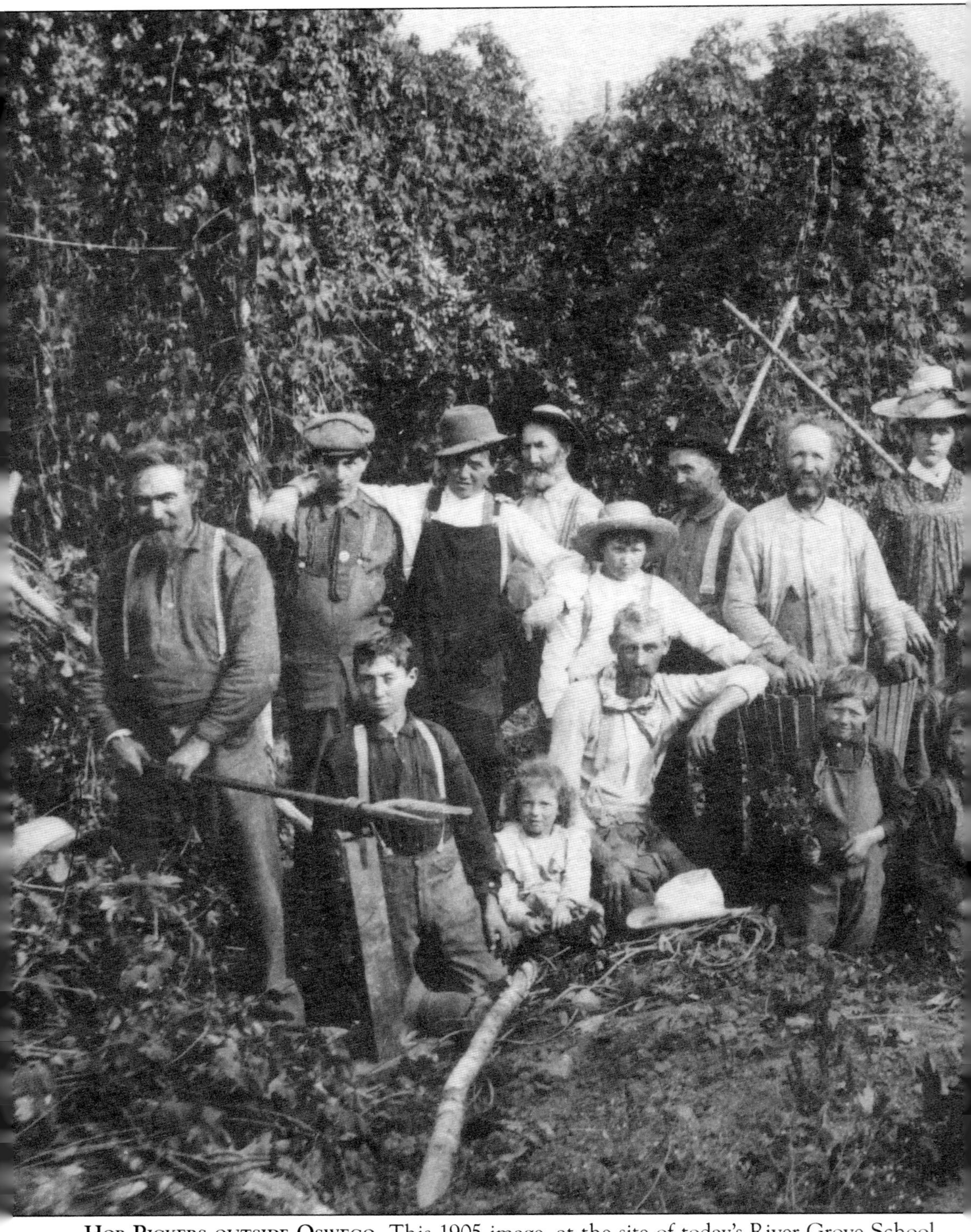

Hop Pickers outside Oswego. This 1905 image, at the site of today's River Grove School, shows people looking festive—one boy holds a bouquet, the man behind seems to be standing in a wooden basket, and a man to his left wears a garland of hops. All ages are seen here; perhaps it was lunchtime during the hop harvest. Before mechanization, the harvests were labor intensive,

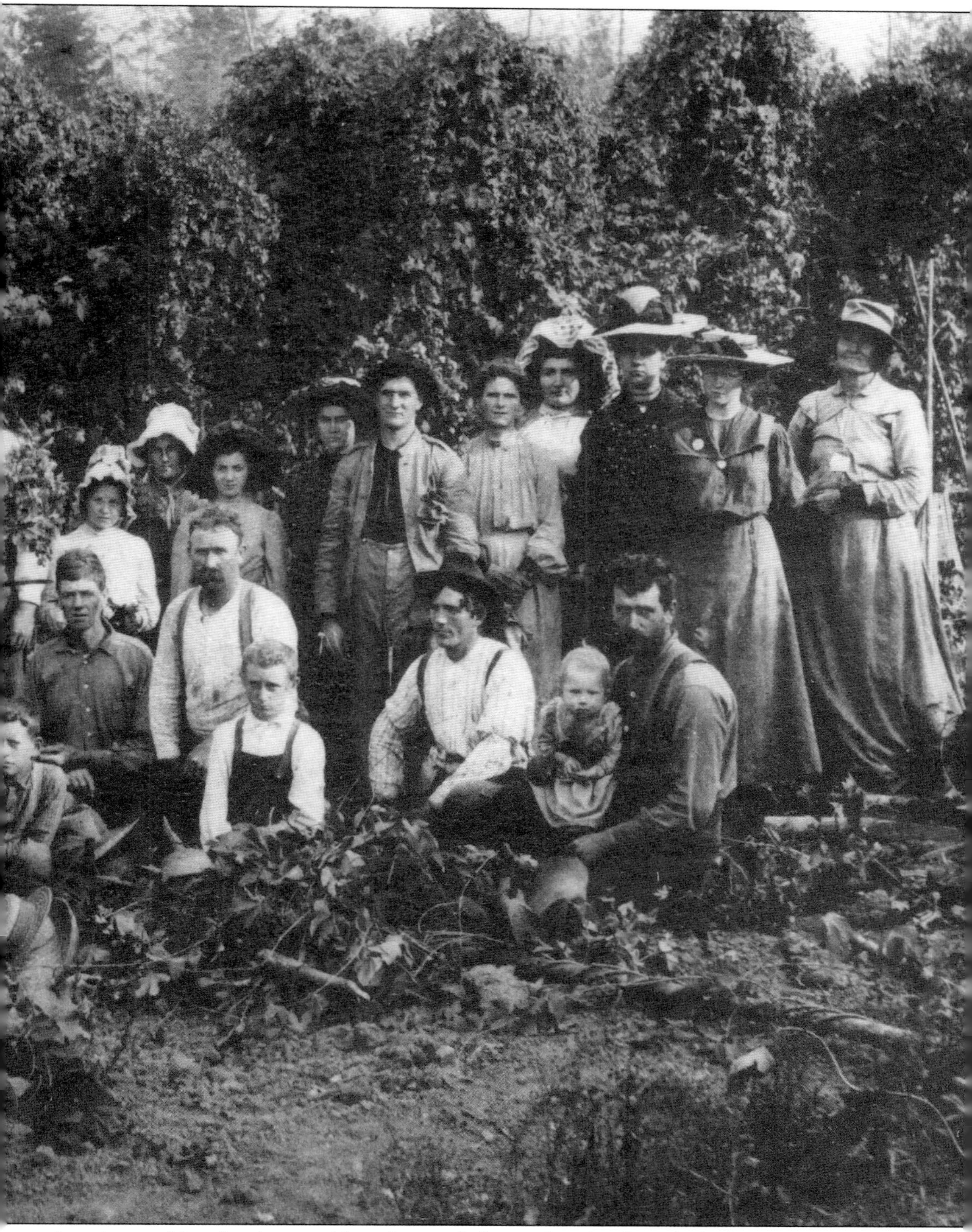

and entire neighbor families would pitch in to help another family pick the hops in August or September. At larger farms, hundreds of itinerant workers would be hired. While this area is now suburban, the Willamette Valley is still one of the world's centers for hop production. Germany is the leader in hop production.

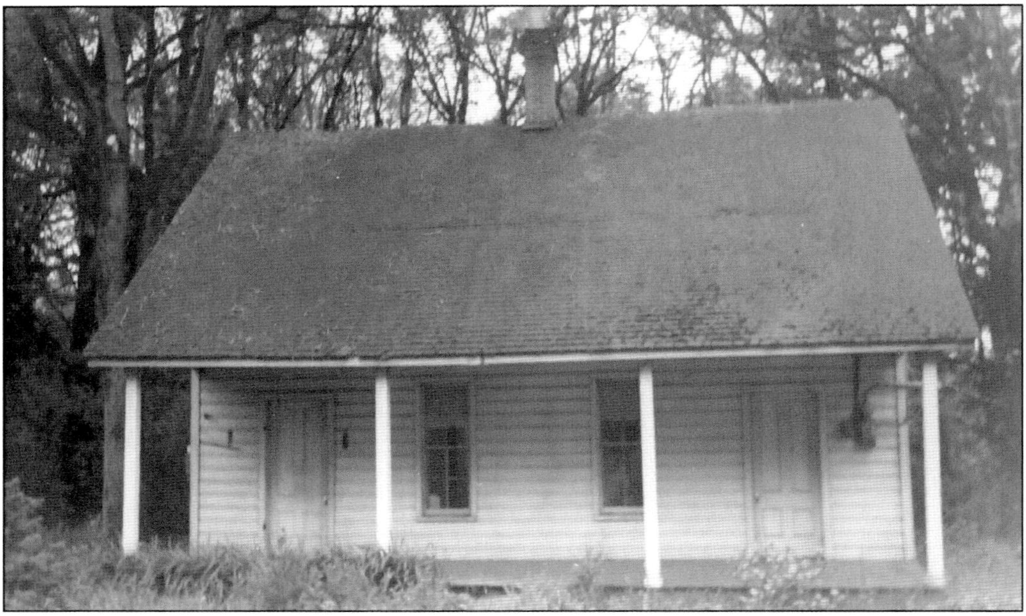

Kruse Farmhouse, Carman Drive. This was the original Kruse homestead house, built in the 1850s by Otto and Frances Kruse who came from Germany via the California Gold Rush. It was torn down in the 1950s and a new family home built. That in turn was demolished when the Pearl at Kruse Way, a longterm residential care facility, was constructed. "Pearl" honors Pearl Padberg Kruse.

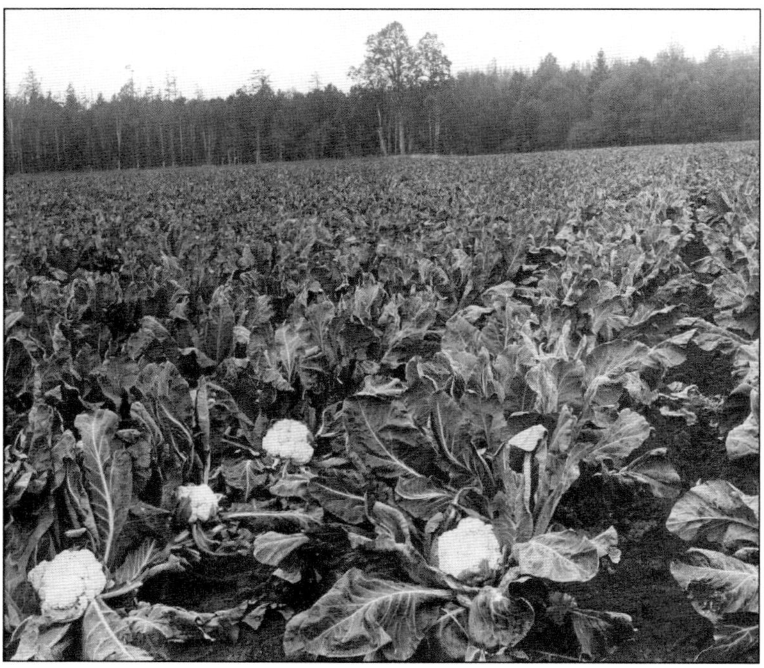

Cauliflower, Kruse Farm. Soils at the west end of the lake, where the Kruse family settled, were rich and deep. In 1913, the *Oregonian* ran a photograph of the Kruse cauliflower crop, a new product for Oregon: "New Industry is Thriving in this State." Other crops raised on the Kruse farm were cabbage, broccoli, and potatoes.

POND, KRUSE FARM. This photograph shows the site of today's Mormon Temple on Kruse Oaks Boulevard. Though this photograph was taken in 1953, it shows a timeless scene. Today I-5 runs just to the west of this once peaceful spot in the woods.

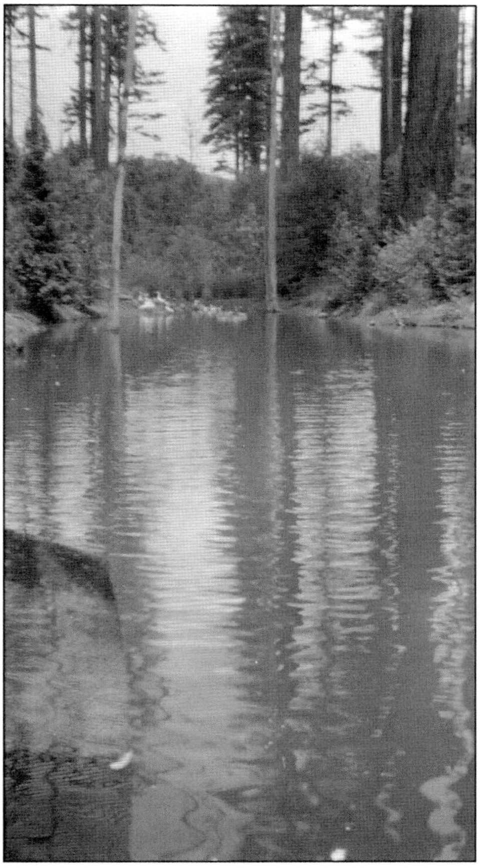

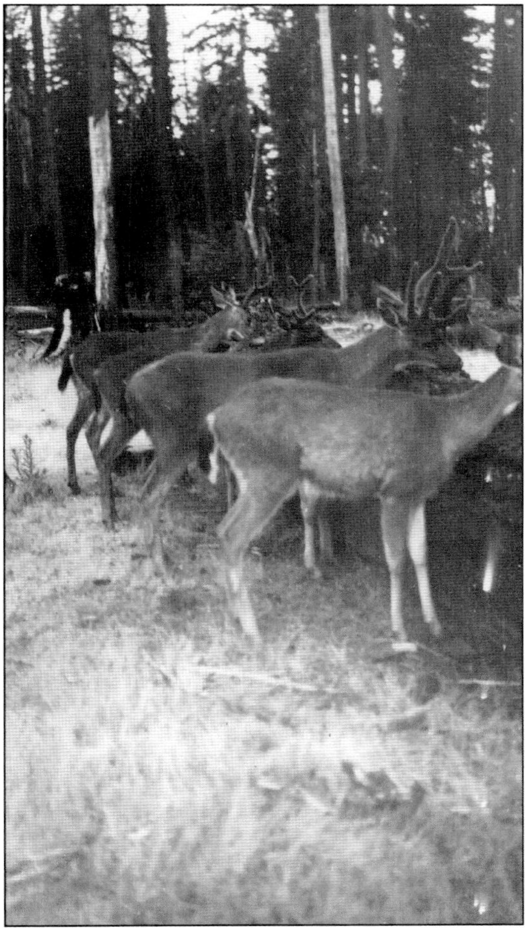

DEER PARK, KRUSE FARM. Deer browse within the fenced deer park in the Kruse family's woods. The family did not hunt the deer, according to Karen Kruse Pong, but others did at times. She recalled her dad coming back from the barbershop one day in the 1940s; the man in the next chair over, he reported, was getting a shave and regaling the barber with how he had bagged some deer at "old man Kruse's deer park."

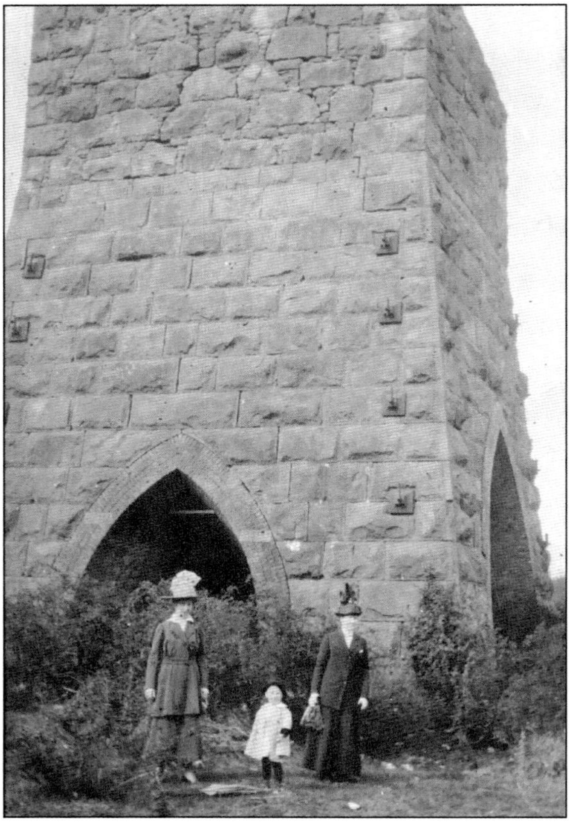

SIGHTSEERS, OLD FURNACE STACK. Two women and a child visit the old industrial site in 1916. The iron hooks, now absent, are still present at that time. Note the cruder stonework at the top of the stack. In 1878, when the furnace was 12 years old, its height was increased to make it more productive.

OSWEGO MAILMAN. Jesse Coon was Oswego's first rural mail carrier, from 1905 to 1910. Here he is stopped in front of a mailbox, perhaps letting his horse drink from the nearby rain barrel.

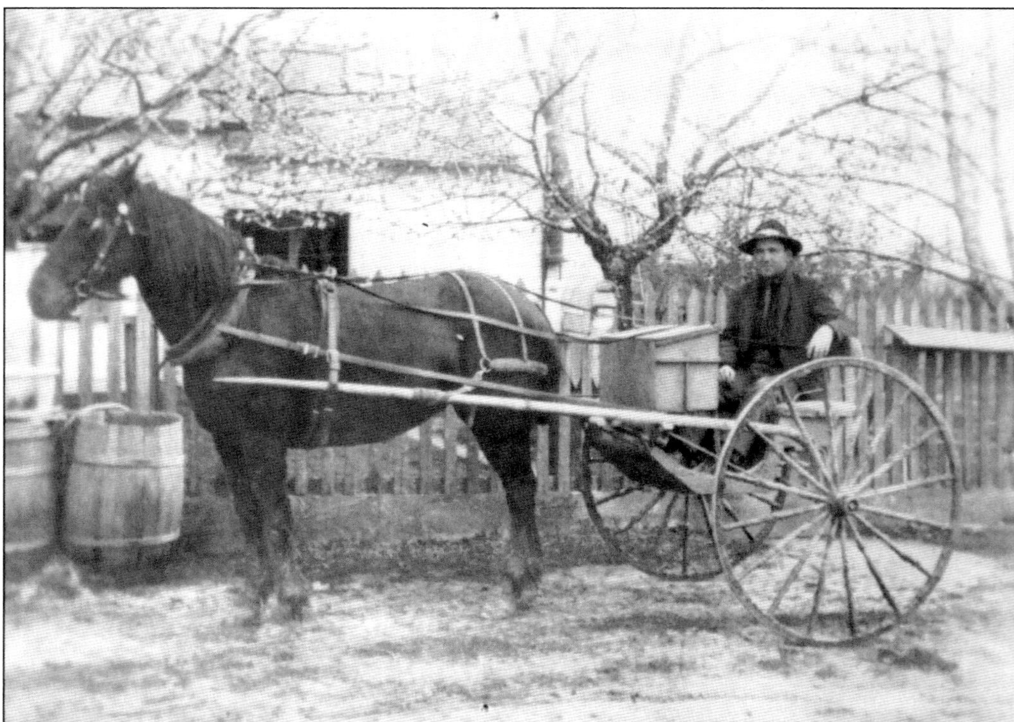

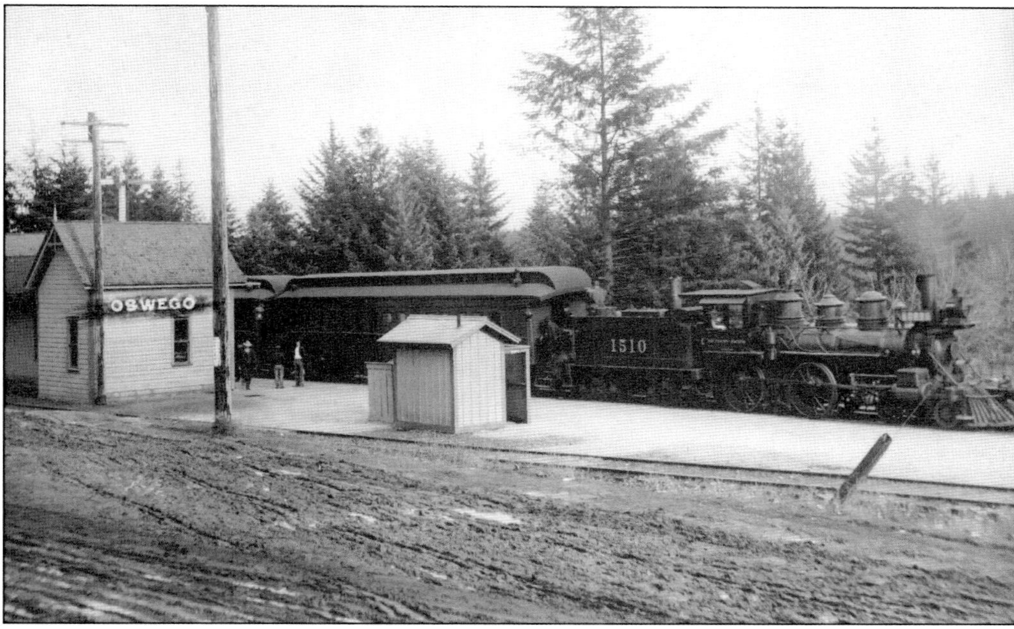

Train at Oswego Depot. The conductor leans out to watch passengers disembark. A businessman climbs down the steps at Oswego Station sometime before 1912, when this rail line was electrified and the steam engines went elsewhere. The name on the engine reads "Southern Pacific."

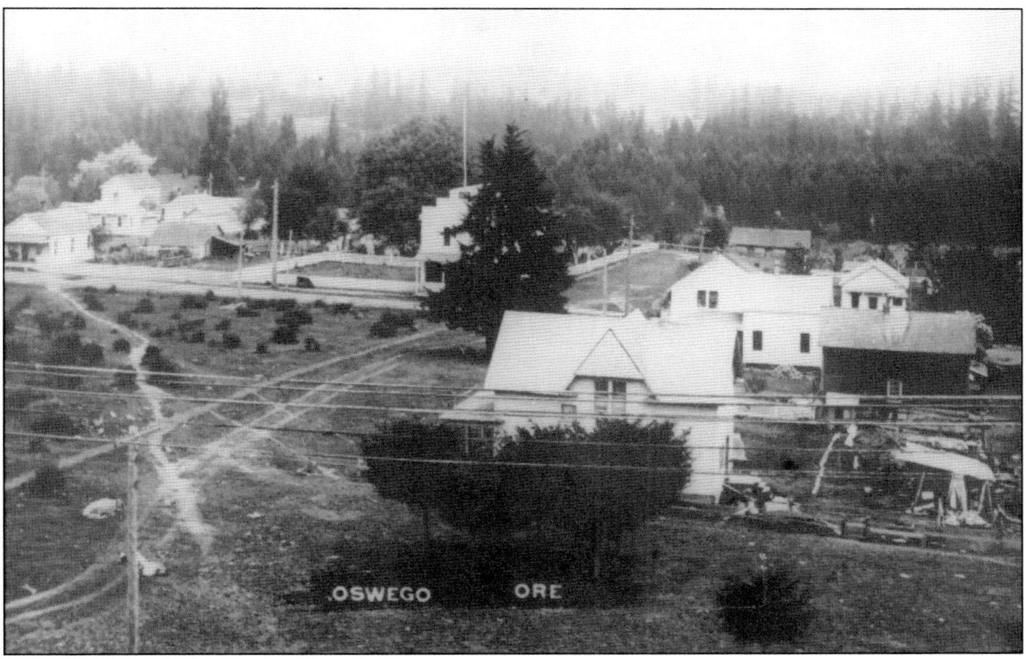

Old Town Oswego, Looking East. This 1900 photograph was probably taken from the public school at State and Wilbur Streets. The path leads to the post office at Prosser's Store on Durham Street. The Odd Fellows Hall is in the center top, partly obscured by a Douglas fir. At this point in time, the town was in the doldrums, with only the pipe foundry working, and intermittently at that.

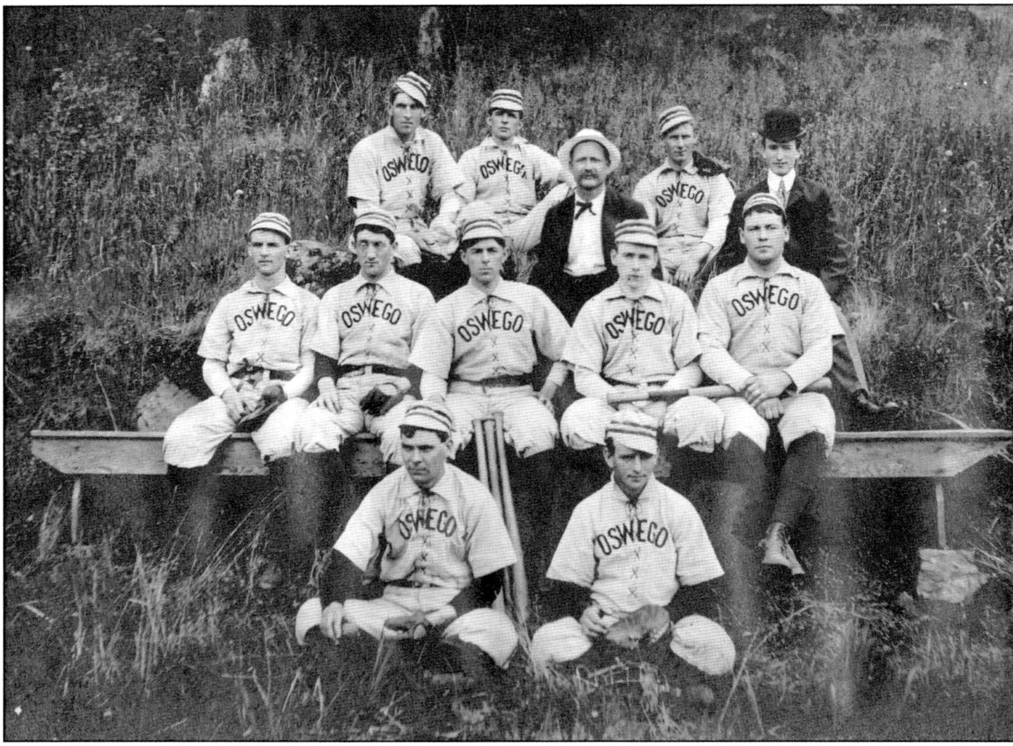

OSWEGO BALL PLAYERS. Note the lace-up uniforms on this 1900 team of ballplayers. The gentleman on the right top is dressed smartly; perhaps he is the businessman who sponsors the team. Modern baseball caps had not yet evolved. Ball games were played on the field seen on the next page.

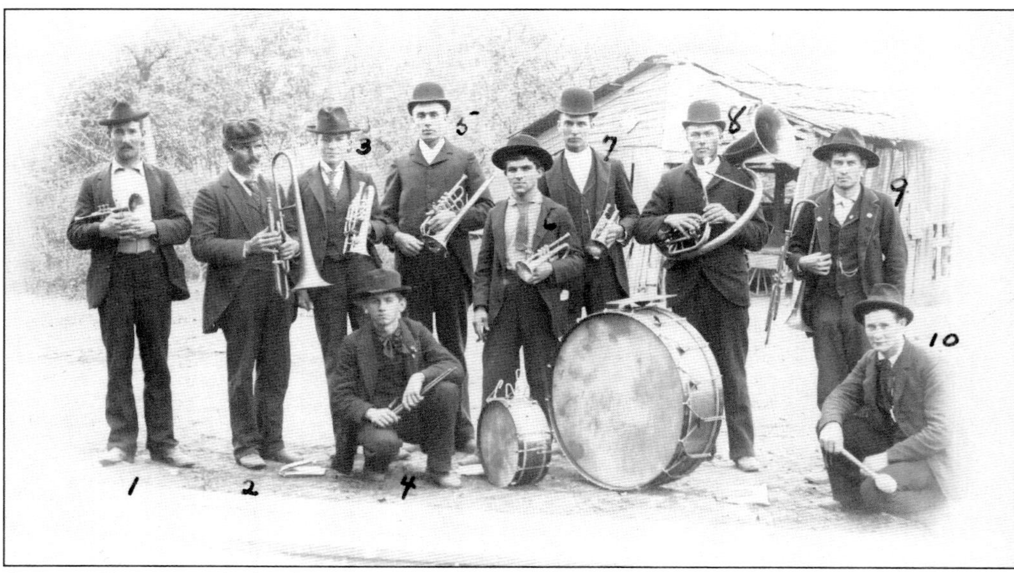

OSWEGO BAND. With the furnace closing in 1894, the men in this 1896 band may have taken much comfort in their music and camaraderie. Their names, as corresponding to the numbers on the image, are Tom Clinefeller, Cornelius DeBauw, John Bickner, Deward Fox, Henry Bickner, Mort Edwards, William Bickner, Joe Bickner, Walter Todd, and John Fox.

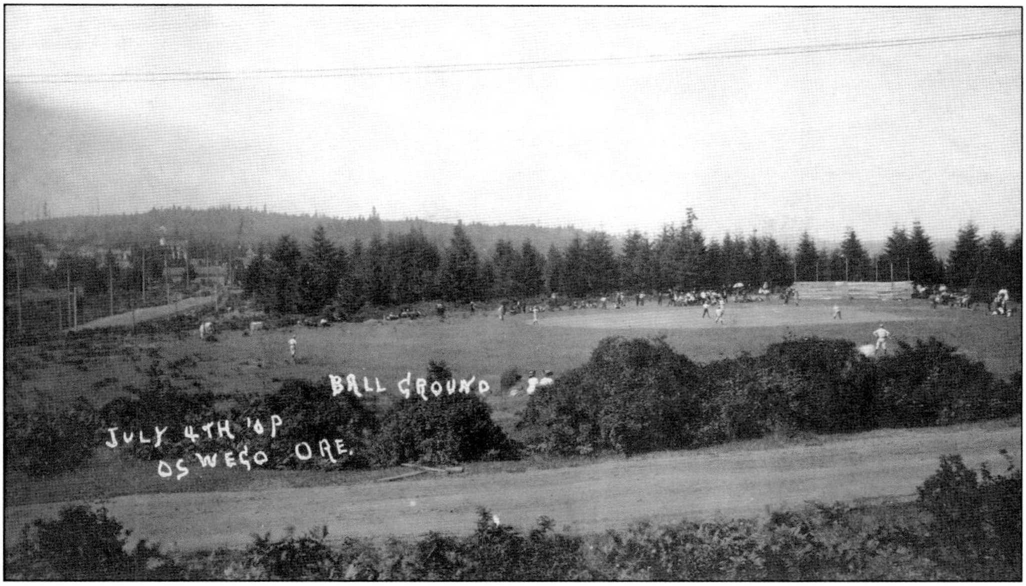

BALL FIELD, OLD TOWN. This scene was photographed on July 4, 1909, in Old Town, looking north. State Street is on the left. A good-size crowd watches, including a few cows just beyond right field. Note the crude backstop of haphazardly nailed boards.

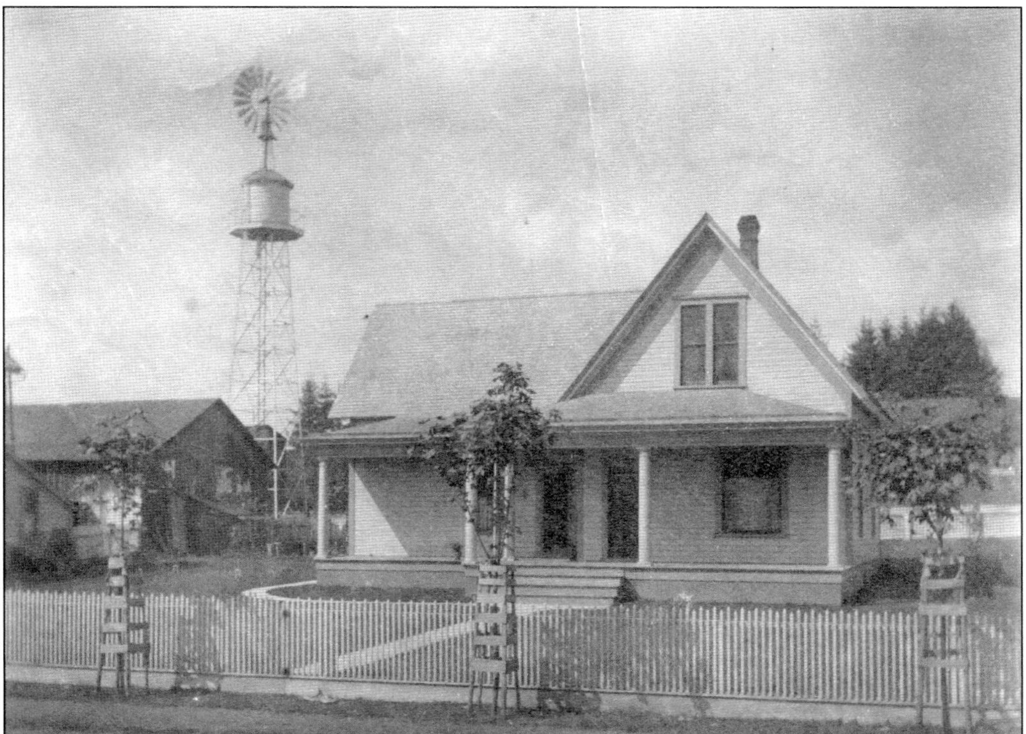

NEW TOWN HOUSE, WATER TOWER. This is the John Bickner home at the corner of State Street and B Avenue in New Town in 1905. John is seen on page 54 in the band. The water tower indicates the Bickners had their own well. Many homes in New Town still relied on wells at this time.

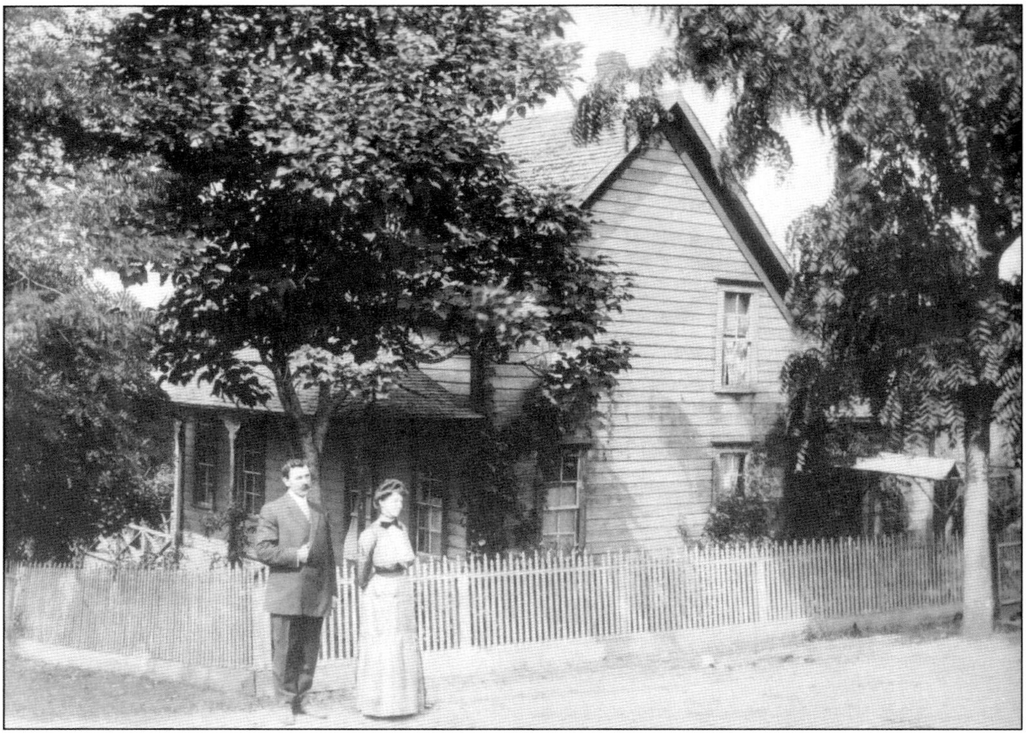

Fenced Yard in Town. Agnes Nelson Cox and her husband, Samuel, stand in front of their South Town home on Ash Street in 1910. Note the fenced yard, common for town houses at this time to keep the family cow from wandering.

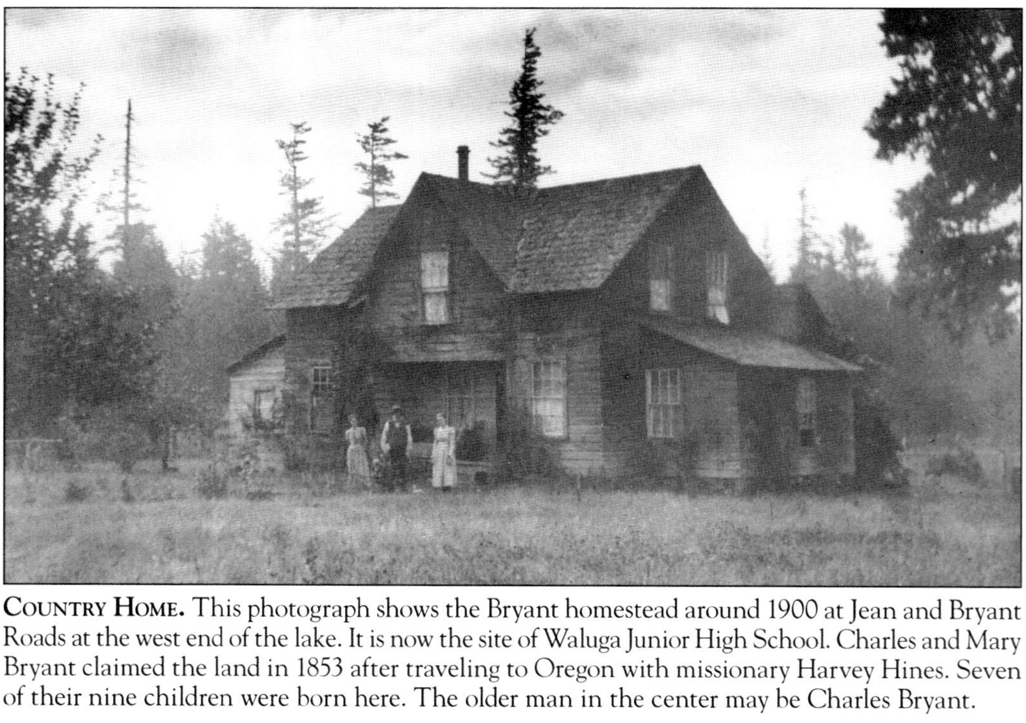

Country Home. This photograph shows the Bryant homestead around 1900 at Jean and Bryant Roads at the west end of the lake. It is now the site of Waluga Junior High School. Charles and Mary Bryant claimed the land in 1853 after traveling to Oregon with missionary Harvey Hines. Seven of their nine children were born here. The older man in the center may be Charles Bryant.

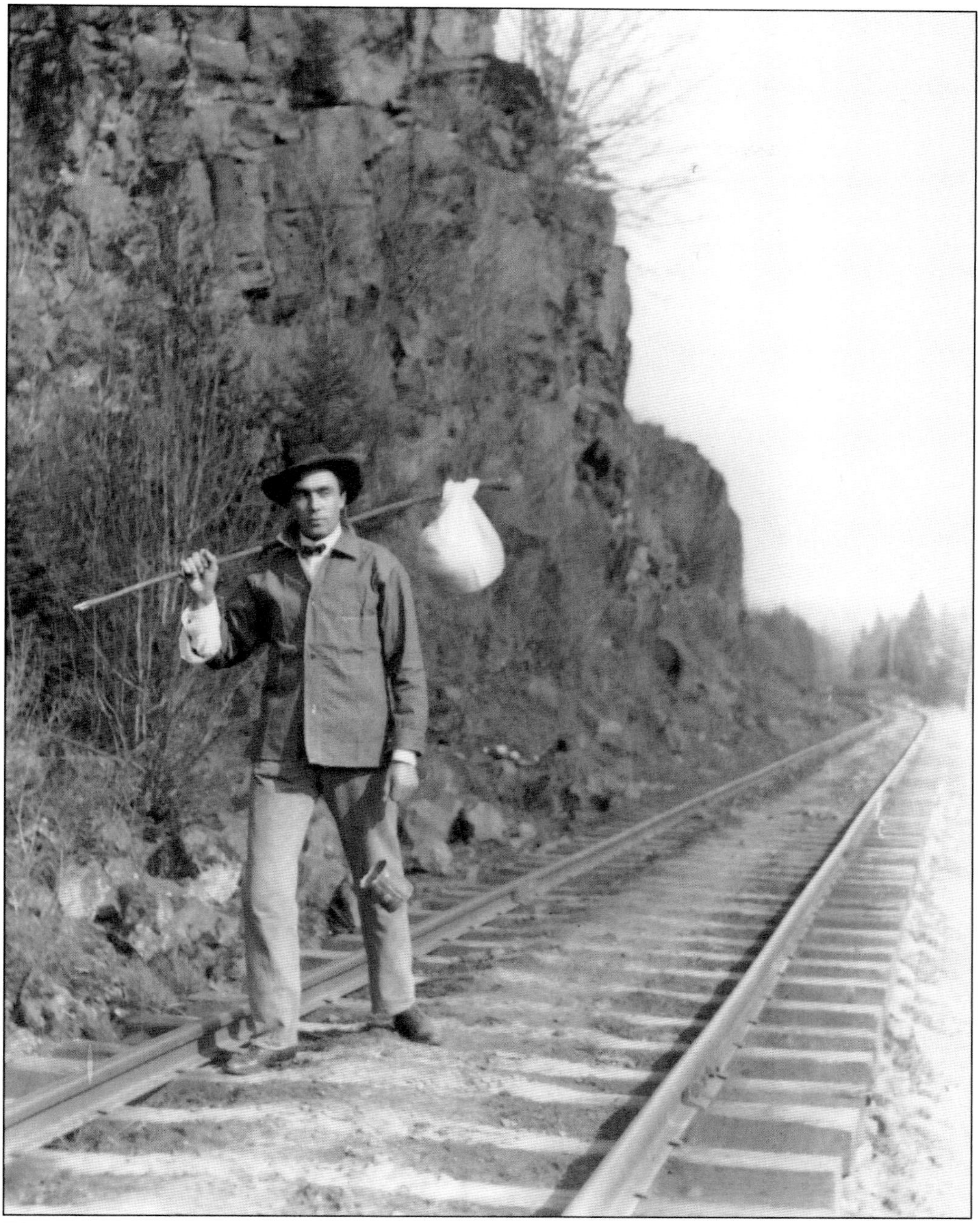

WALKING THE RAILS. In the 1890s, the nation was in recession and Oswego was suffering from hundreds of jobs lost when the iron furnace closed for good. Men would often walk 5 miles one way to Oregon City for work at the mills there. It was also common to walk into Portland, a distance of 7 miles, simply for a Sunday outing with friends. This gentleman appears to be too well dressed to be a hobo. His collar is freshly starched, he wears a tie, and his sleeves have tidy cuffs. With his cup and his lunch, presumably, tied to a stick, he looks to be out for a daylong adventure or perhaps is walking to find work for the day. He would have found water at the many springs or streams entering the Willamette from the hills on its west bank.

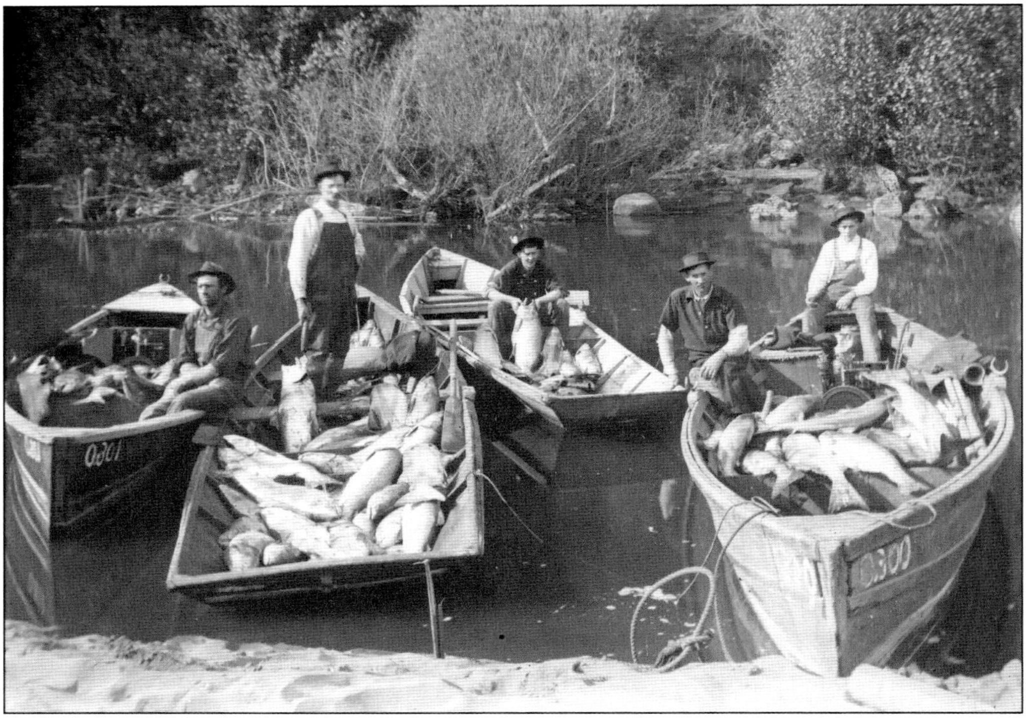

SALMON, SUCKER CREEK. Longtime Oswego resident Charlie Didzun remembered that around 1900 fishermen at the mouth of Sucker Creek (Oswego Creek) would catch one ton of salmon each night at the beginning of salmon season. The meat sold for 10¢ to 15¢ per pound. This photograph dates from 1905. The men are, from left to right, Rollie Worthington, Isaac "Ike" Austin, Ed Erickson, Otto Larson, and Willie Austin.

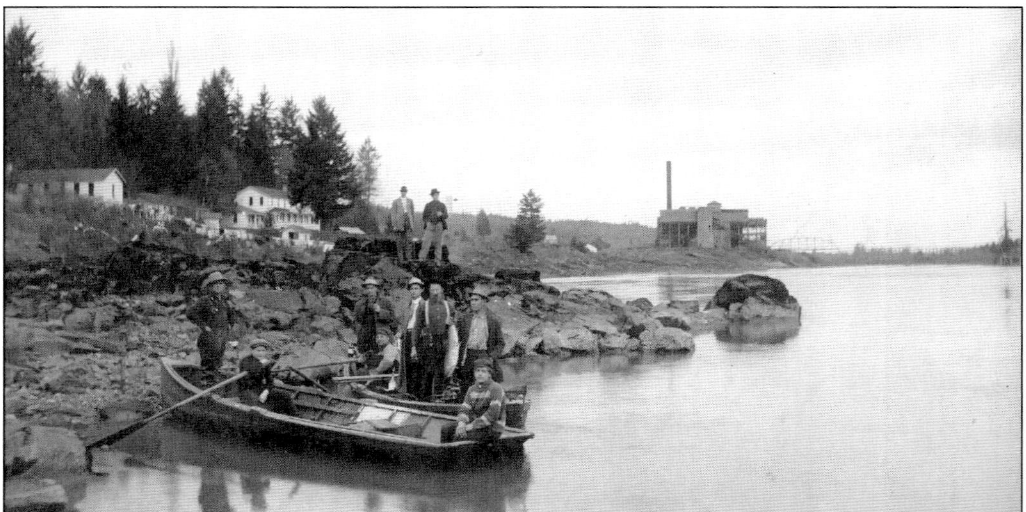

FISHING THE WILLAMETTE. The second furnace, shut down at this point (around 1910–1920), is in the background. Men, with liquor bottles in the boat and in hand, show off the catch. Not all appear to be fishermen; some are dressed in formal collars and ties. In the background, houses of Old Town Oswego are visible, with clothes on a clothesline. The 1909 rail bridge is in the distance.

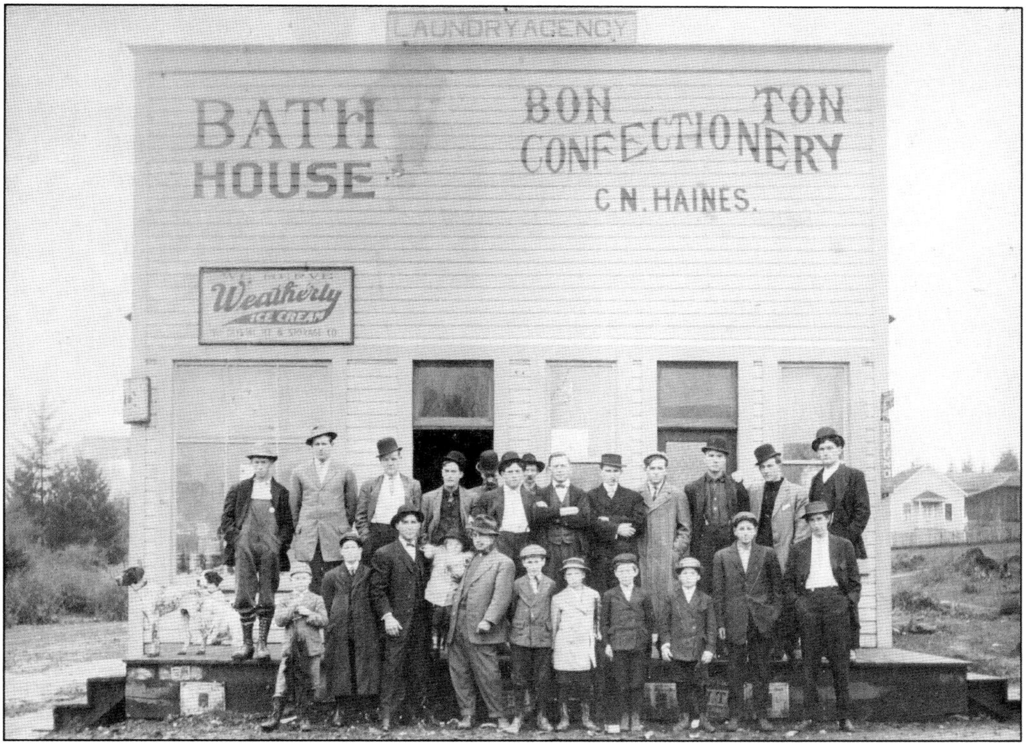

Bathhouse and More. This multitasking building was on the northwest corner of First Street and A Avenue. The photographer did not label the people's names, but the dogs are Sport and Heinie. Men living in Oswego's hotels for single workers could have their clothes cleaned at the laundry while they took care of their personal hygiene at the bathhouse. Afterwards, Weatherly Ice cream capped off the day.

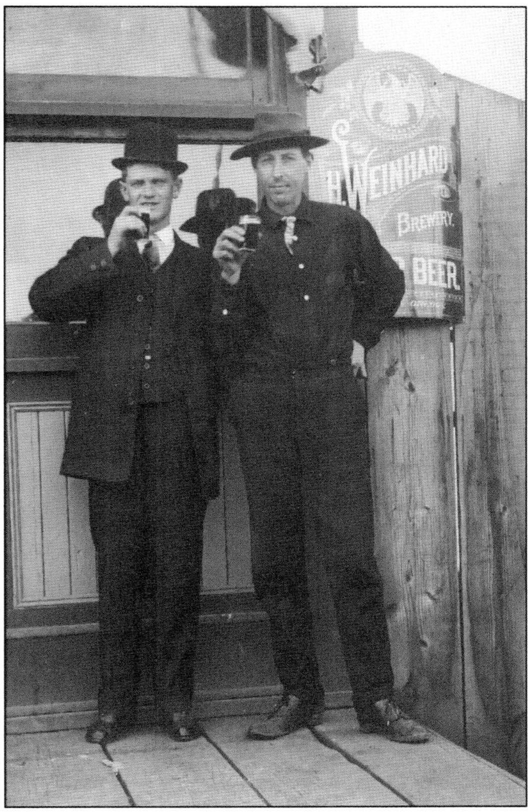

Percy Mosier's Saloon. At this saloon at State Street and A Avenue (later the site of George Rogers's store), men raise a toast. Mrs. Howard Pettinger remembered in a 1973 interview about a similar saloon: "It was to McFarland's saloon the men from the furnaces and the foundry flocked on pay-day nights to cash their checks . . . few got out with enough money to pay the grocery bill or to buy shoes for the children."

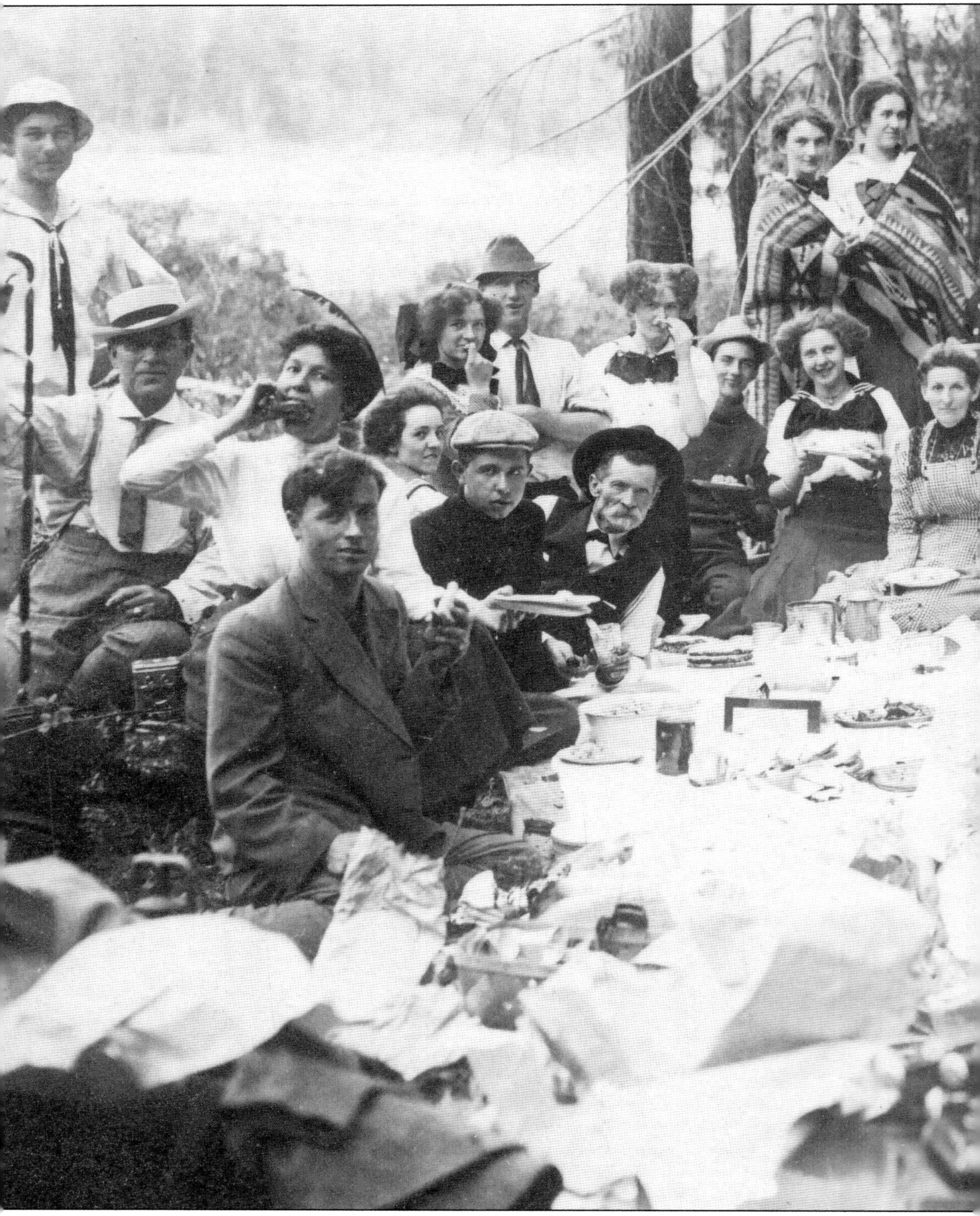

A Lakeshore Picnic. In 1908, friends gather for a picnic. Note the two women in back wrapped in Pendleton blankets, the Victrola at the bottom right, and the dog sleeping in front of it. It was at such a picnic in 1910, Herbert Nelson recalled, that the Ladds and Corbetts, of the Ladd Estate Company, first hatched the plan to develop the lake. They hired Herbert and his friends to row them up the lake that day. "We rowed them up to the head of the lake three miles. Being thrifty

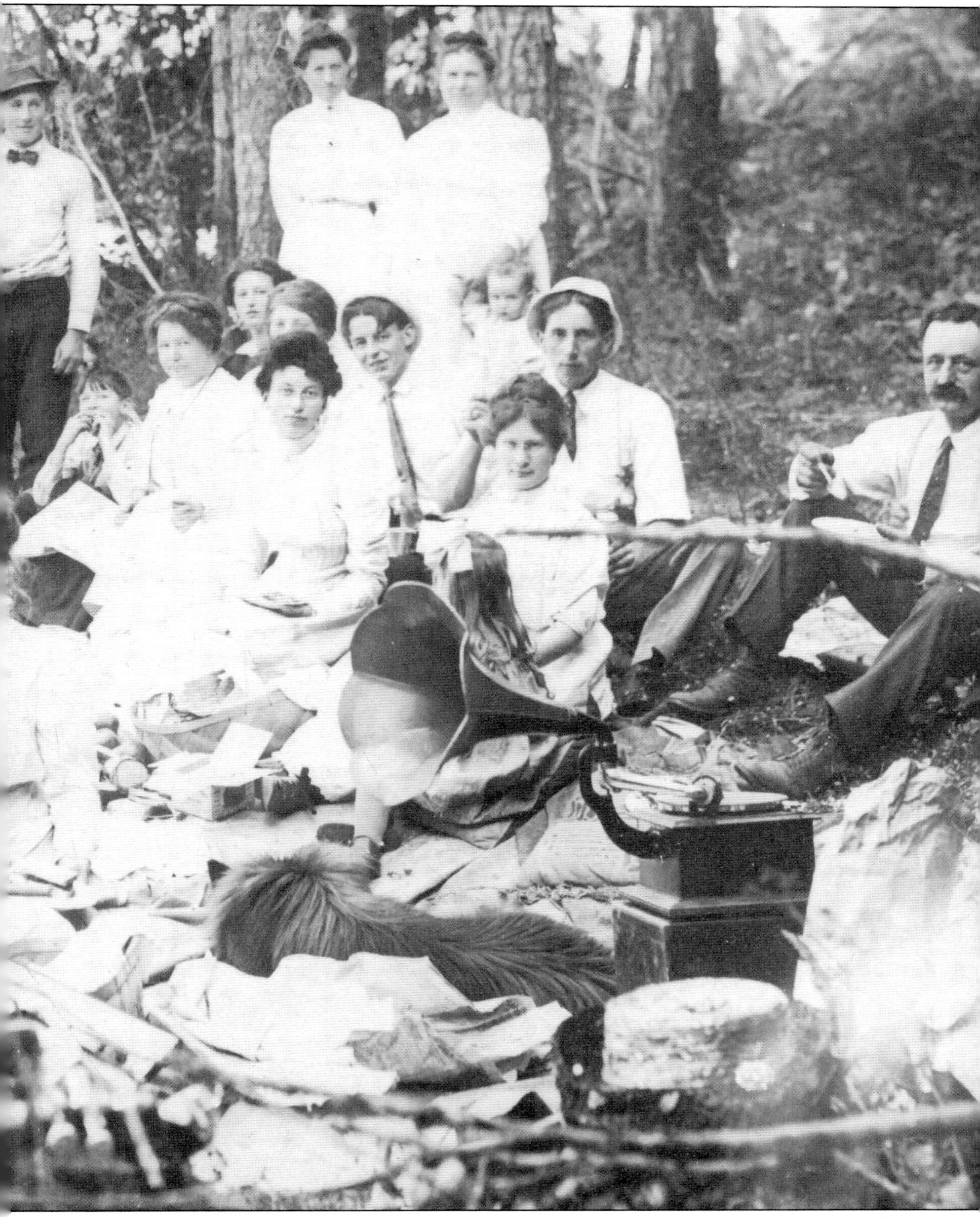

people, they wouldn't have any use for the boats during the day so they let us take the two big boats back. I think on that date the Ladds and the Corbetts had a picnic . . . to see if anything could be done with Oswego Lake, if it was worth anything. The next year they hired surveyors and in 1912 they put it on the market."

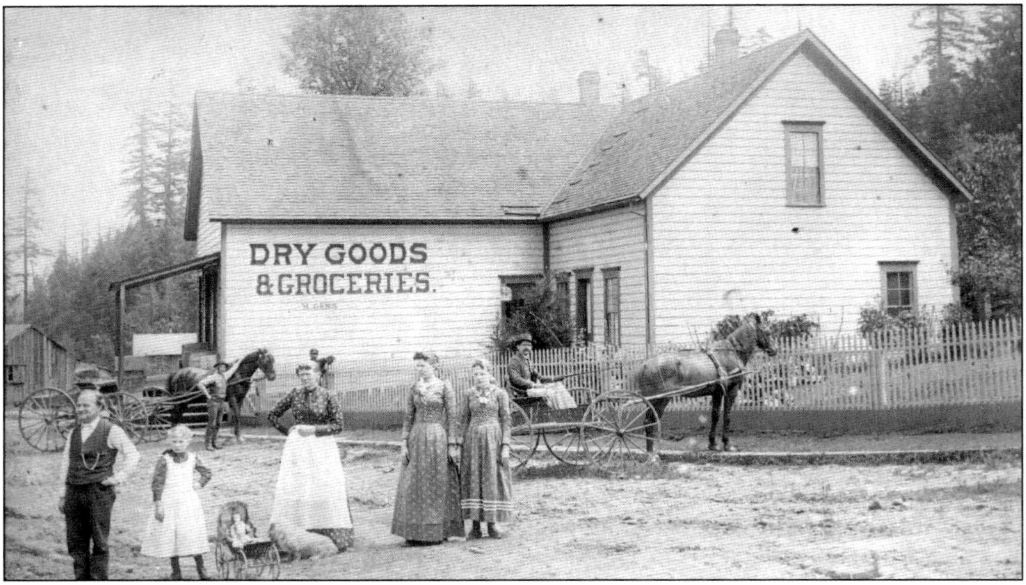

South Town Store. This photograph from 1890 shows the Bickner store in South Oswego. "H. Gans" is painted on it, the name of the former owner. Dr. Sullivan is in the buggy; standing left to right are Henry, Rose, and Clara Gans; Mary Bickner; and Lillian Gans.

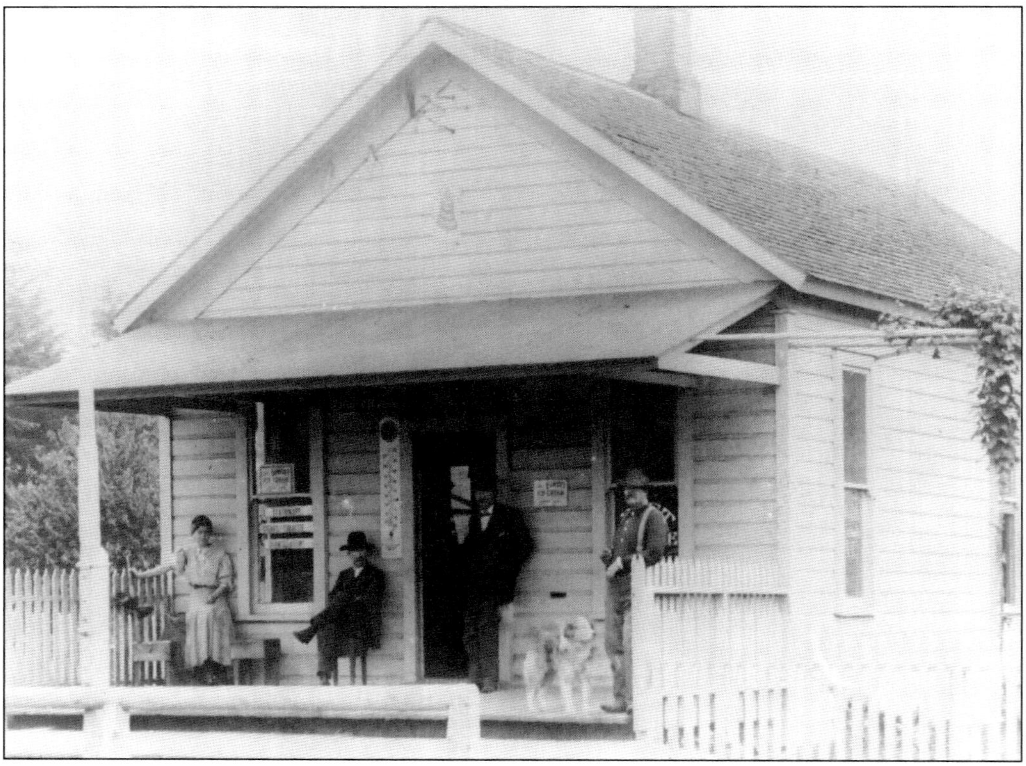

First Post Office. The Prosser store and post office was on Durham Street between Church and Leonard Streets and is seen here *c.* 1910. It can be seen on page 53 from a greater distance. A bell sign, likely to indicate telephone access was inside, is at the gable end; above it, telephone lines are attached to the building.

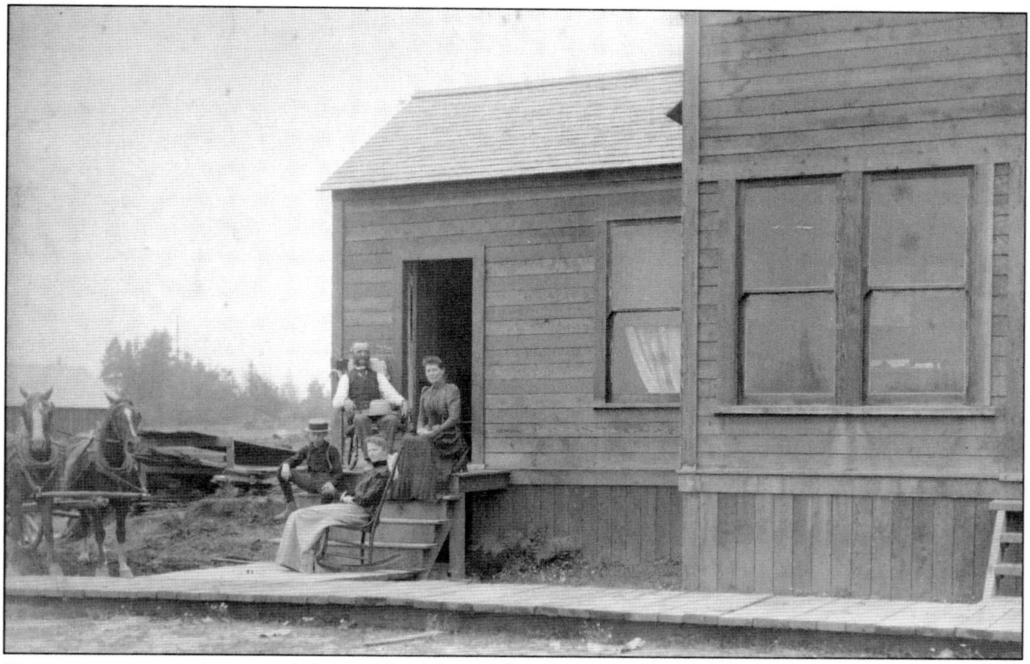

Relaxing at the Lumber Yard. The Mintie family owned the lumberyard on State Street. In this *c.* 1900 photograph, Eleanor Mintie relaxes on a wooden sidewalk in her rocker in front of her parents, Mr. and Mrs. Fergus Mintie. They lived above the store until they built a home on Fourth Street and A Avenue in New Town.

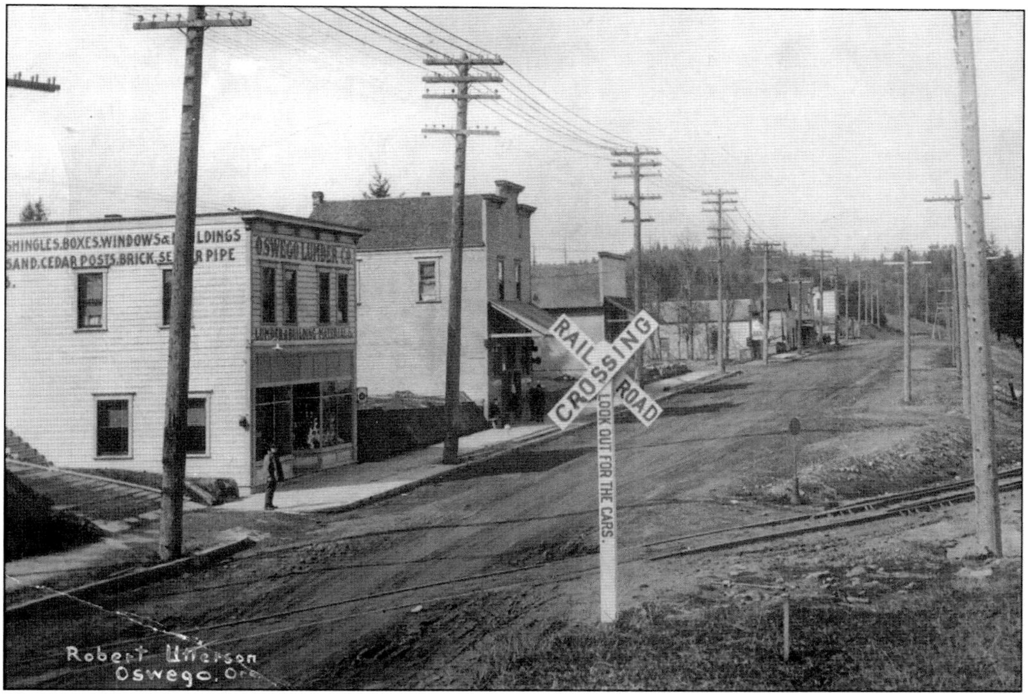

State Street Looking North. Oswego Lumber Company is on the left of this 1910 photograph in a new and improved store building from the one pictured above. Note the new concrete sidewalk. The road would not be paved for another 10 years.

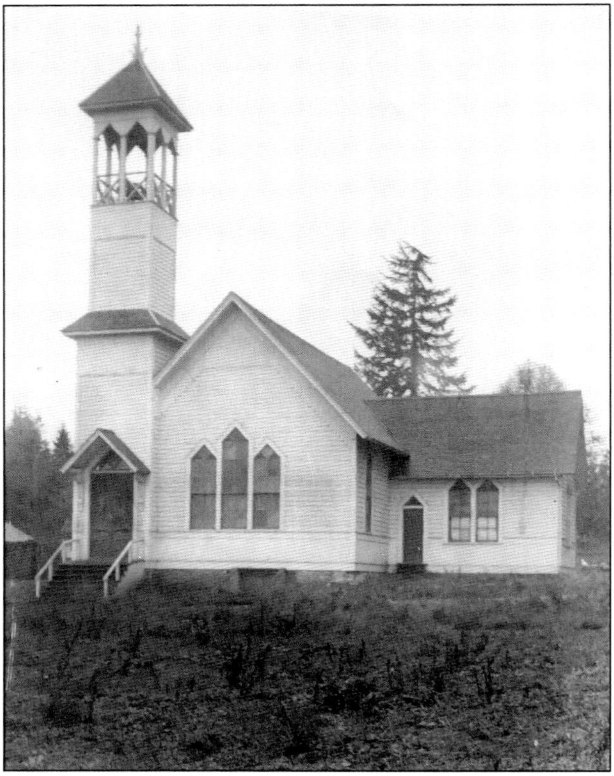

Congregational Church. The beautiful Carpenter Gothic style was used for the Congregational Church at Fourth Street and D Avenue. The site is now the Lake Oswego Public Library.

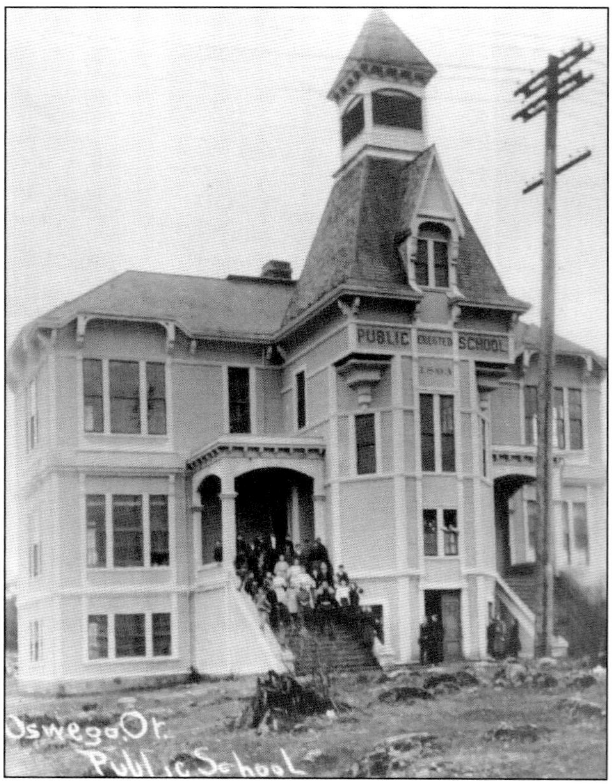

Oswego Public School. This building replaced the Grange Hall School. It was built in 1893; note the stumps in the front yard, likely grubbed out soon after this by some of the school's bigger boys. The site today is the Lakewood Center for the Arts, on State Street.

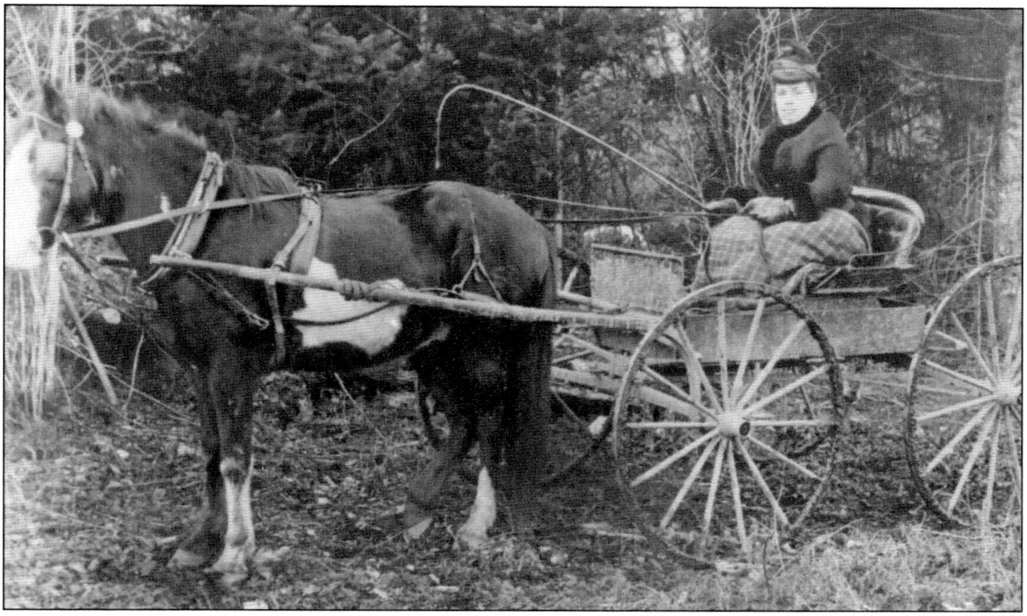

Mrs. Marks and Carriage. This 1893 photograph shows the raw state of Oswego roads before the use of rock aggregate paving materials. The lack of a smooth ride does not seem to intimidate Mrs. Marks, a formidable-looking woman.

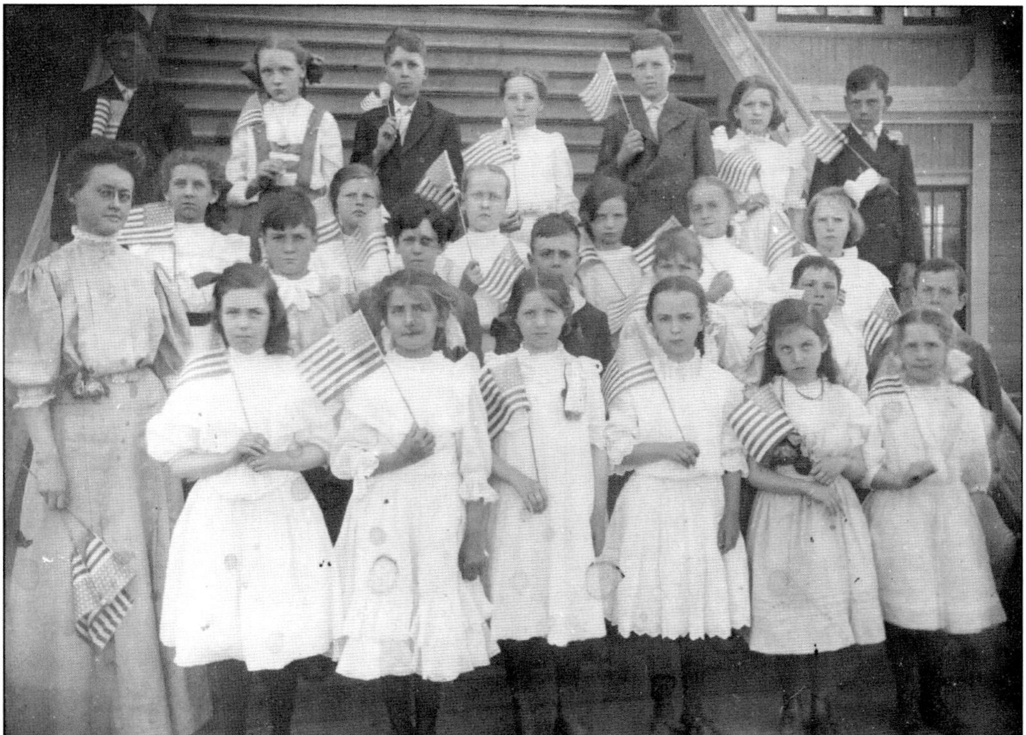

Third Graders and Teacher. This 1906 class of identically dressed third graders was taught by Edna Kincaid, who after she married William Bickner (seen on page 54 with his band) stopped teaching, a typical move for a woman of that era.

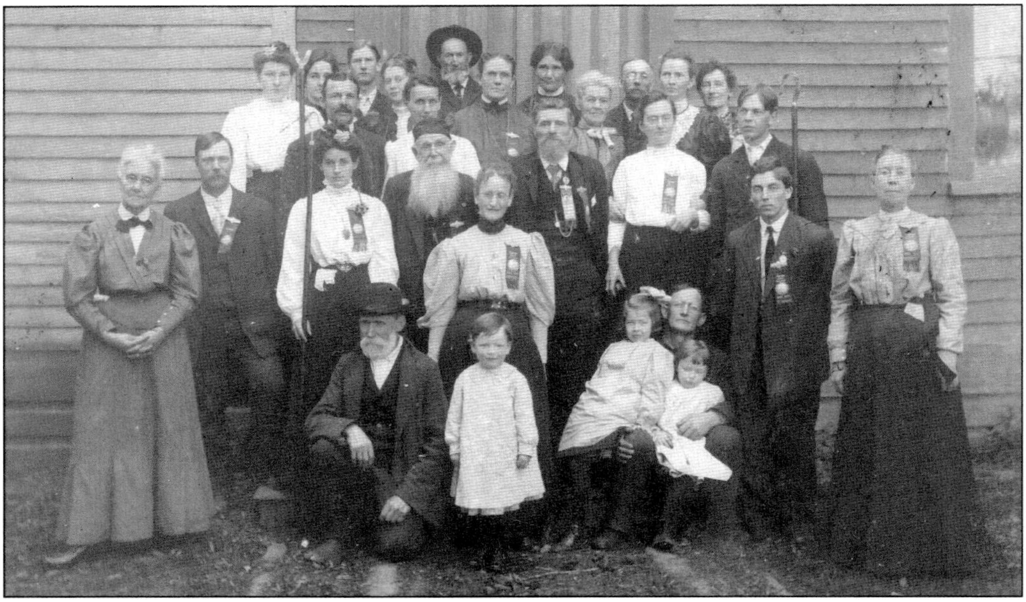

Oswego Grange Members. Oswego's Grange Hall was on Furnace and Leonard Streets. The Grange (or the Order of Patrons of Husbandry) is a fraternal organization for farmers. Founded in 1867, peak membership came in the 1890s to 1950s. "Grange" derives from the Latin for "grain." In this c. 1895 photograph (based on the leg o' mutton sleeves on one woman), members pose with shepherd's staffs, typical of the small, ceremonial farm tools often displayed at Grange functions.

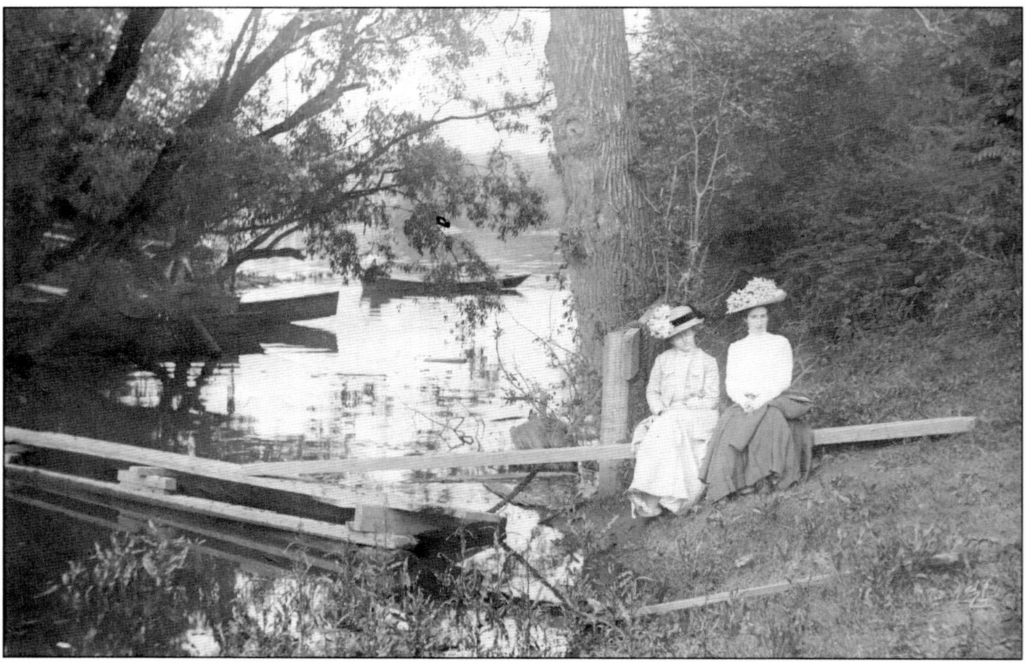

Friends at Tryon Creek. Edna Bickner and Maude Zimmerman enjoy a picturesque setting in 1908 a short walk from Edna's home (seen on page 84.) Today the creek just above its confluence with the Willamette River travels through a culvert under Highway 43 and the railroad tracks. Note the large black cottonwood behind the women, a common tree along waterways.

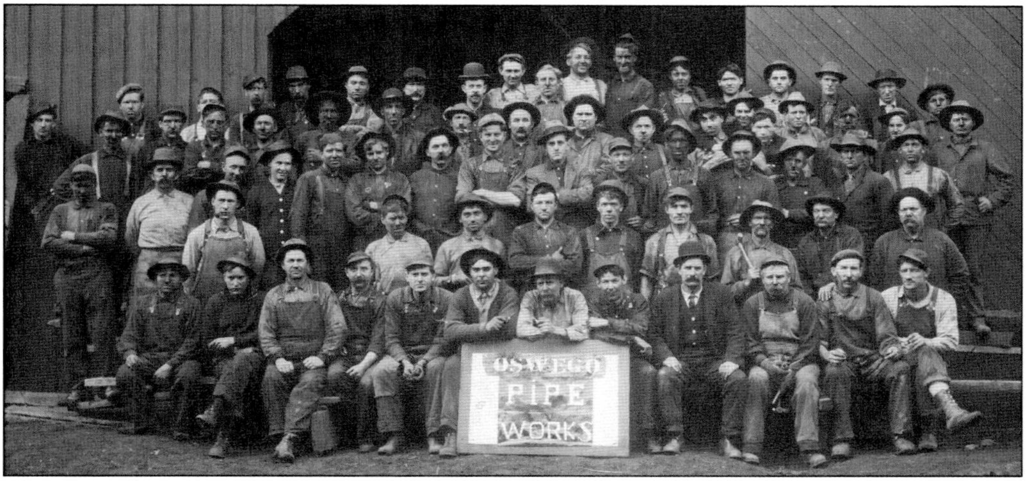

PIPE FOUNDRY MEN AFTER WORK. Some of the men's faces are totally blackened with soot. The plant manager sits in the front row.

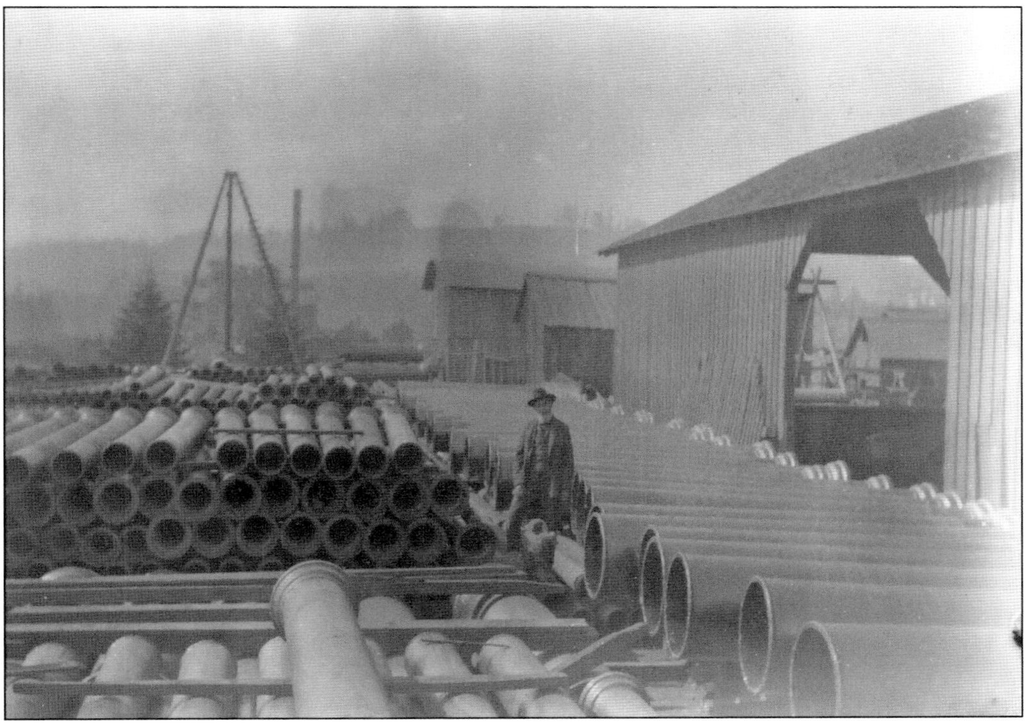

PIPE FOUNDRY OUTPUT. After the red-hot iron was poured in the mold and around the clay core, the pipe would set in the mold a few hours to cool. When the pipe was pulled out of the mold, the clay had to be beaten out of its center with a large wooden hammer. (The clay was reused.) After removal of the clay, the pipe would be tarred. Each pipe was dipped into the tar pit on site and a crane would lift it out. It would be tested under water pressure, then weighed and shipped by rail. Besides the water pipe it purchased from the foundry, Seattle bought gas and gasoline pipe as well.

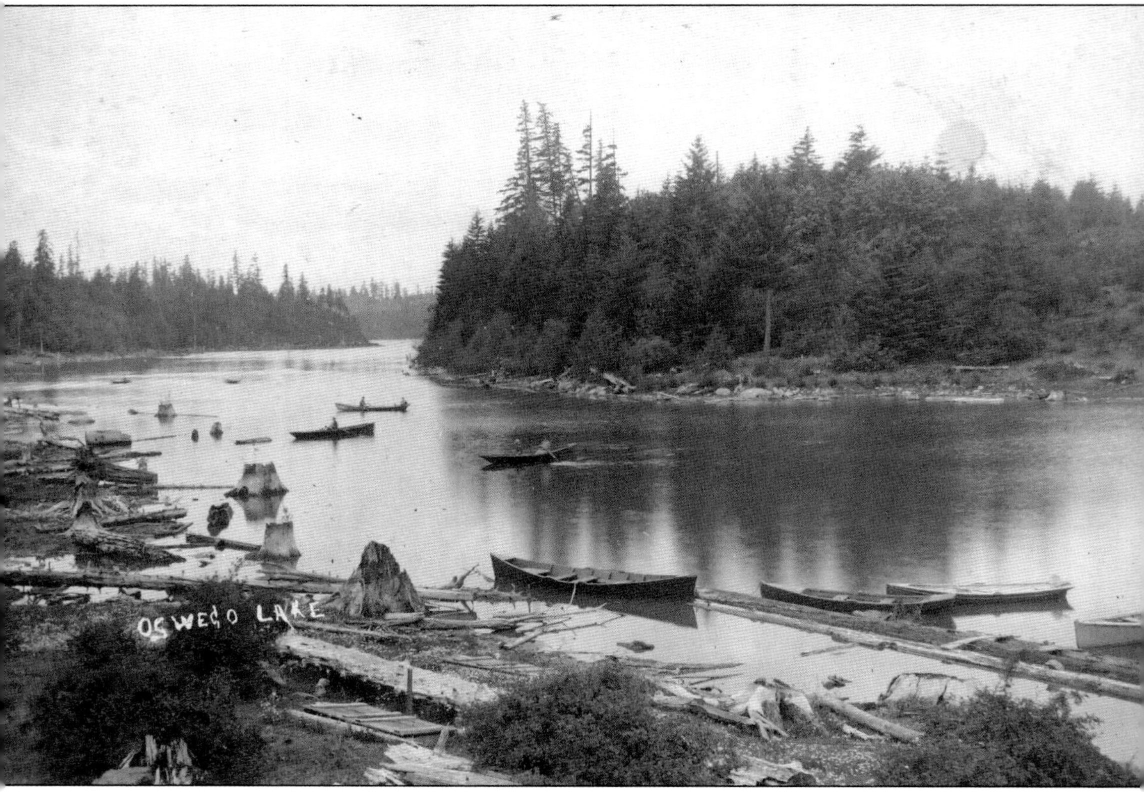

Boats upon the Lake. This *c.* 1910 image shows a still-wild lake with boats rented from David Nelson's concession dotting the waters near the lake's east end. In 1973, David's son Herbert Nelson remembered, "Since we lived so near the lake, only a couple of blocks away, eventually we got hold of an old boat and for a long time we had the only boat around there because the lake was absolutely neglected. Oswego people never went near the lake." He said someone stocked it with bass, which provided more impetus for sport fishermen from Portland to visit the lake. "They would come out on Sunday morning and would race to see who would be there first to get our boat. So my mother said, 'I believe some money could be made by putting some boats on the lake.'" In this image, there is not even a dock yet; boats are chained up and float among the downed trees.

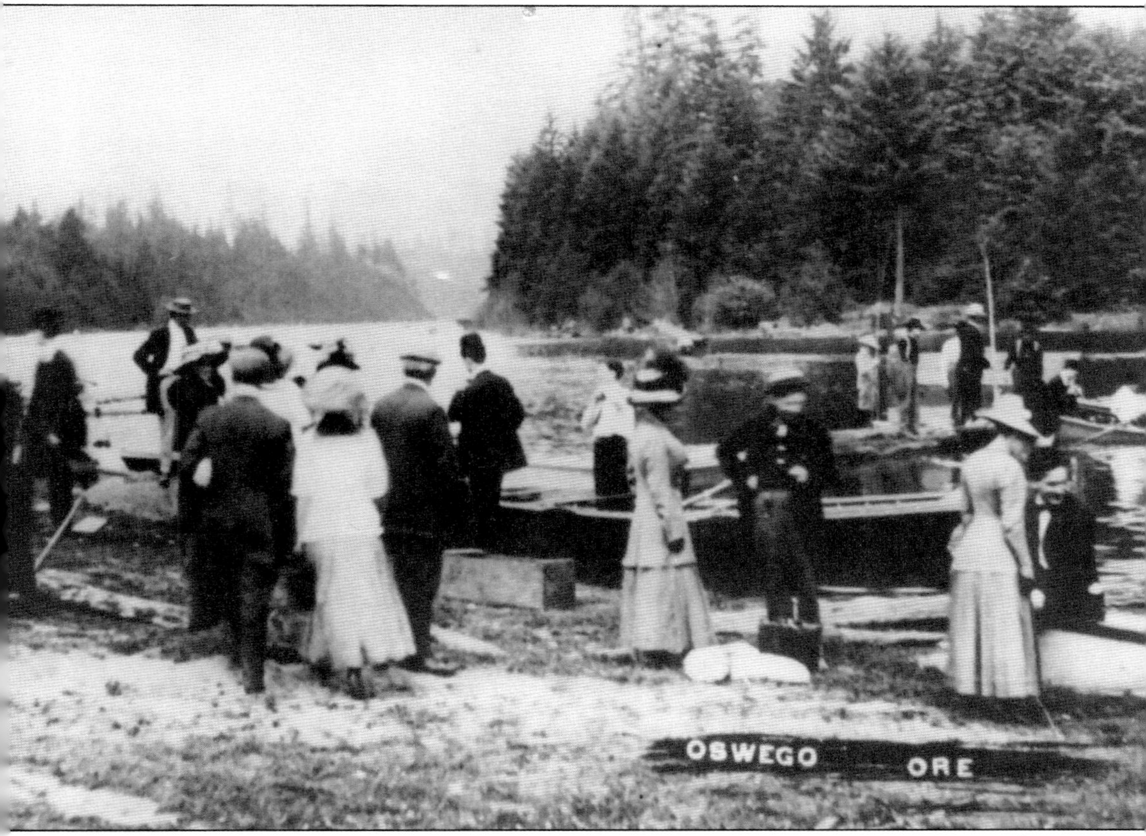

Renting Boats. Oregon Iron and Steel made David Nelson caretaker of the lake. Herbert Nelson said, "Dad could collect money from everybody who wanted to come up there and squat on the lake and charge them a small amount for ground rent. So a lot of people went around in the brush and put up a shack or maybe just a tent to camp for a few days. Some of them put up regular shacks and some were occupied for years."

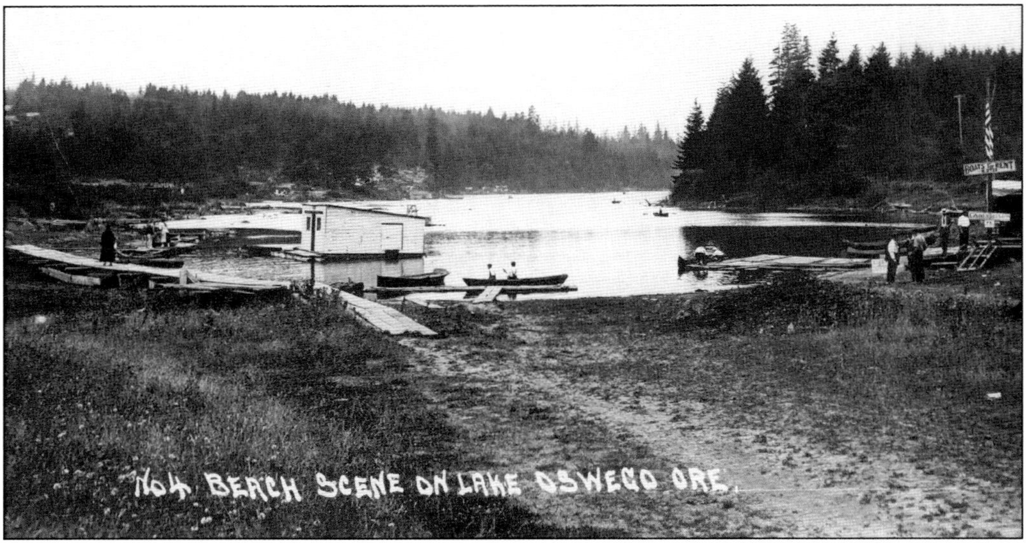

Boat Concession, Lake's East End. Here the boating concession has advanced a bit, with wooden docks and a small boathouse, and there is some evidence of crude structures in the woods. On the far right under an American flag, signs read: "Live Minnows for Sale," "Canoes for Rent," and "Boats for Rent–H. Dyer." Houses of South Oswego are visible on the hillside to the left.

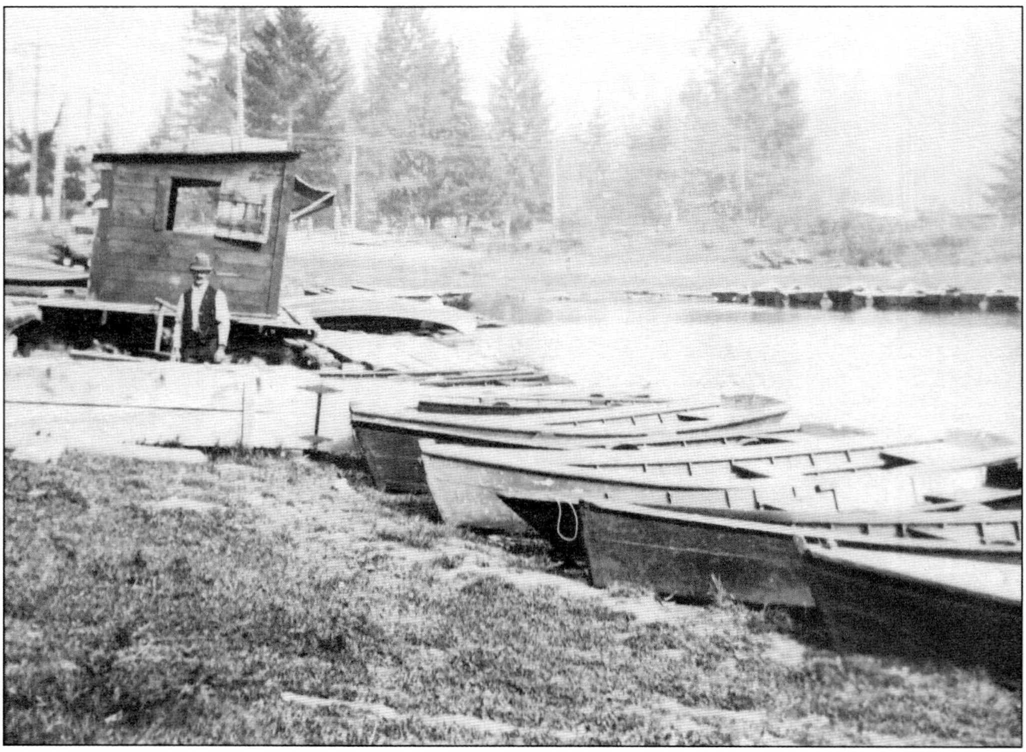

Before the Tourists Arrive. Nellie Nelson Kyle recalled that her family had the first telephone in town, in 1910, because of the booming boat business: "The telephone was a necessity because of our lake business with the reservations that the people had to make in order for them to get their boats and canoes and to reserve the tents and cottages for the summer."

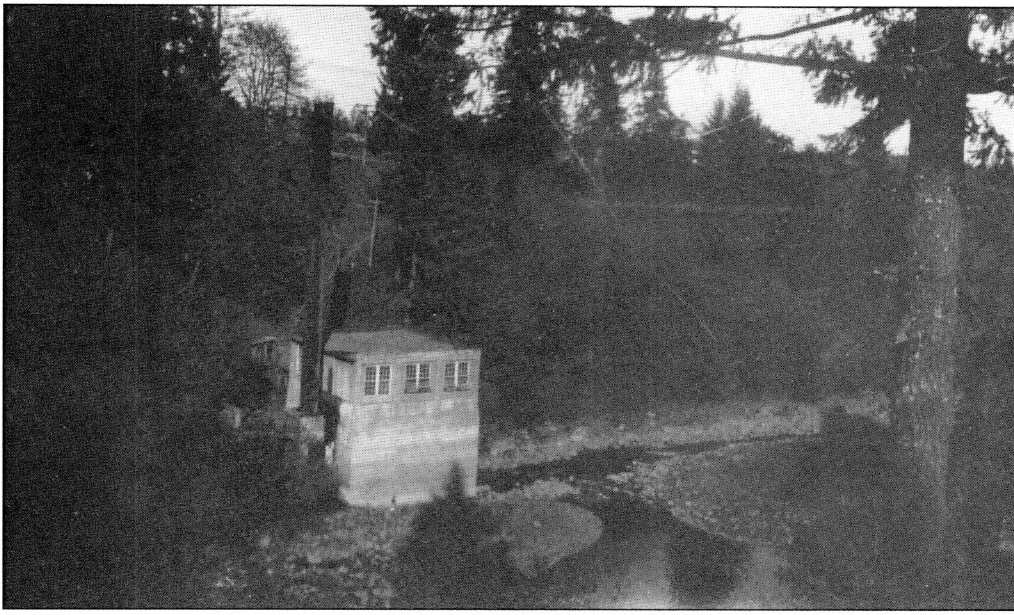

Electric Power Plant. Built around 1910 by Oregon Iron and Steel, this power plant generated Oswego's first electricity and continues to do so using water from Oswego Creek. It is owned by the Lake Oswego Corporation today, which has a Tualatin River water right to generate power at this site. Although in Oswego power lines had been part of the landscape for a few decades, bringing power to Portland from Willamette Falls, it was not until 1910 that Oswego itself was electrified.

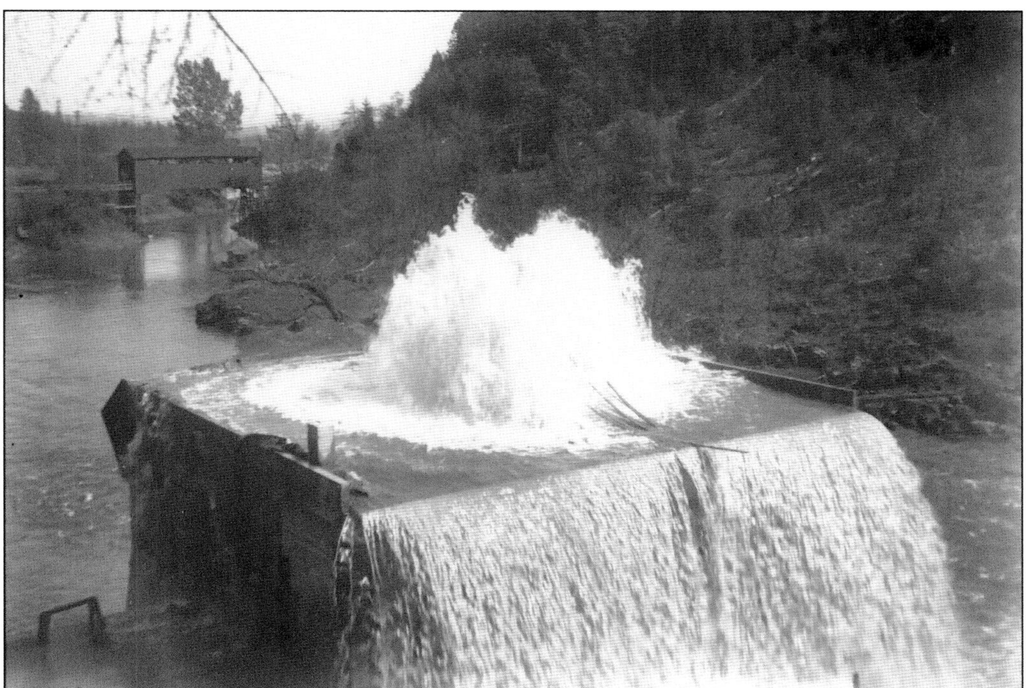

Power Plant Overwhelmed. The power plant, lacking a surge protector, so to speak, has its top blown out during high water. The bridge over McVey Avenue is in the background.

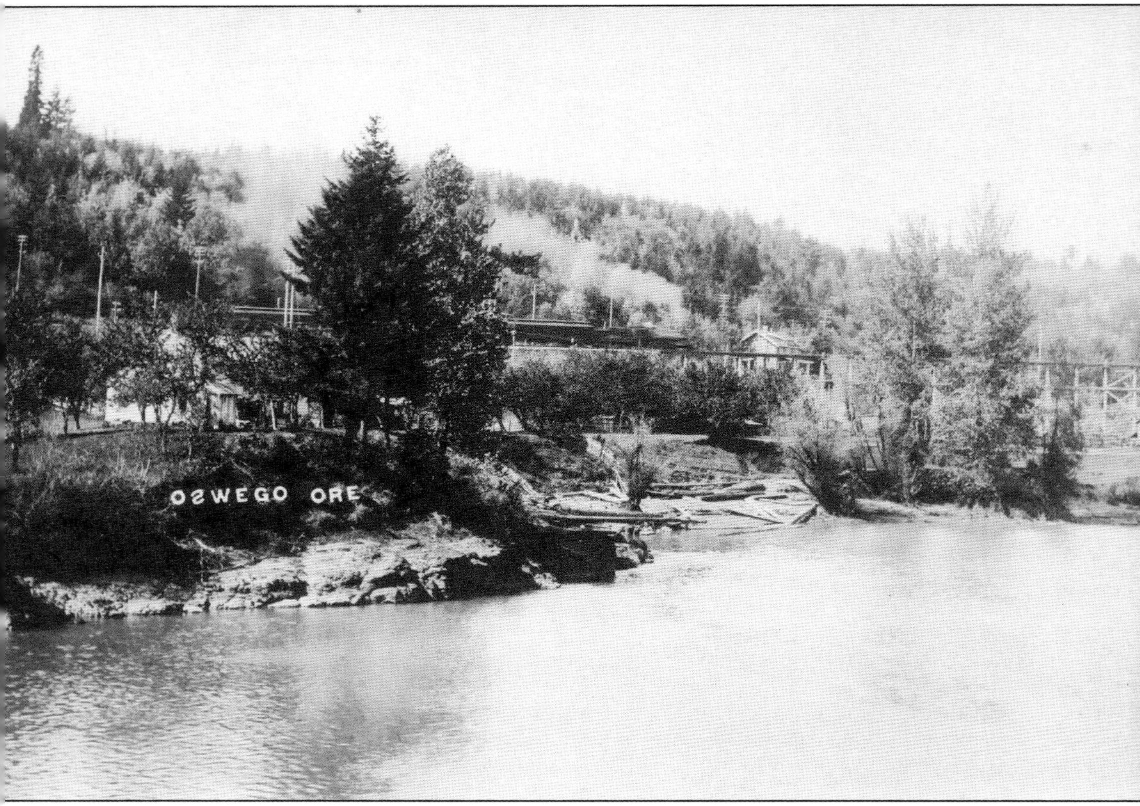

Bridge Crosses Willamette. In 1910, a cement plant was planned for the former Oregon Iron and Steel furnace works site, and the economy began to look up. Tangible evidence of this was the new Southern Pacific Railroad bridge from Oswego to Milwaukie. It was built because Portland city planners did not want freight traffic rumbling through downtown Portland. After this bridge was built, northbound traffic would cross the river at Oswego, travel the east bank of the Willamette, and cross back over it on the Steel Bridge (built in 1912) to the rail yards (or continue north to the Albina yards on the east bank). It crosses the Willamette just north of the mouth of Tryon Creek. Here a train is on a trestle over the bottomland next to the river, just west of the bridge.

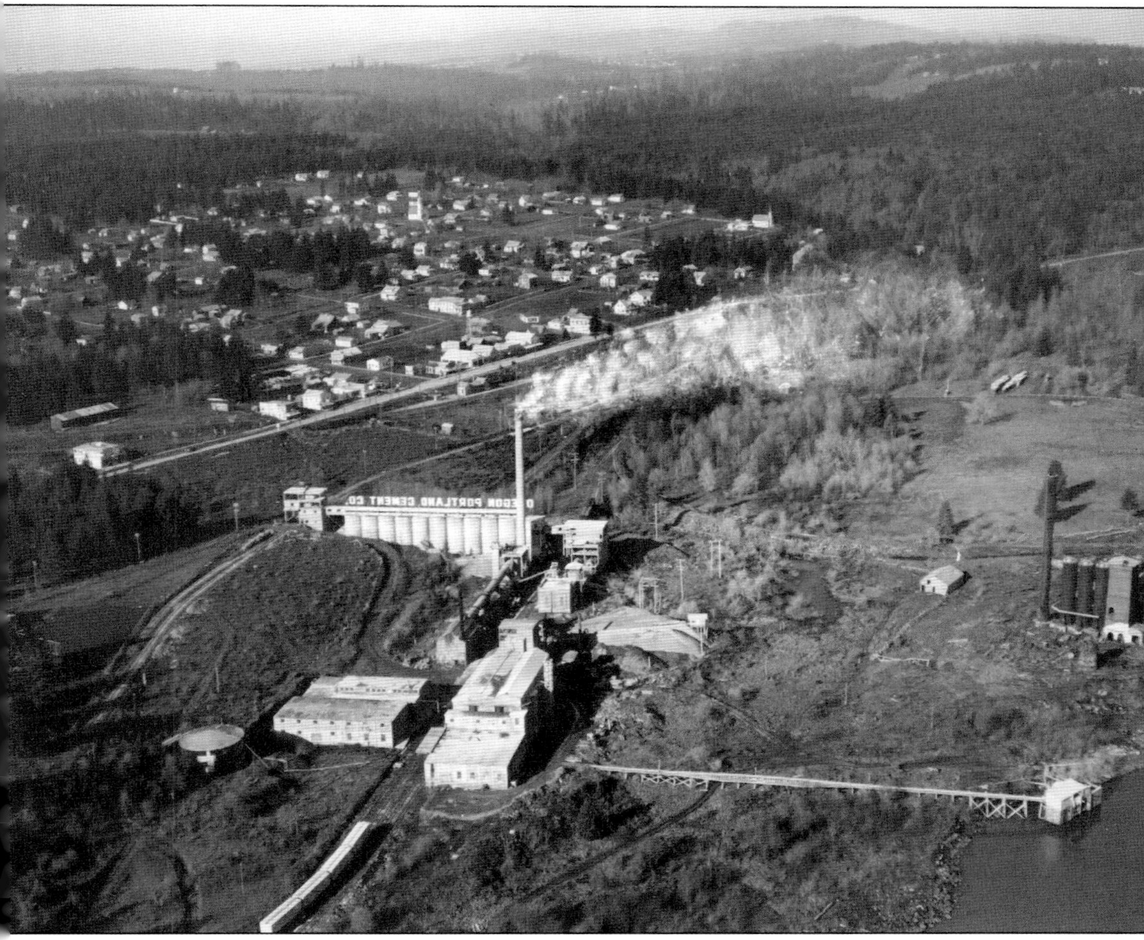

CEMENT PLANT. The cement plant was Oswego's first new industry in over two decades. In 1916, the plant produced its first batch of cement. Despite the dust and noise, the town was elated at the presence of a large new employer. One investor was Robert Butchart, whose wife Jennie created the now-famous Butchart Gardens from a former quarry on Vancouver Island. The plant's name, the Oregon Portland Cement Company, had nothing to do with the town of Portland, Oregon. Portland Cement was developed in England in the early 1800s; the name comes from the cement's similarity to Portland stone, a white-gray limestone quarried on the Isle of Portland in Dorset, England.

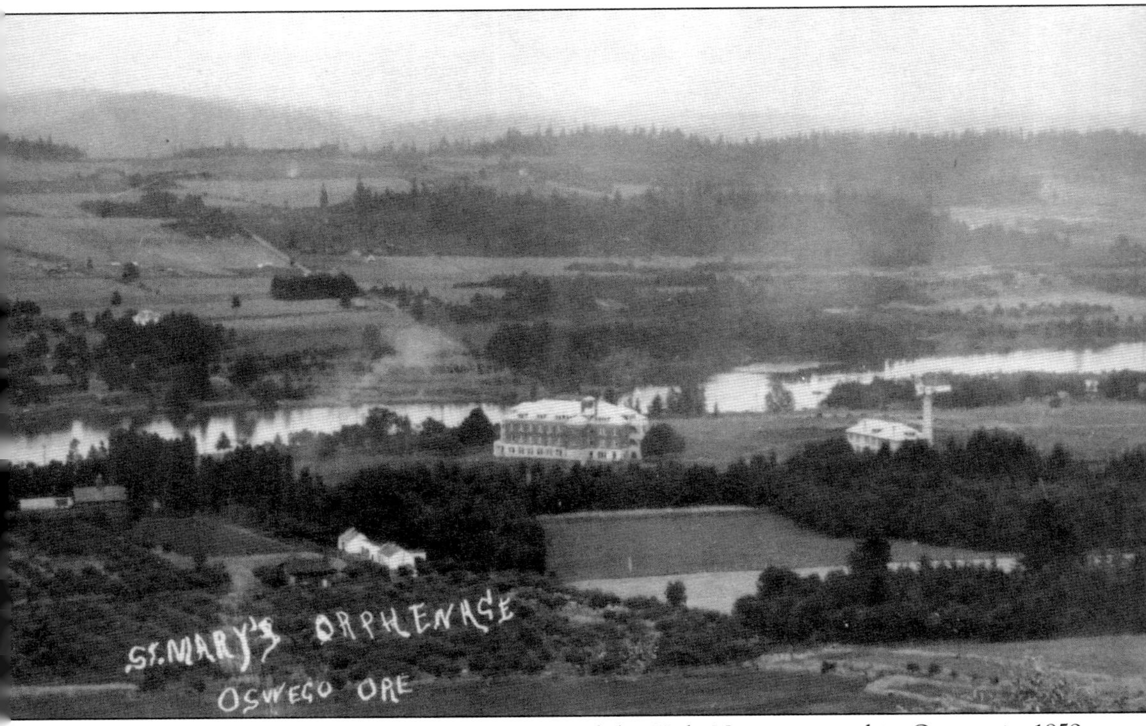

ST. MARY'S NOW MARYLHURST. The Sisters of the Holy Names arrived in Oregon in 1859 to establish a school and fulfill any other missions that might arise. One of the first that did was the care of infants and children abandoned at their doorstep in Portland. This land was purchased in 1908 for an orphanage, administrative office of the order, and a convent. Horticulturist Albert Walling owned the land; his orchards are seen in this photograph. The land continued to be used by the sisters as a subsistence farm. Archbishop Alexander Christie called the land "Villa Marie" but changed it to Marylhurst in 1913 (German for "Mary's Woods"). In 1912, the sisters opened the Holy Names Normal School (a teacher training school), a sister institution to St. Mary's College in Portland. In 1919, the normal school became Marylhurst Normal School. In 1930, St. Mary's College moved to Villa Marie and became Marylhurst College. (The schools joined in 1950; today they are Marylhurst University.)

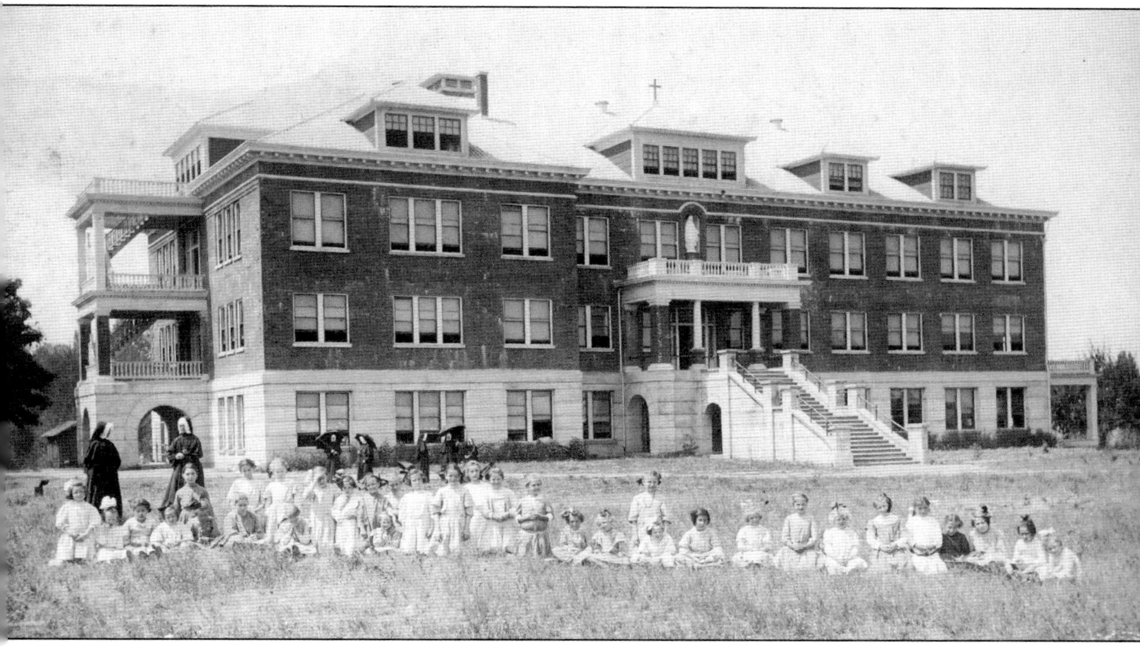

ORPHAN GIRLS, NUNS IN SUMMER. This *c.* 1920 photograph of the Christie School (formerly known as the Christie Orphanage) shows well-dressed orphan girls sitting on the lawn. Many wear hair ribbons, and their calm, sweet faces reveal nothing about the sufferings inherent in their status as orphans. This building was constructed in 1908. The sisters' first orphanage was in Portland at the site of today's Portland Plaza (the building west of the Ira Keller Fountain). It later moved to St. Paul, Oregon, but a diphtheria epidemic prompted Catholic archbishop Alexander Christie to move the orphanage to land closer to Portland in case of another medical emergency.

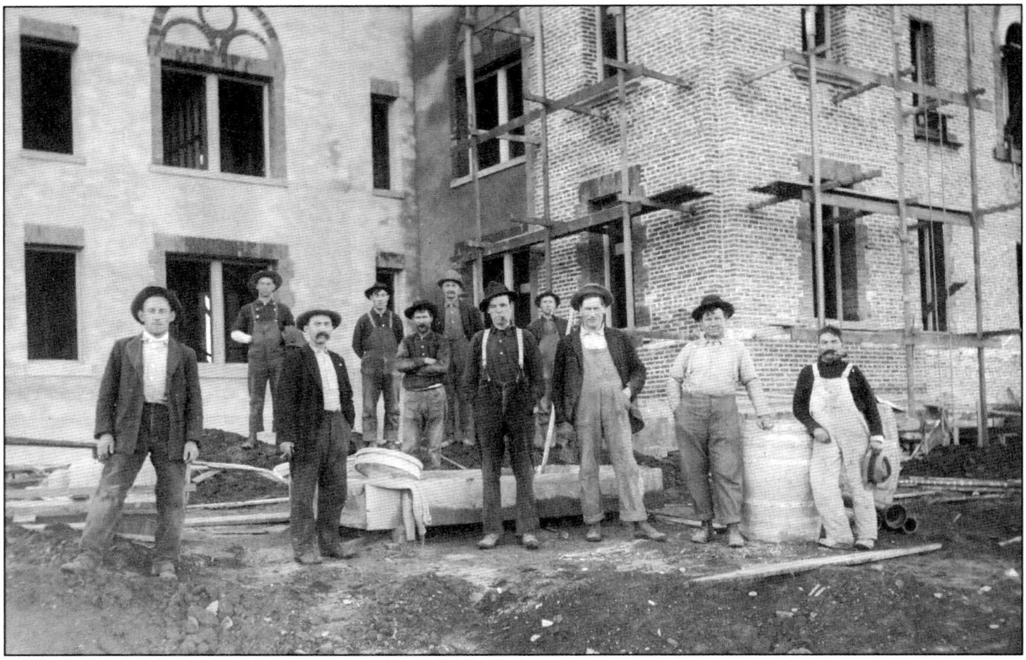

Convent of the Holy Names and Provincial House. The convent's center and south wing were built in 1911 in the Italian villa style. The building also included a novitiate and infirmary. The cost was $75,000. Here the scaffolding is still up on the structure. Reportedly, the brick in the structure may have been recycled from the Oswego iron furnace. The construction workers wear overalls or suspenders, clothing styles that perhaps should be revived to prevent the sort of inadvertent exposure often suffered today by construction workers, especially plumbers.

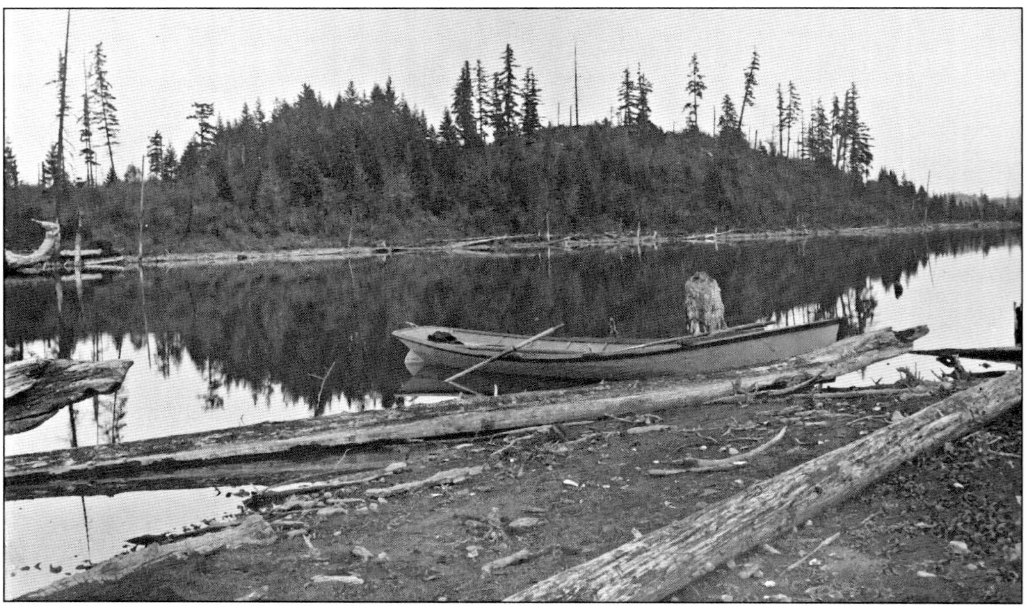

Oswego Lake. This photograph from the 1910s evokes a quieter time. Even before its name was officially changed from Sucker Lake, locals often called it Oswego Lake. As Herbert Nelson recalled in 1973, "Of course, we never called it anything but Oswego Lake, because we didn't like the name of 'Sucker' because it branded all of us in a way."

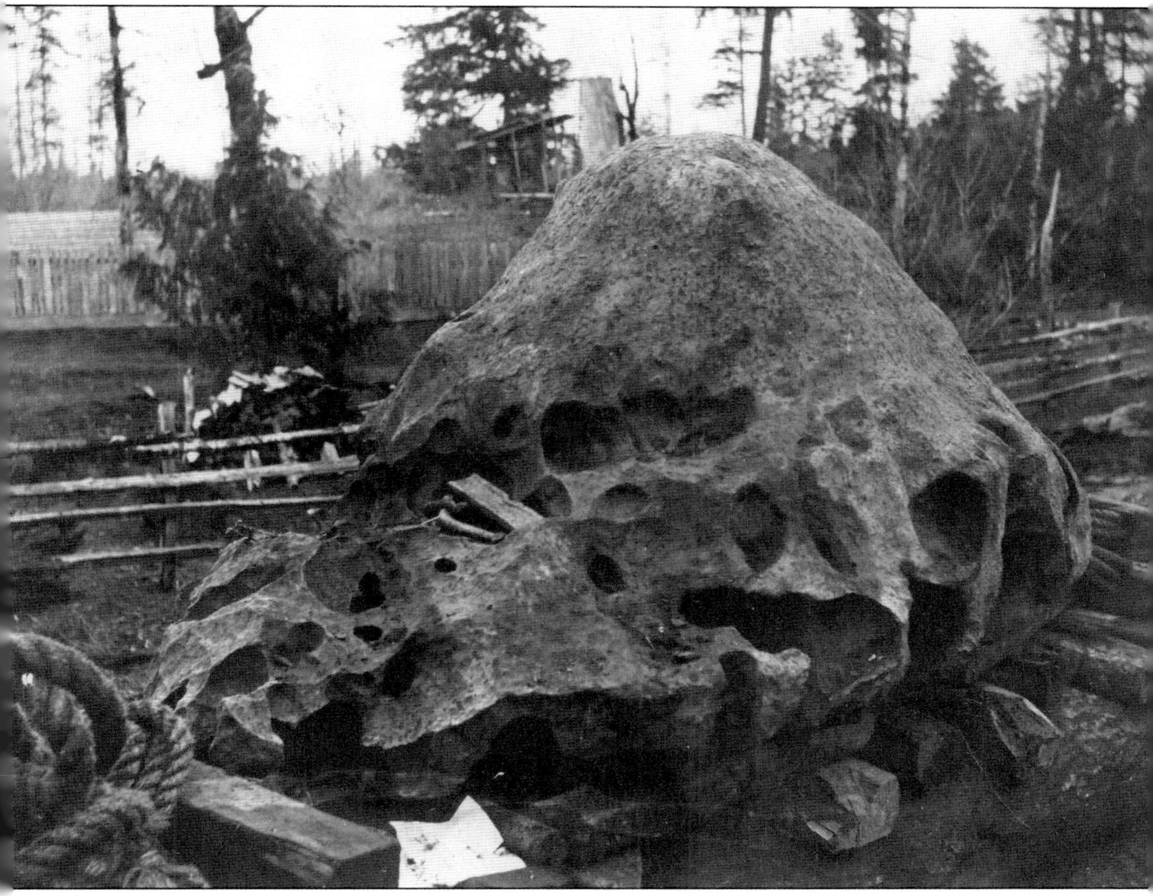

Willamette Meteorite. The meteorite is the largest ever found in the United States. It was partly embedded in the earth for millennia and was revered by native people, who called it *Tomanowos*. The site showed no impact crater, so it may have been transported here in ice sheets or in massive floods. In 1902, the meteorite was found by farmer Elias Hughes south of the lake, near the intersection of Grapevine and Sweetbriar Roads, just south of Rosemont Road. Though that land was owned by Oregon Iron and Steel, Hughes built a crude truck with wooden wheels to haul it to his farm, where he charged 25¢ to see it. His theft was discovered and a lawsuit followed. Hughes lost. The meteorite was shown at Portland's 1905 Lewis and Clark Exposition; soon after a private investor bought it and donated it to New York's American Museum of Natural History, where it sits today.

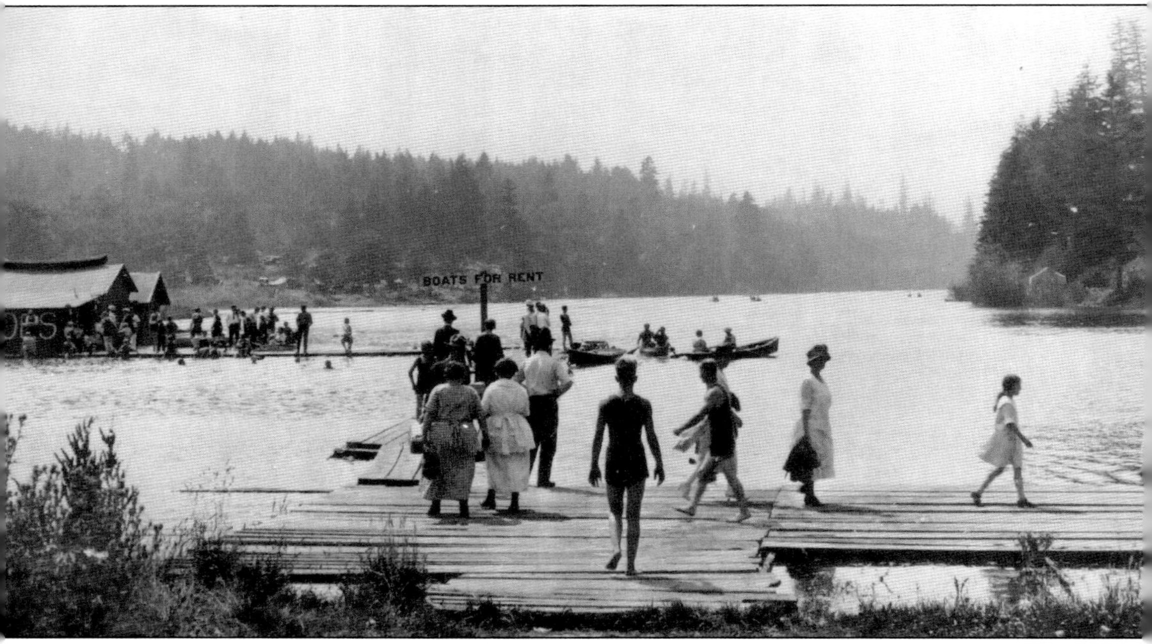

A Day on the Lake. The boating concession, well developed at this point in the 1920s, has a canoe mounted on its roof. Beyond the swimmers, in South Oswego, cars and tent camping sites are visible. On the opposite shore is a rustic cabin, one of the many rustic homes for which the Nelsons collected ground rent. The Douglas firs around the shoreline have grown up since the last commercial cutting of the woods in the early 1890s for charcoal, and the landscape is softening and becoming parklike again. Around this time, the many day-trippers coming from Portland wearing little more than their swimsuits precipitated a law: no swimwear on the streets of Oswego. The Nelson swim concession, seen here and in previous pages, was on the site of condominiums at State Street and McVey Avenue that were built in the 1960s as the Bay Roc apartments.

Four

The Lake Inspires a New Venture, Residential Real Estate 1910–1960

The Ladd family, who controlled Oregon Iron and Steel interests after the company had defaulted on loans, had hired David Nelson as caretaker of the lake after realizing that hundreds of people were using it for swimming, boating, fishing, and even camping. With demand seemingly high for the lake, at least recreationally, and with its holdings now being taxed by the newly incorporated City of Oswego, the Ladd Estate Company began selling off land. In 1912, Paul Murphy, fresh from his success developing both Seattle and Portland's Laurelhurst neighborhoods, bought 3,000 acres of land around the lake. Lake View Villas was the first platted subdivision of this era, located at the lake's west end (the Lake Grove area). It was platted in 1912. Tour boats took prospective buyers to view lakeside lots, and OIS built Lake View Park (today's Lake Grove Swim Park) to entice visitors. Development stuttered, however, because while rail service was good, the area had no good roads leading to it. In 1913, OIS began planning the boulevard system of scenic roads around the lake that exist today. For the next 40 years, Oswego continued to develop as a unique suburban community, alone in Western Oregon with a lake as its defining attraction.

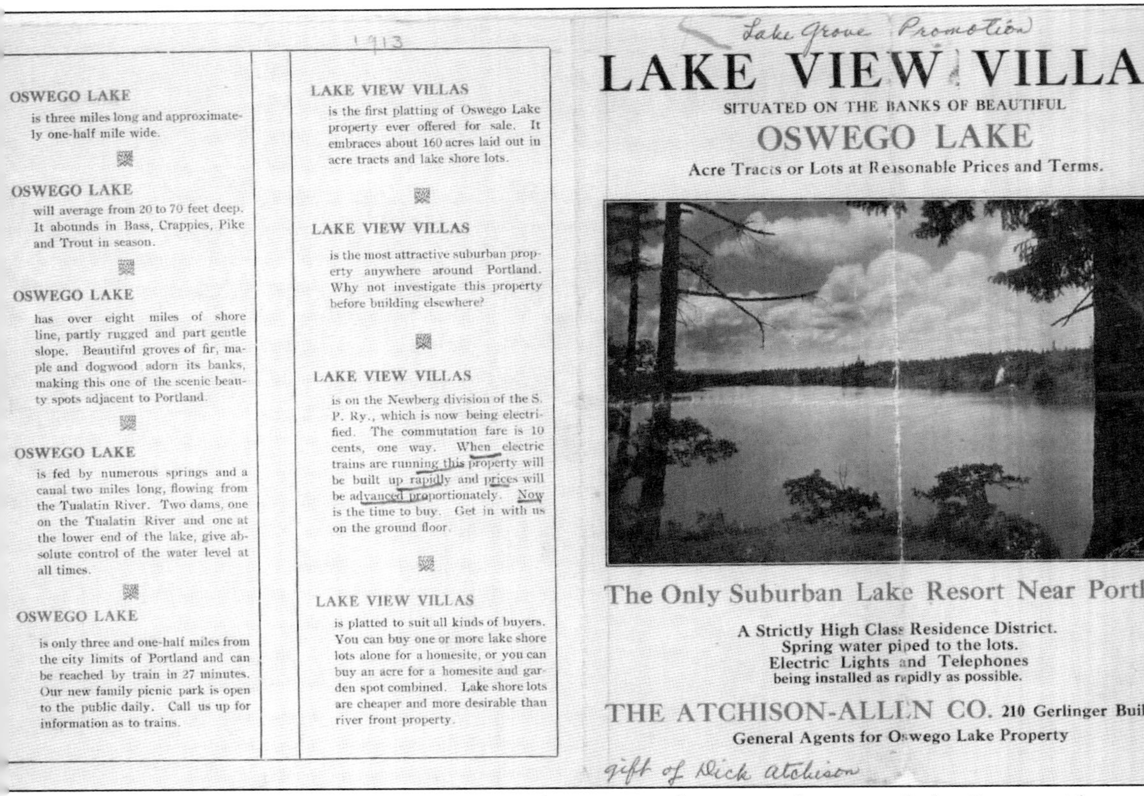

1913

OSWEGO LAKE
is three miles long and approximately one-half mile wide.

OSWEGO LAKE
will average from 20 to 70 feet deep. It abounds in Bass, Crappies, Pike and Trout in season.

OSWEGO LAKE
has over eight miles of shore line, partly rugged and part gentle slope. Beautiful groves of fir, maple and dogwood adorn its banks, making this one of the scenic beauty spots adjacent to Portland.

OSWEGO LAKE
is fed by numerous springs and a canal two miles long, flowing from the Tualatin River. Two dams, one on the Tualatin River and one at the lower end of the lake, give absolute control of the water level at all times.

OSWEGO LAKE
is only three and one-half miles from the city limits of Portland and can be reached by train in 27 minutes. Our new family picnic park is open to the public daily. Call us up for information as to trains.

LAKE VIEW VILLAS
is the first platting of Oswego Lake property ever offered for sale. It embraces about 160 acres laid out in acre tracts and lake shore lots.

LAKE VIEW VILLAS
is the most attractive suburban property anywhere around Portland. Why not investigate this property before building elsewhere?

LAKE VIEW VILLAS
is on the Newberg division of the S. P. Ry., which is now being electrified. The commutation fare is 10 cents, one way. When electric trains are running this property will be built up rapidly and prices will be advanced proportionately. Now is the time to buy. Get in with us on the ground floor.

LAKE VIEW VILLAS
is platted to suit all kinds of buyers. You can buy one or more lake shore lots alone for a homesite, or you can buy an acre for a homesite and garden spot combined. Lake shore lots are cheaper and more desirable than river front property.

Lake Grove Promotion

LAKE VIEW VILLA
SITUATED ON THE BANKS OF BEAUTIFUL
OSWEGO LAKE
Acre Tracts or Lots at Reasonable Prices and Terms.

The Only Suburban Lake Resort Near Portl
A Strictly High Class Residence District.
Spring water piped to the lots.
Electric Lights and Telephones
being installed as rapidly as possible.
THE ATCHISON-ALLEN CO. 210 Gerlinger Buil
General Agents for Oswego Lake Property

gift of Dick Atchison

LAKE VIEW VILLAS BROCHURE. By 1916, there were a dozen or so houses in Lake Grove, with a concentration along Reese Road and Upper Drive. The business section was laid out along Boones Ferry Road, the "highway" as it was sometimes called, although in the 1910s few people owned cars and instead relied on the train to reach Lake Grove.

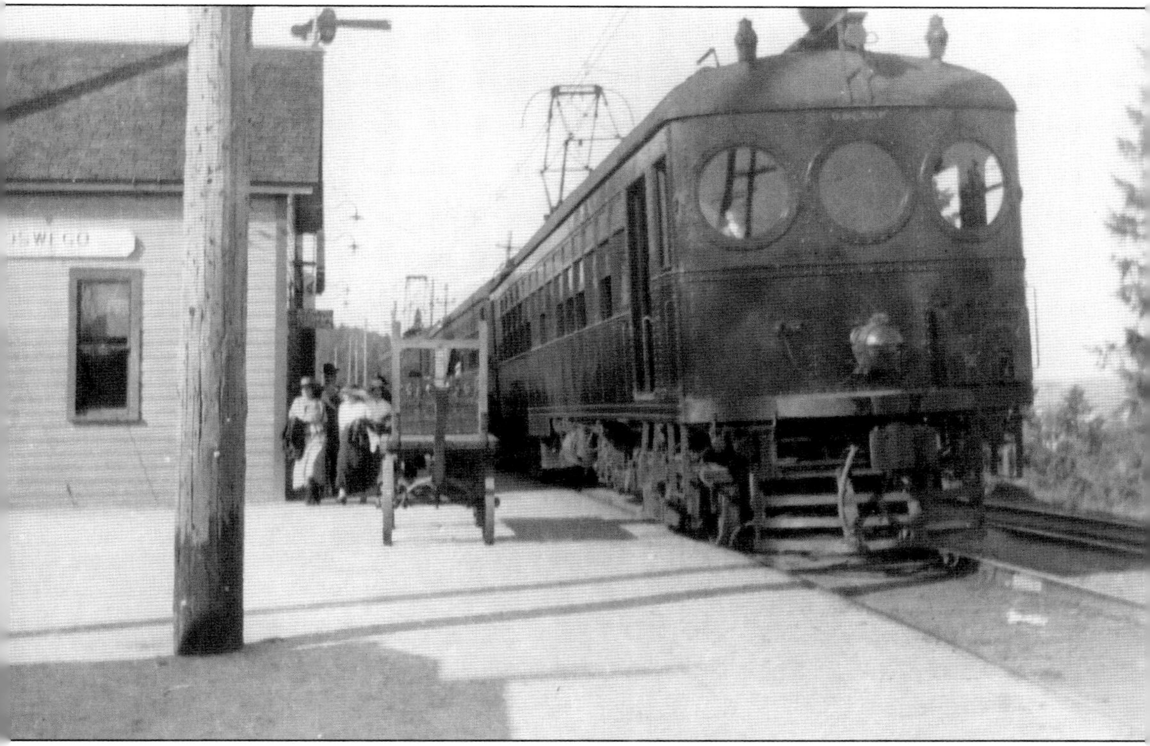

THE TRAIN FROM PORTLAND. Longtime Lake Oswego resident Herbert Nelson recalled: "It seemed that every mile [in the Lake Grove area] or so the Red Electric had a station to pick up local people." The frequency of stops no doubt was designed to compensate for the lack of roads. This photograph shows the Red Electric train at Oswego Depot. From here it turned west toward the west end of the lake. The line once used by the Red Electric between Portland and Oswego is used now by the Willamette Shore Trolley, an excursion train that runs from spring through fall.

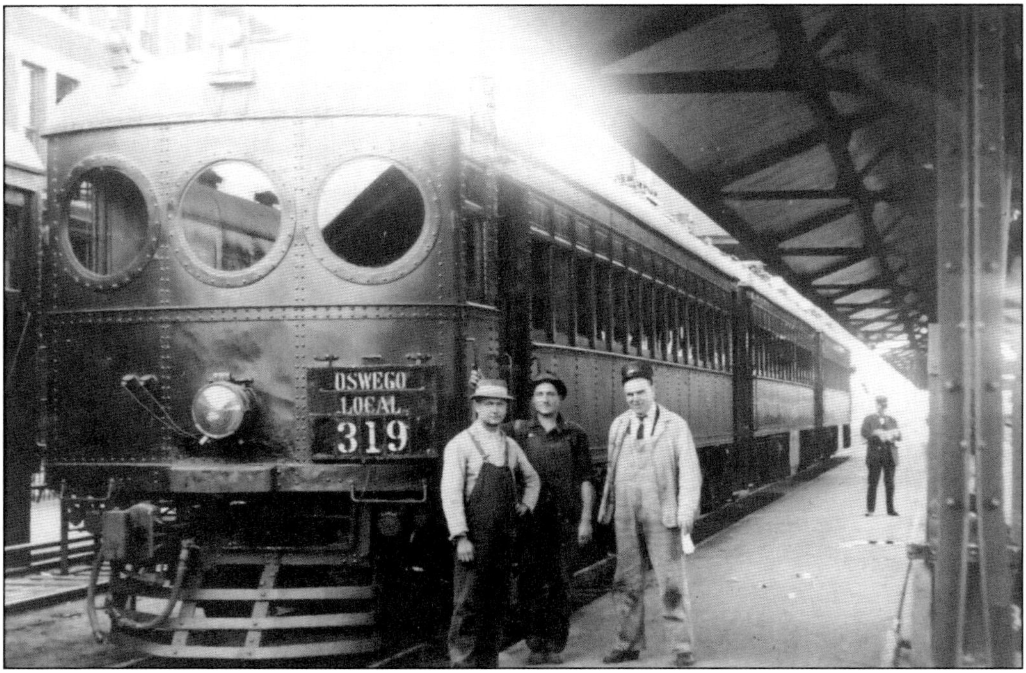

The Red Electric and Crew. In 1914, the rail line between Portland and Oswego was electrified. The rail line became a commuter line with 64 trains each day, part of the web of streetcars and commuter rail lines in the Portland metropolitan area.

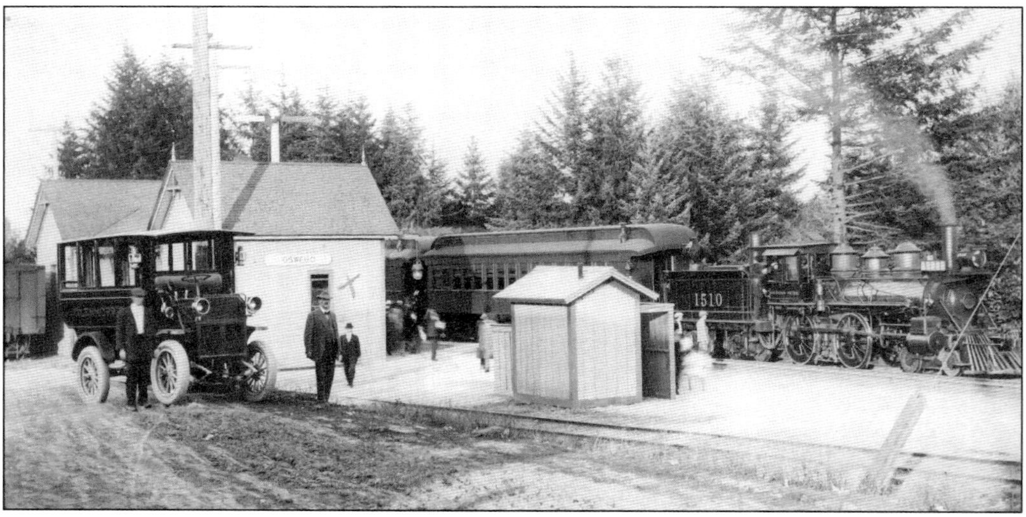

Depot with Glenmorrie Bus. The Glenmorrie Bus waits at the Oswego Depot in the early 1910s. Glenmorrie was the former riverside estate of P. F. Morey, head of Portland General Electric. It is located between River Road and Highway 43, just north of Marylhurst. After Morey's death, his son platted the property in 1910 with the hopes of developing it with upscale homes. It was not a success, and the neighborhood did not develop much until after World War I.

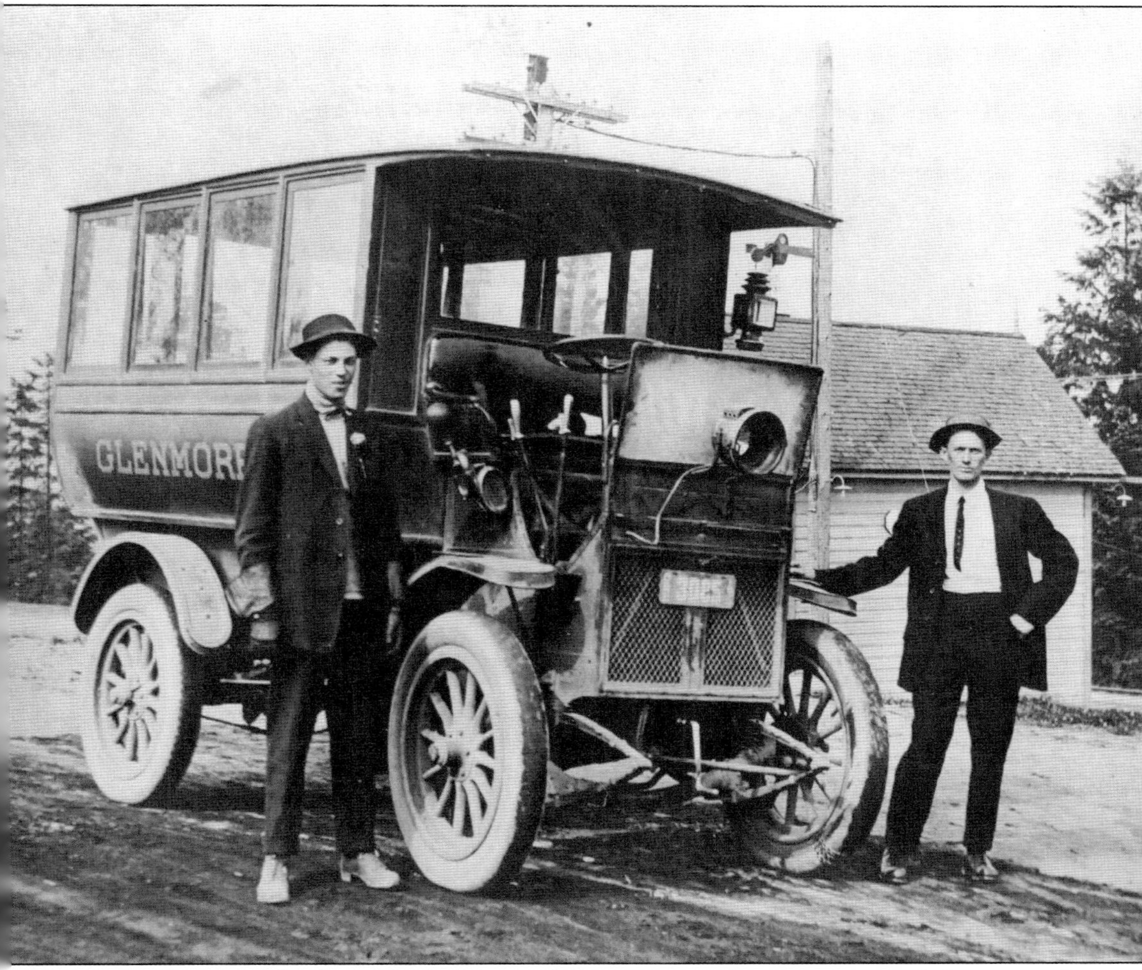

GLENMORRIE BUS. This bus, which ran just for a few years, sometimes carried the nuns of Marylhurst, next-door neighbors to Glenmorrie, to and from the train depot when they made trips into Portland, though some preferred to walk the quiet river road into Oswego. Glenmorrie, developed by P. F. Morey as his country estate beginning in the late 1880s, was 640 acres, much of it intensively worked with a 50-acre orchard, crops such as potatoes and wheat, hand-wrought stone walls, and a bridge over a creek. Morey was a collector of plants and reputedly planted 400 varieties of trees, shrubs, and vines on his land.

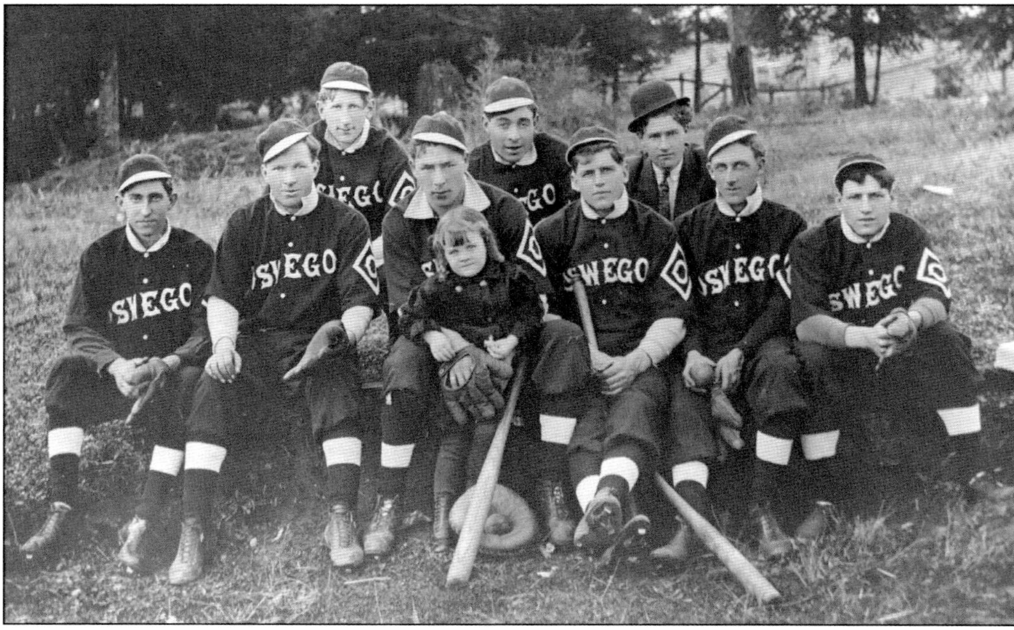

Ball Team and Mascot. Compare the more modern uniforms of this 1914 team with uniforms on page 54. Cleats, padded mitts, and visor caps are not too different from today's baseball uniforms and equipment. Ollie Worthington was on the construction crew at Marylhurst. He is second from the left in the top row here and in the construction crew photograph on page 76.

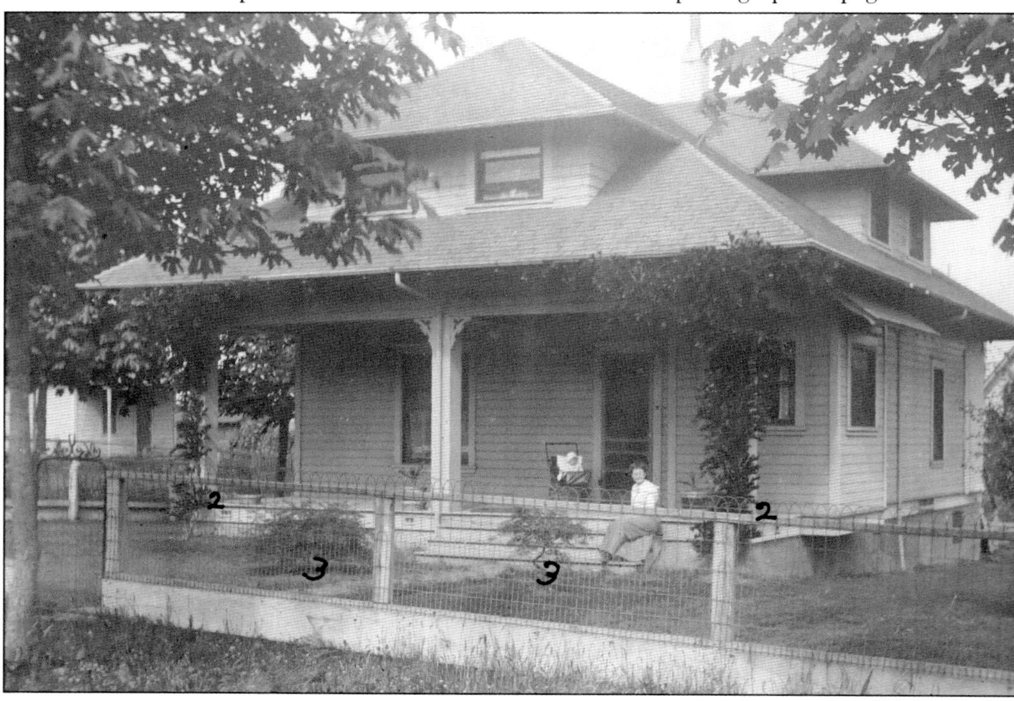

First Addition Home. This 1914 photograph shows the Bickner home at A Avenue and First Street. Baby Ava is six months old, and the proud homeowner labeled with numbers the plants on the property: No. 1 is a Hawthorne, No. 2 is wisteria, and No. 3 is cut leaf maples. This site is now a Safeway.

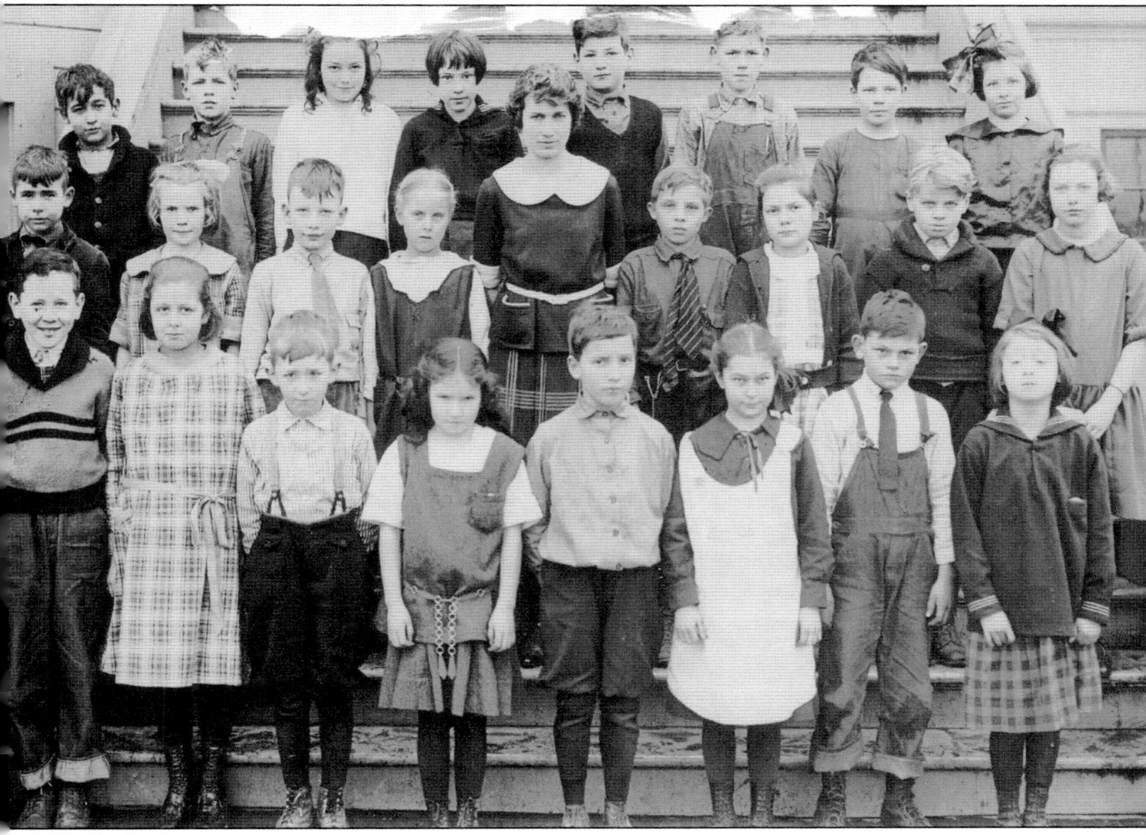

THIRD GRADE AND TEACHER. In this 1921 class of third graders at Oswego Public School, Ava Bickner is second from the left in the first row. She is seen as a baby on her parent's porch on the previous page and on page 92. Her hair is smooth and carefully tended, perhaps what would be expected from the daughter of the town's general storekeeper. Other children look like they have just come in from recess. Note the high, lace-up leather shoes. Of the shoes in the first row, Ava's are by far the shiniest. The boy second from right appears to be a farm boy; his shoes look like they have been much worn by his older brothers. His overall and tie combination is a charming touch. Ava became a first lieutenant in the U. S. Army in World War II. She died in 1973.

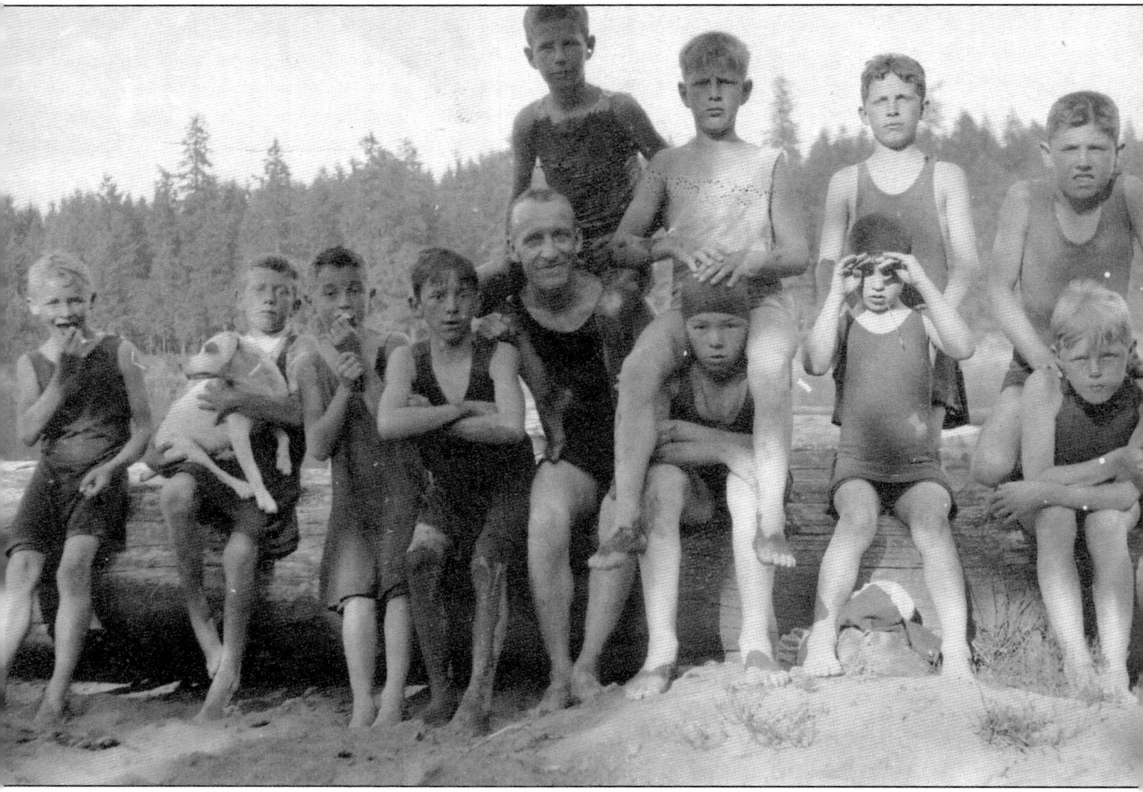

HAPPY CAMPERS. While the lake was being marketed to home buyers, some of the population appears to have been unconcerned about the coming changes to their town. In this c. 1920 photograph, the combination of mud (note the boy on the man's shoulders), water, a dog, and snacks seem to have made for a perfect day of horseplay and camaraderie.

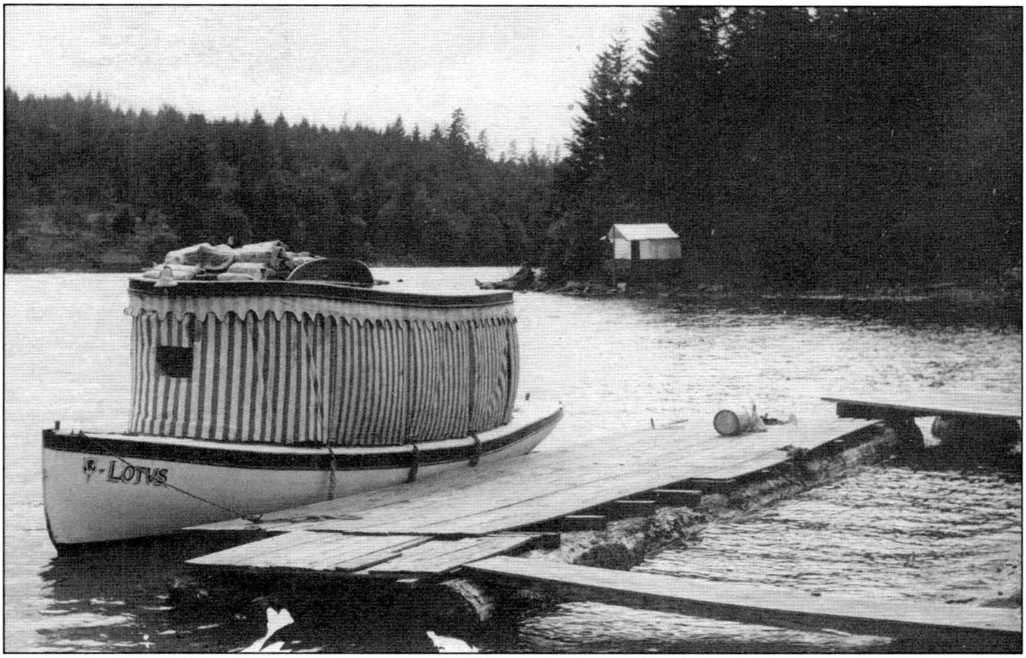

Early Lake Boathouse. These two photographs and the photograph on page 88 date from 1912 or 1913. The *Lotus* was used by developers to take prospective buyers to look at lakefront lots at the west end of the lake—the Lake Grove area. The boat's canvas enclosure was no doubt an accommodation to Oregon's weather. With no roads to lakefront lots, the *Lotus* was an alternative to train access and a walk through the woods. Showing potential lakefront lots from the lake itself must have won the sales agent many easy commissions. A cabin tent is in the background, enjoying the last decade of the lake in its natural state.

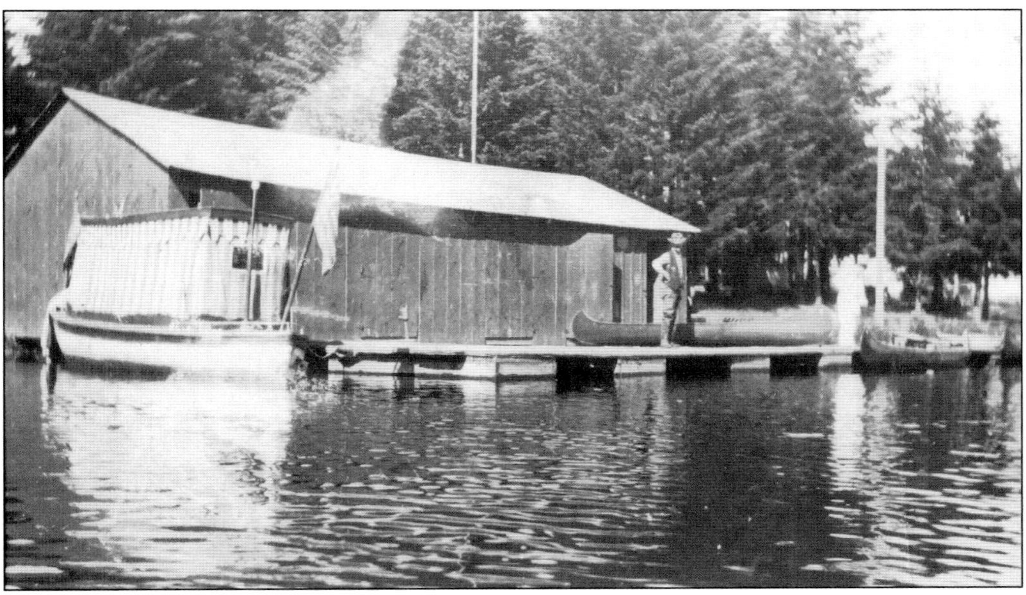

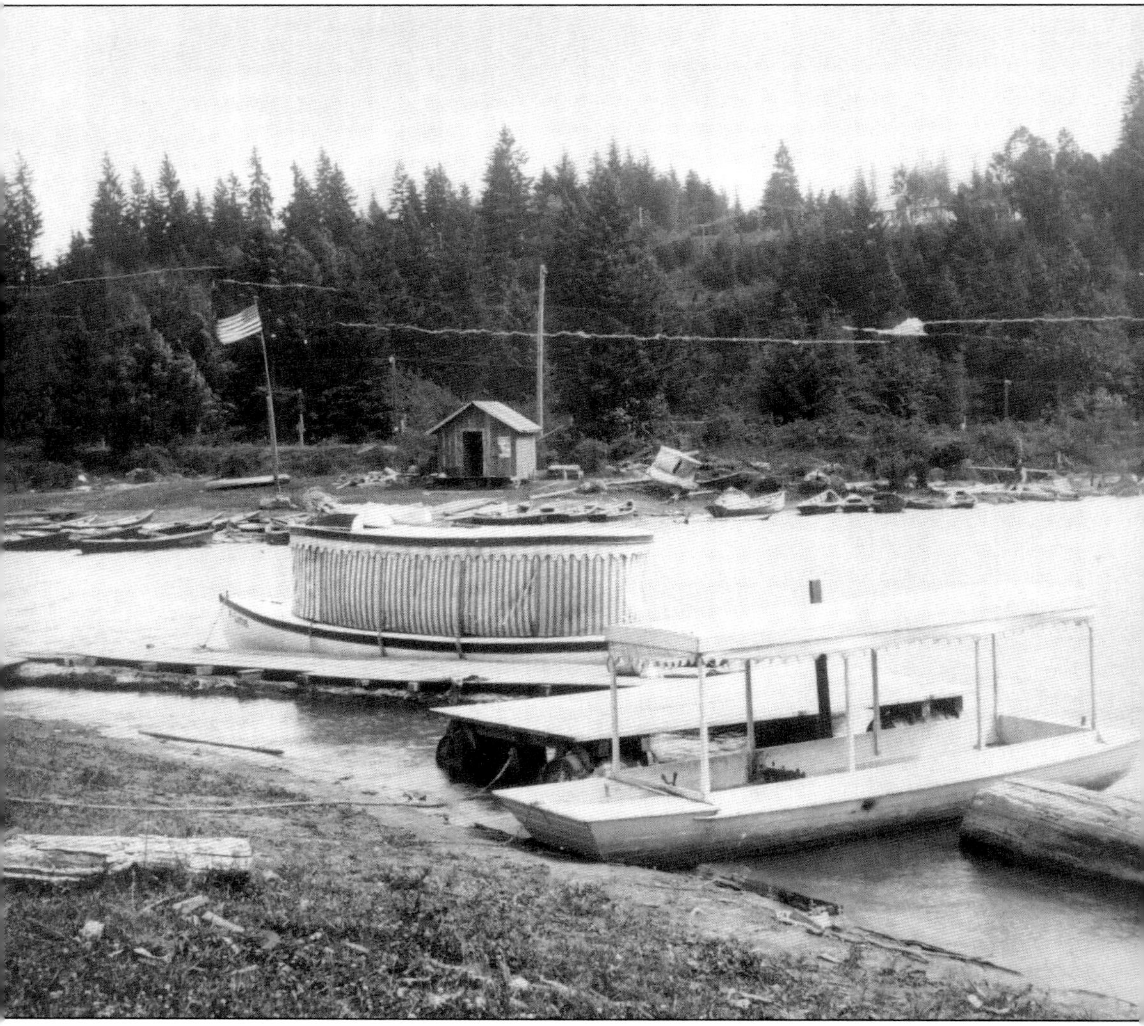

EXCURSION BOAT. Another boat, open to the elements, was available to serve potential buyers when the weather was fine. This scene is of the east end of the lake, looking south, and near the site of today's Oswego Swim Park off Ridgeway Road. Portlanders could take the train out to Oswego and walk a few blocks from the depot south on State Street to get here. Across the water is the boat-rental concession. Beyond it is South Oswego.

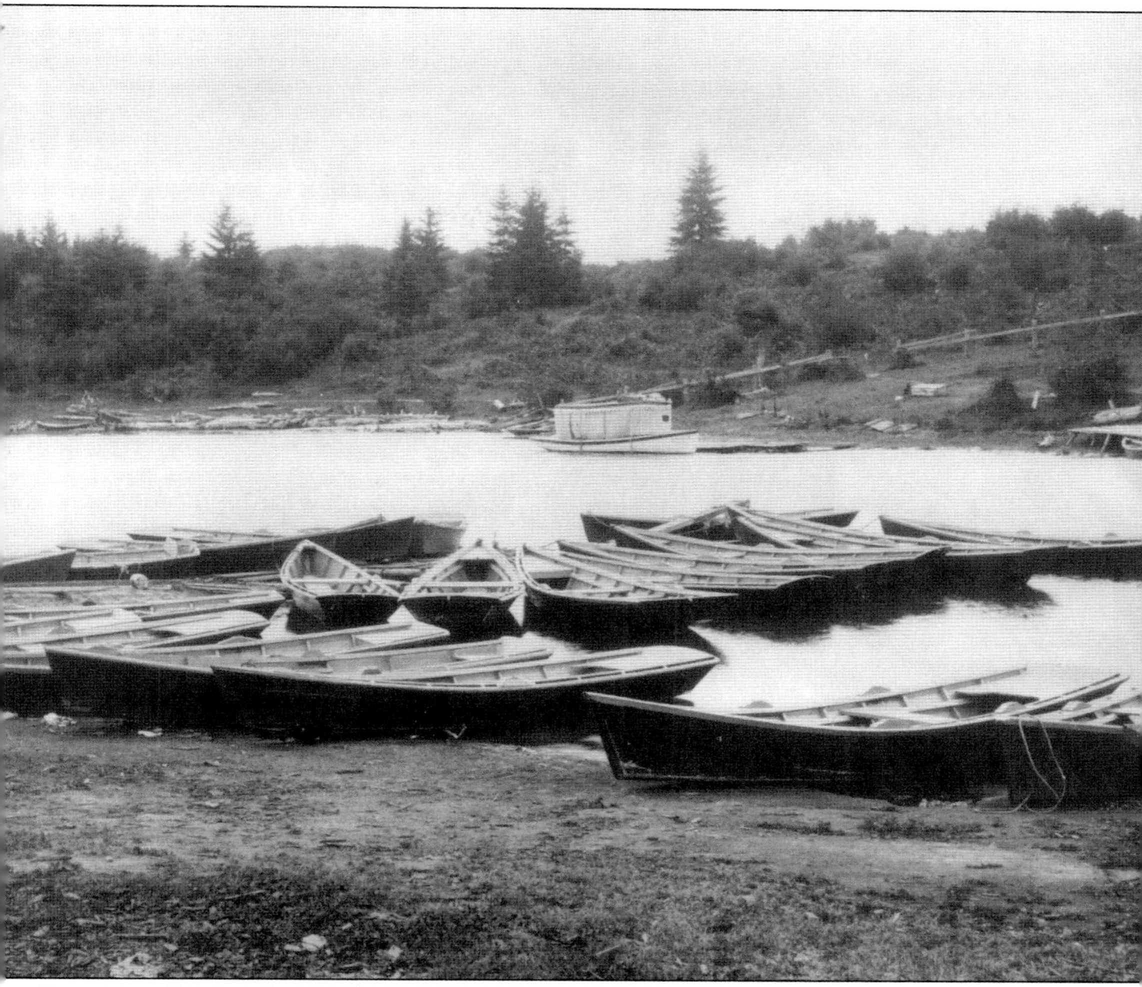

JUMBLE OF BOATS. One early resident remembered about the Nelson boating concession, "They had about 75 boats and 20 canoes. You had to get down there Thursday or Friday or you couldn't even rent one for the weekend." Here the view is looking north toward what is now the Lakewood neighborhood.

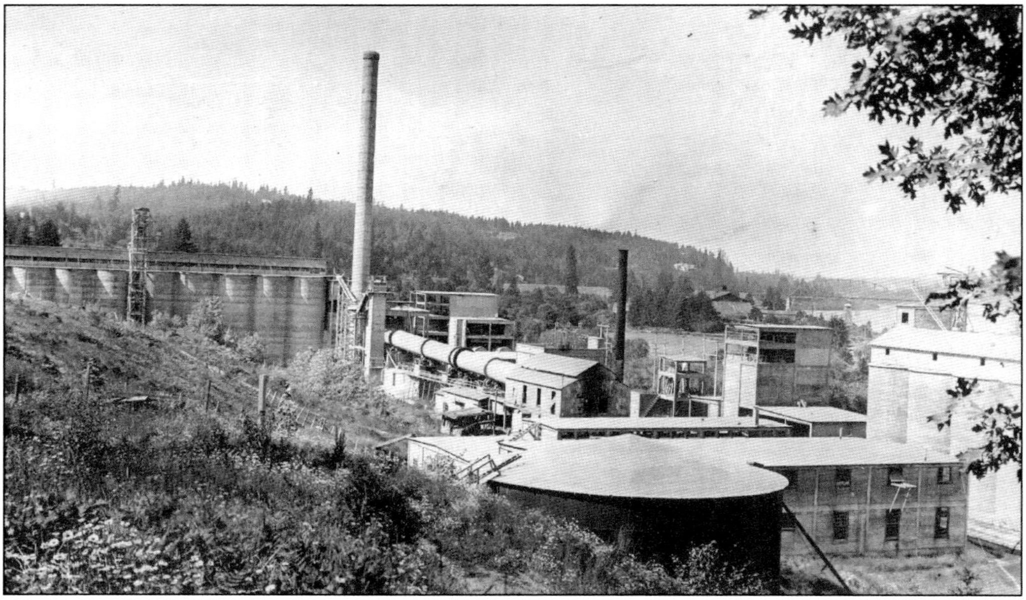

Cement Plant. While lakefront lots were being sold, Oswego had not yet latched on to its later incarnation as a suburb; it still had its own heavy industries, the cement plant and the pipe plant, which kept Oswego men working in Oswego. This view, looking north, shows the Southern Pacific bridge over the Willamette.

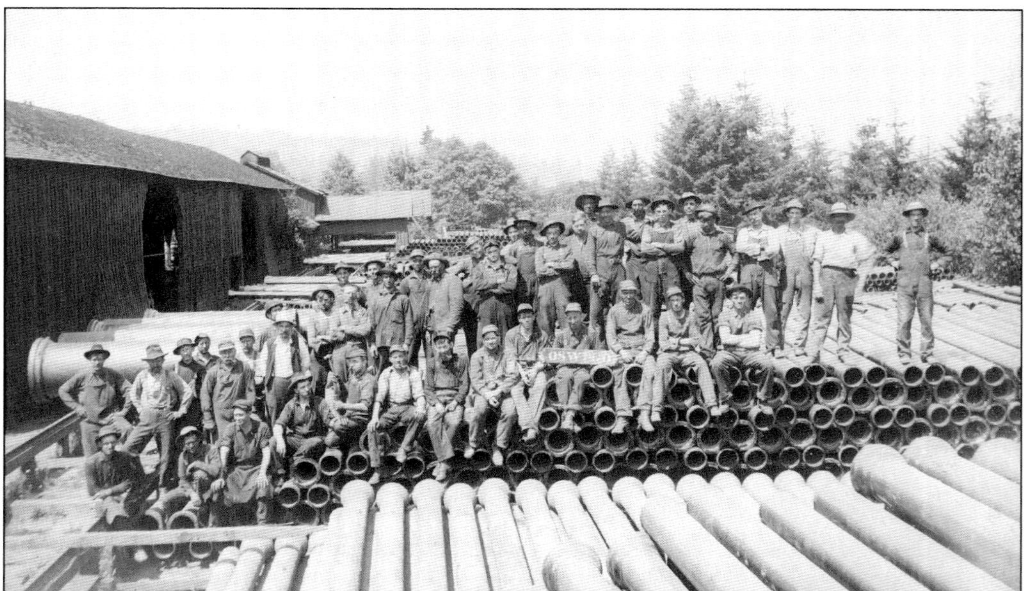

Pipes and Workers. The pipe foundry operated until the mid-1920s. This photograph of workers on a bright summer day shows blackened faces and some horseplay; note the two men—one with a raised hammer and the other with a chisel set into his forearm.

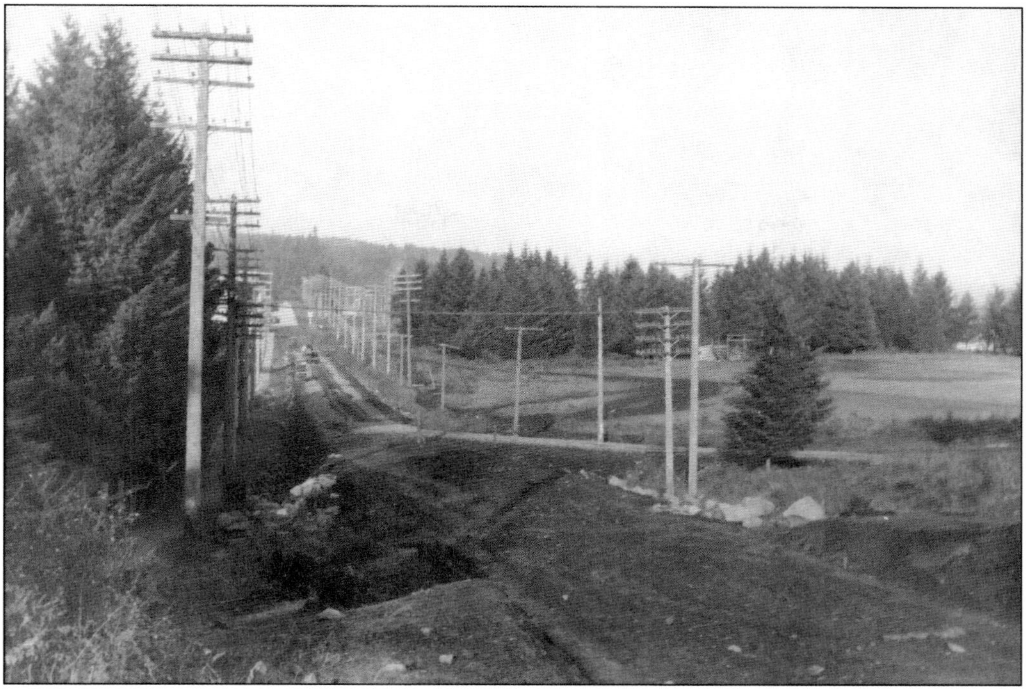

State Street near Old Town. State Street is pictured here in 1919, the year before it was paved. The view is looking north from about the location of today's Lakewood Center for the Arts. The town baseball field is to the right.

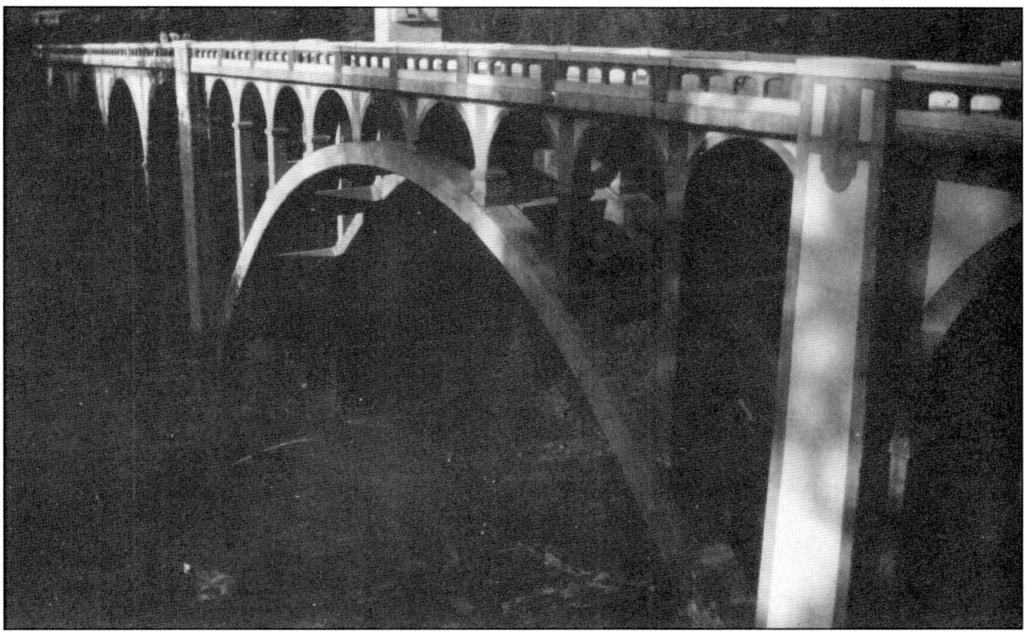

New Highway Bridge. In 1920, this concrete bridge was constructed over Oswego Creek. The bridge still exists, but a second bridge was later built adjacent to it to handle increased traffic. When built, the bridge was part of the Pacific Highway, or Highway 99. In the 1930s, Highway 99 was moved to McLoughlin Boulevard on the Willamette's east bank, and this became Highway 43.

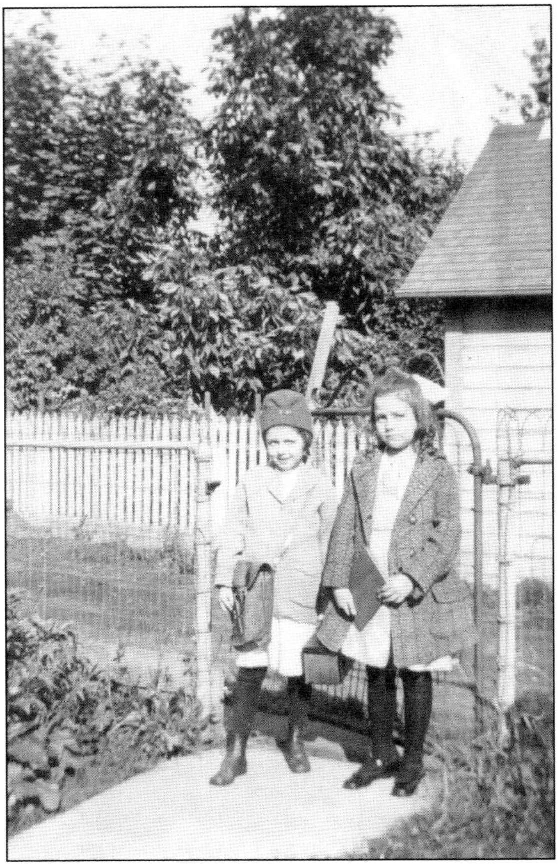

SCHOOL FRIENDS. Ava Bickner (see page 85) and her friend Constance Koehler are pictured in September 1919 as they walked to or from the public school on State Street from their homes in First Addition.

FIRST ADDITION. Looking east on C Avenue at Fifth Street, sidewalks have been paved, but the road is still dirt. The white, hipped-roof house was built *c.* 1925.

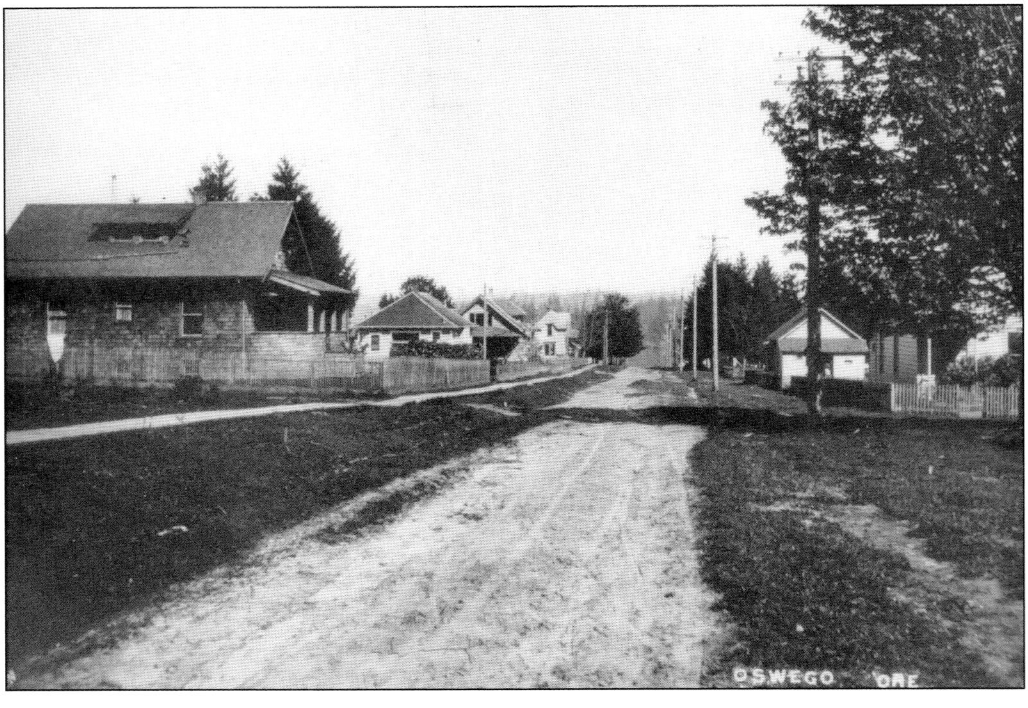

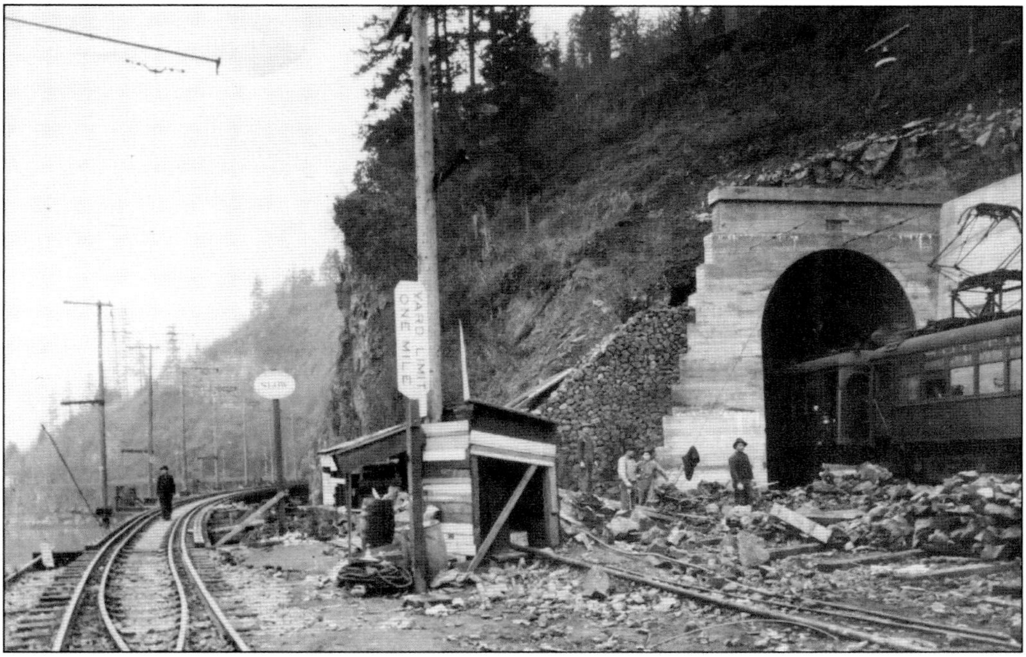

TUNNEL THROUGH ELK ROCK. In 1921, commuters to Portland no longer had to endure the perilous Elk Rock trestle with its falling rocks and precipitous drop to the river. After a rock reputedly crashed through a train one day, hitting Ella Newlands in the head (she survived), it was decided that a tunnel was overdue. This tunnel was bored 1,396 feet through Elk Rock. Today the Willamette Shore Trolley runs excursion trains through the tunnel on its route between Portland and Oswego. The tunnel makes an S curve between its two portals.

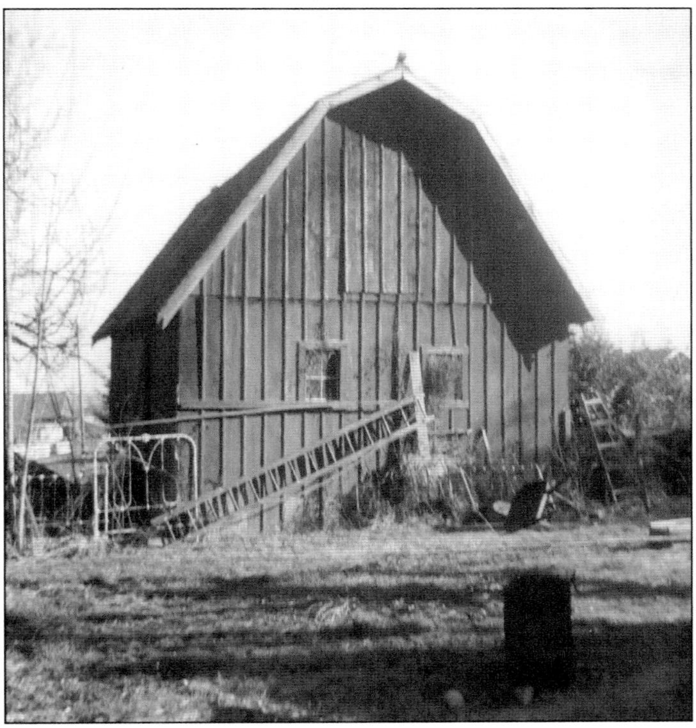

AN URBAN BARN. The Clifford Johnson barn at Fifth Avenue and G Street is the last urban barn in the First Addition neighborhood, once a neighborhood of widely scattered houses. Built in 1910, the barn was part of a farm complex between Fourth and Fifth Avenues.

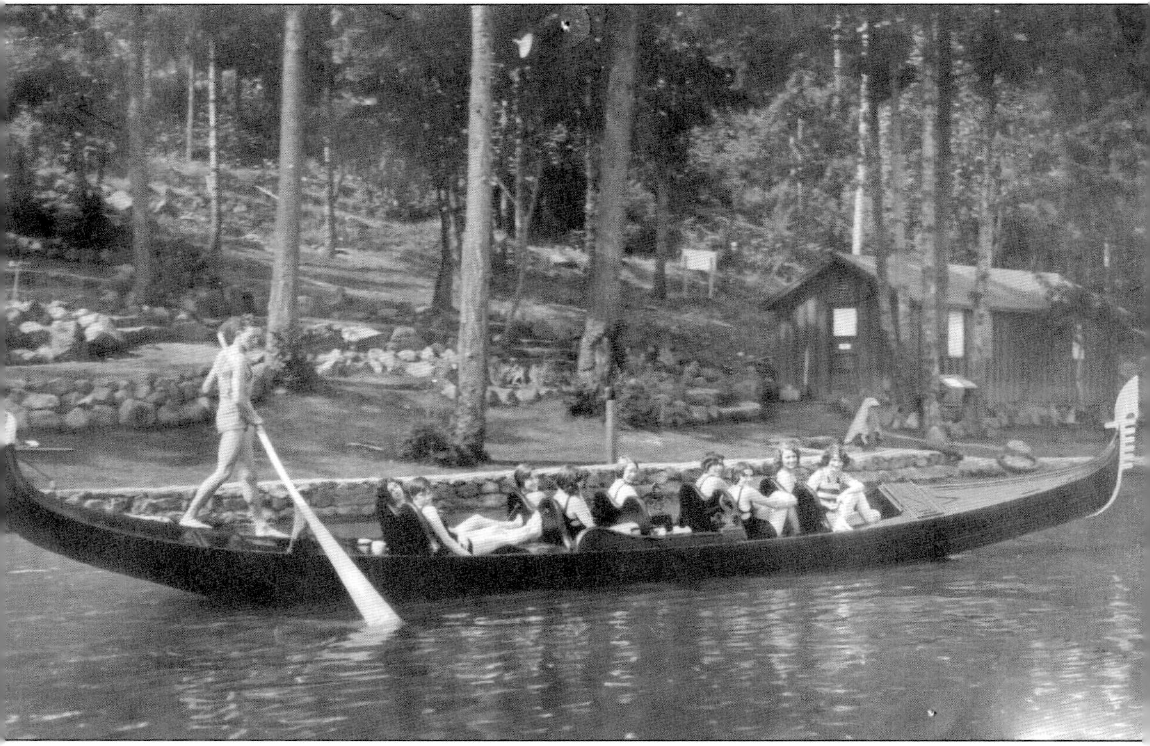

VENICE MEETS OREGON. In 1920, at what is called "Lake Oswego Park" on the image, likely today's Lake Grove Swim Park, nine young women ride in a gondola being paddled by a handsome man. The young man, however, has his eyes on his work. The scenery on shore is so beautiful it is almost surreal. According to notes on the photograph, the gondola later sank in the lake. Lake Grove Swim Park is today one of only two swim areas open to Lake Oswego residents who do not own lakefront property or a lake easement.

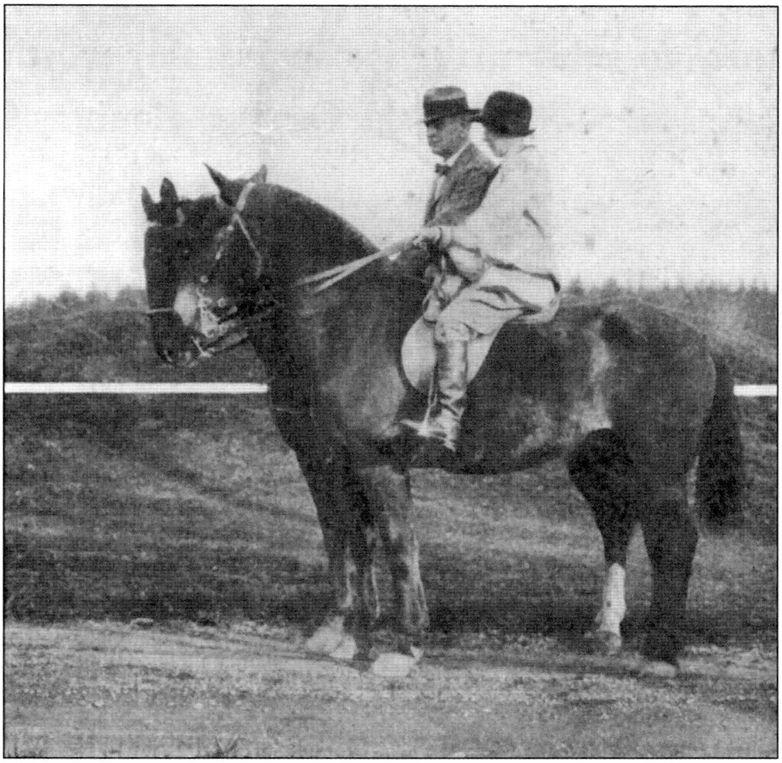

ON BRIDLE TRAILS, COUNTRY CLUB DISTRICT. This photograph and the three that follow were in a promotional brochure from the 1920s inviting people to "LIVE where you PLAY" in the Lake Oswego Country Club District, an idyllic setting where "trails urge you on." Bridle paths ran throughout the district in the early days on easements granted by Oregon Iron and Steel.

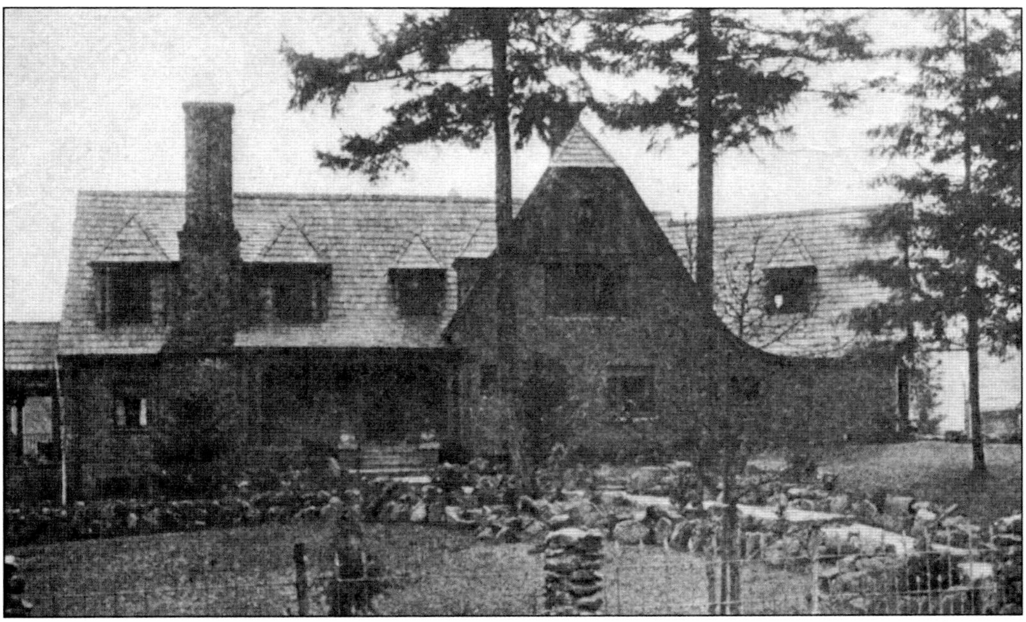

A SHOW HOME ON THE LAKE. Madrona Place is shown here, the home of architect Charles Ertz, who designed Carl Jantzen's nearby home on Jantzen Island. The home is in the Arts and Crafts style with a steeply pitched roof and an asymmetric composition, both elements that give it the romantic, Naturalistic style encouraged by the early real estate developers. This home on North Shore Road was razed in 2000 and a new home constructed, a common occurrence in Lake Oswego after about 1990.

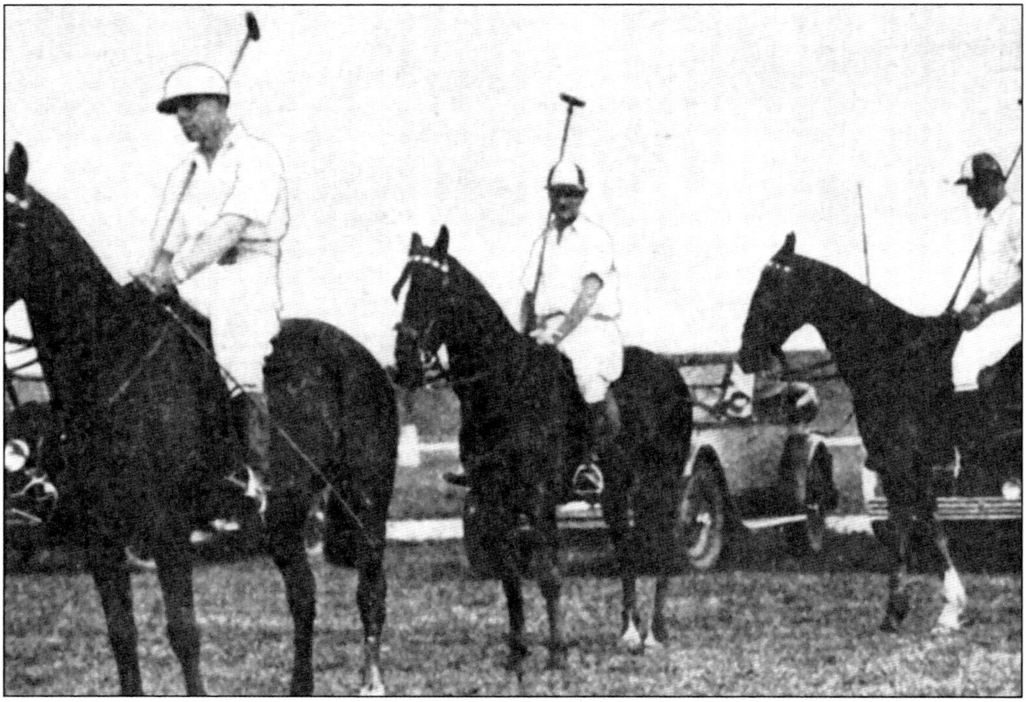

Polo at Oswego. This image shows players at the Forest Hills Polo Club, part of the Lake Oswego Country Club. This polo club merged in the 1930s with Portland's Multnomah Hunt to form the Lake Oswego Hunt Club when 19 acres were set aside for equestrian activities. See pages 104–105 for more on the hunt club.

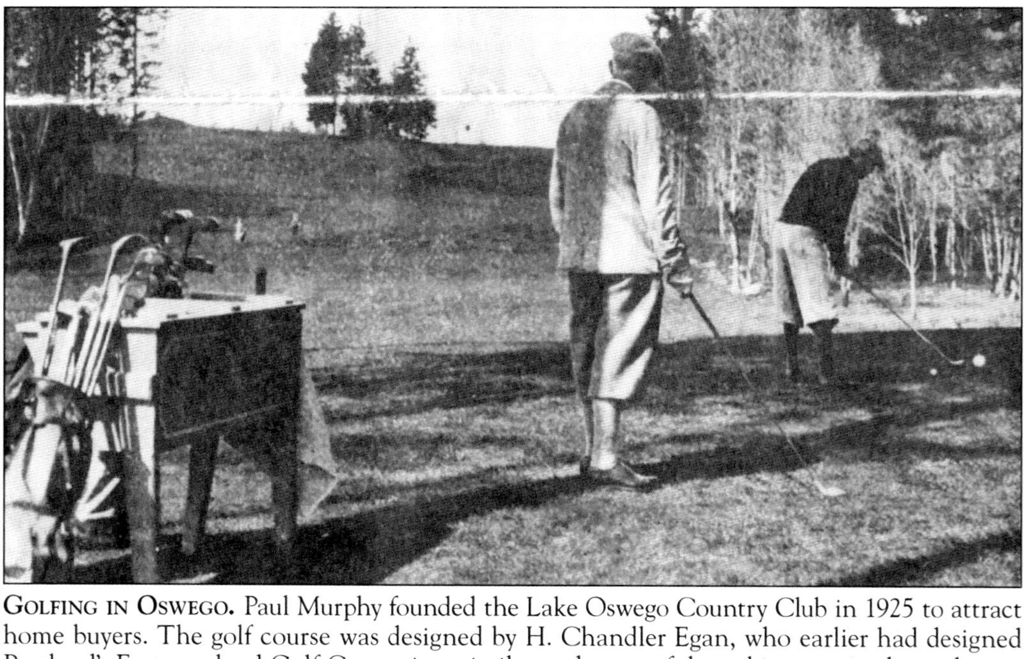

Golfing in Oswego. Paul Murphy founded the Lake Oswego Country Club in 1925 to attract home buyers. The golf course was designed by H. Chandler Egan, who earlier had designed Portland's Eastmoreland Golf Course in a similar and successful gambit to entice home buyers into a new subdivision. This course is hilly and challenging; originally the 17th tee had a Pierce Arrow open touring car, attached to cables, to take golfers to the top of the hill.

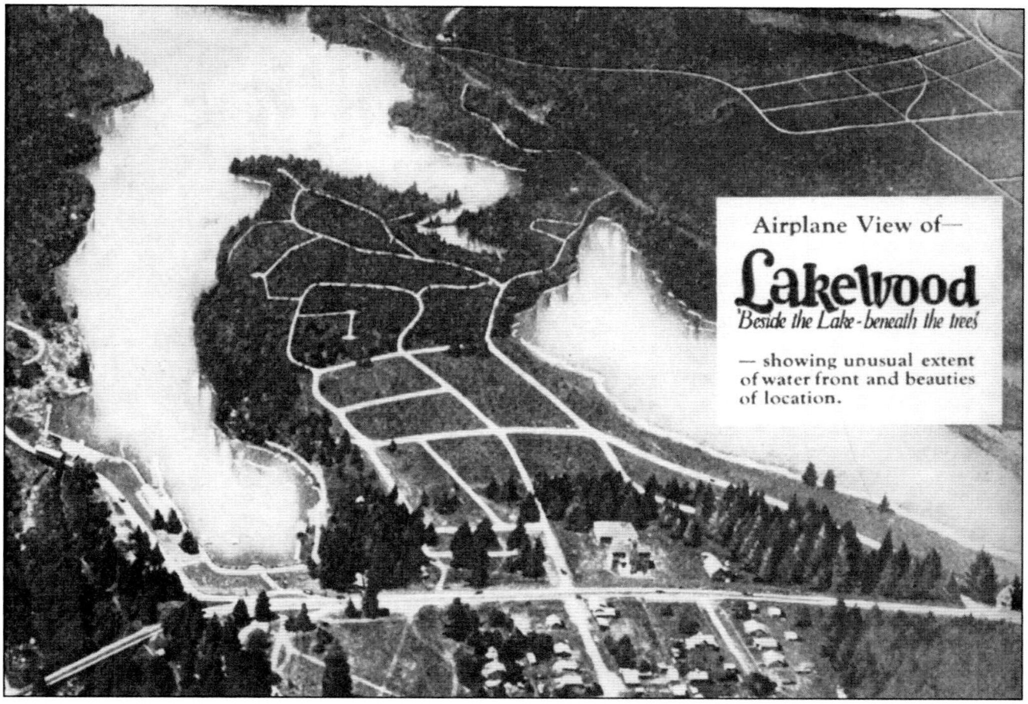

A New Subdivision. With the success of Lake View Villas and the Country Club District, developers saw opportunity for more waterfront lots along the swampy, pockmarked duck pond to the east of the lake. A channel was dug to connect the pond with the main lake, and the swamp was flooded and renamed Lakewood Bay. Oswego residents were warned that fines would be levied if the old name passed their lips.

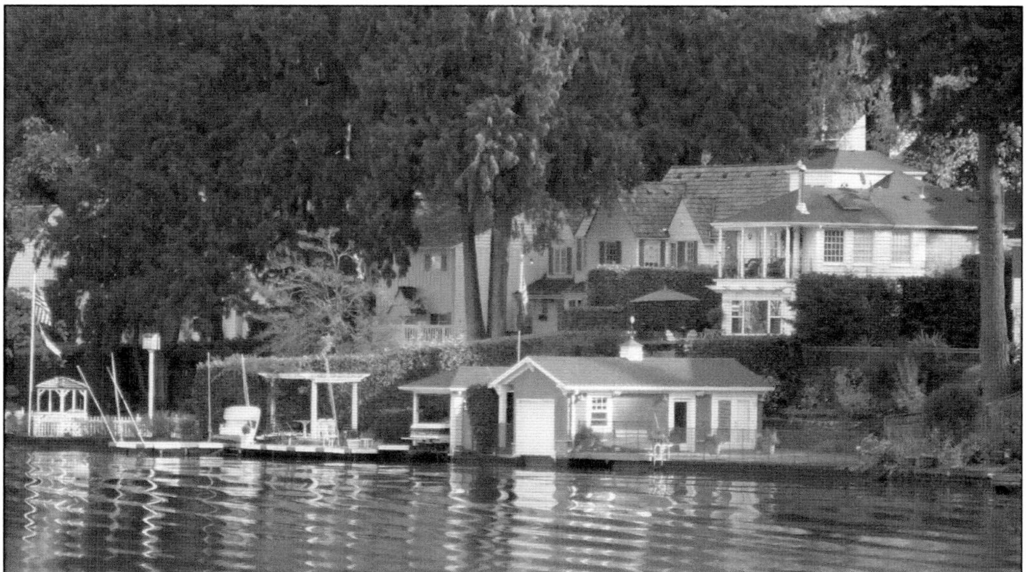

The Former Duck Pond. Today Lakewood Bay is lined with homes, boathouses, and docks. During draw downs of the lake, its swampy origins are evident as it becomes totally drained. It is the only part of the lake readily seen by passersby from park space along State Street and a multiuse path along its north shore. (Author's collection.)

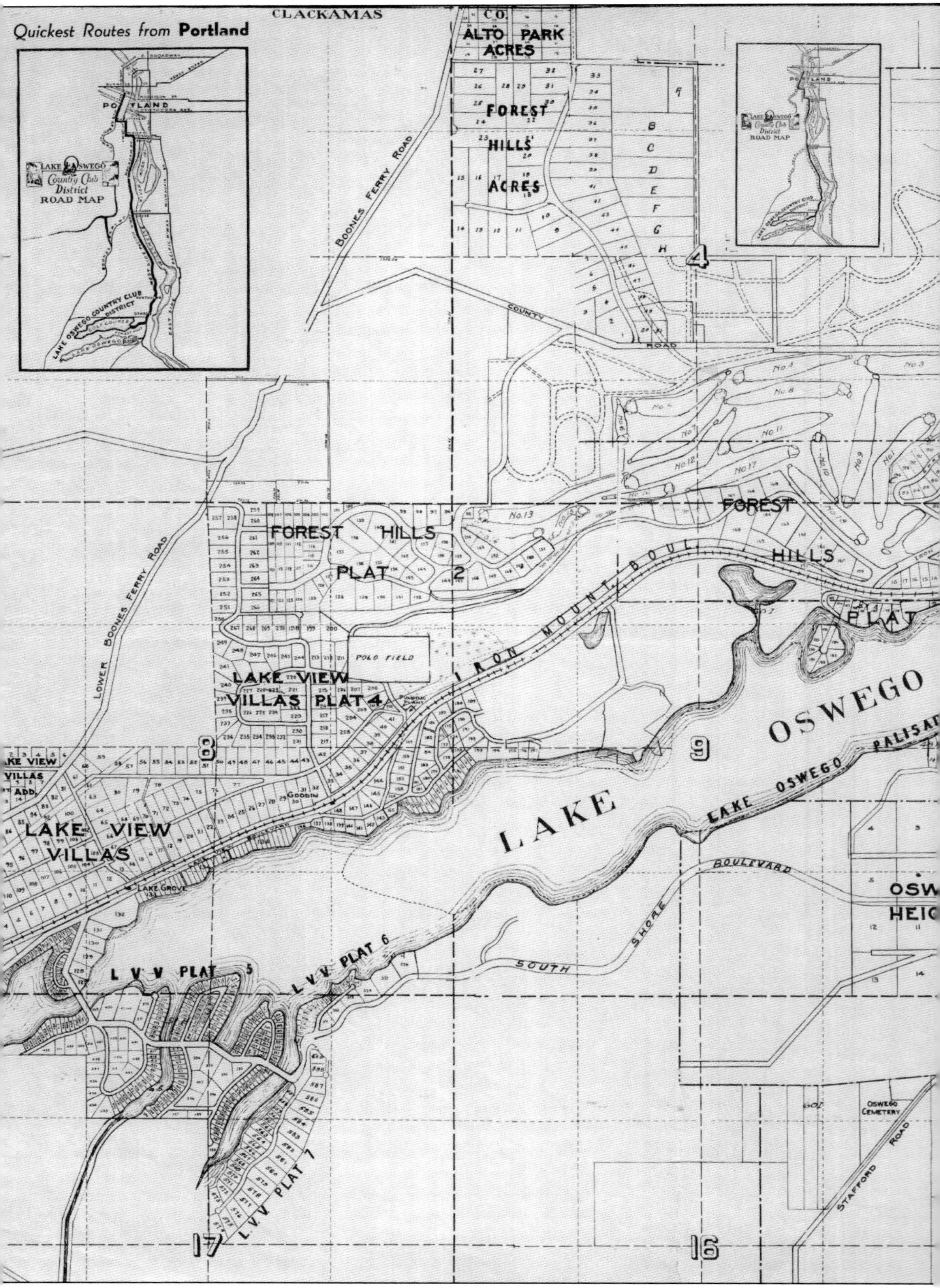
CLACKAMAS CO.
Quickest Routes from Portland
Lake Oswego Country Club District Road Map
ALTO PARK ACRES
FOREST HILLS ACRES
BOONES FERRY ROAD
COUNTY ROAD
FOREST HILLS PLAT 2
LOWER BOONES FERRY ROAD
POLO FIELD
IRON MOUNT BOUL
FOREST HILLS
LAKE VIEW VILLAS PLAT 4
LAKE VIEW VILLAS
LAKE OSWEGO
LAKE OSWEGO BOULEVARD
OSWEGO PALISADES
SOUTH SHORE BOULEVARD
OSWEGO HEIGHTS
L V V PLAT 5
L V V PLAT 6
L V V PLAT 7
OSWEGO CEMETERY
STAFFORD ROAD
4
8
9
16
17

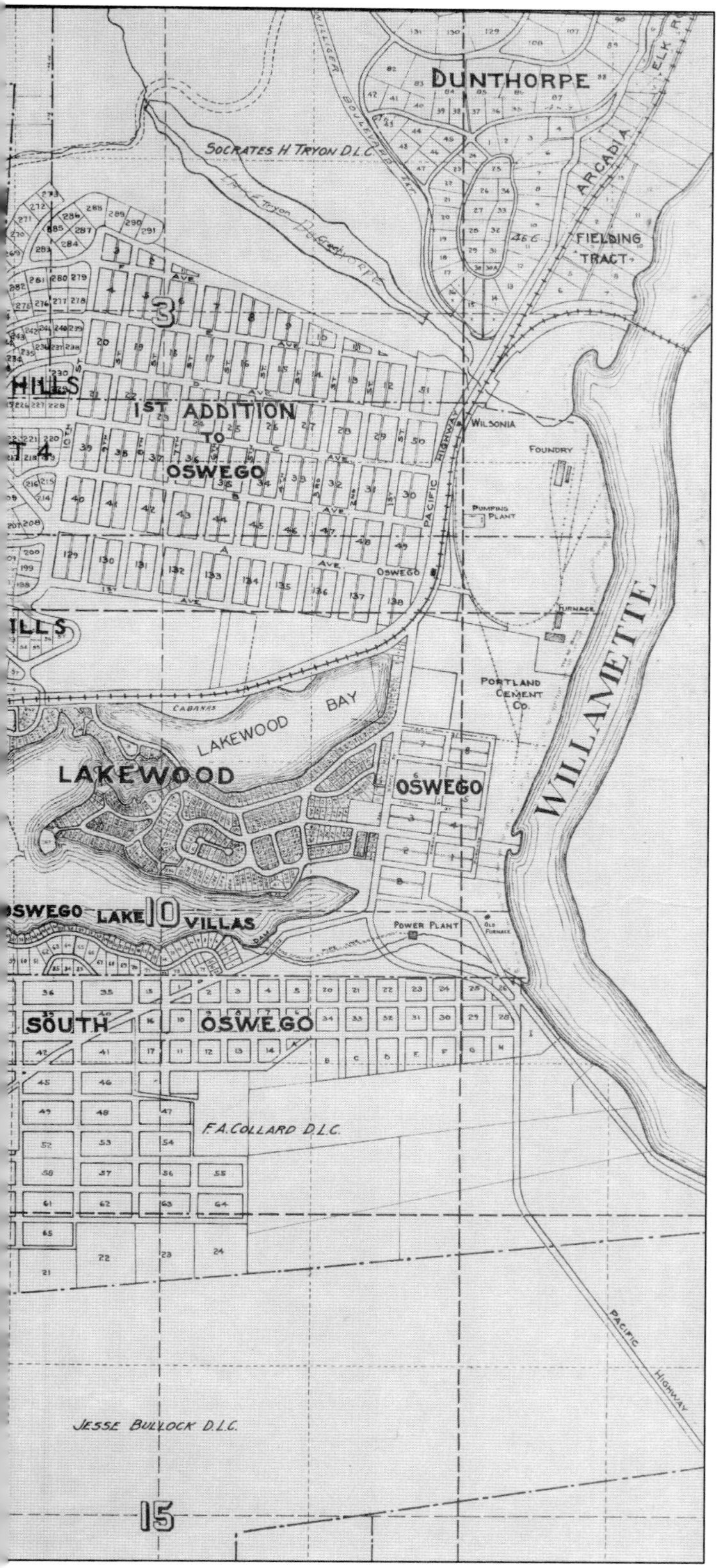

OSWEGO MAP, 1920S. In marketing lots around the lake, roads were a big selling point, as early real estate sales had been stymied by their absence. A 1920s real estate brochure notes that the Country Club District is "only twenty minutes from the city over paved boulevards" with "all the conveniences of the city . . . electricity, gas and macadam are in and paid for." The roadways, designed to follow the land's contours were in contrast to the grid pattern of most urban streets: "The winding roadways afford you access, yet detract nothing from the native state of the district." Never mind that the native state had been logged and mined, it was still a compelling and successful argument. Compare the earlier plats of South Oswego, Oswego, and First Addition with their right angles to the sinuous contours of the new developments.

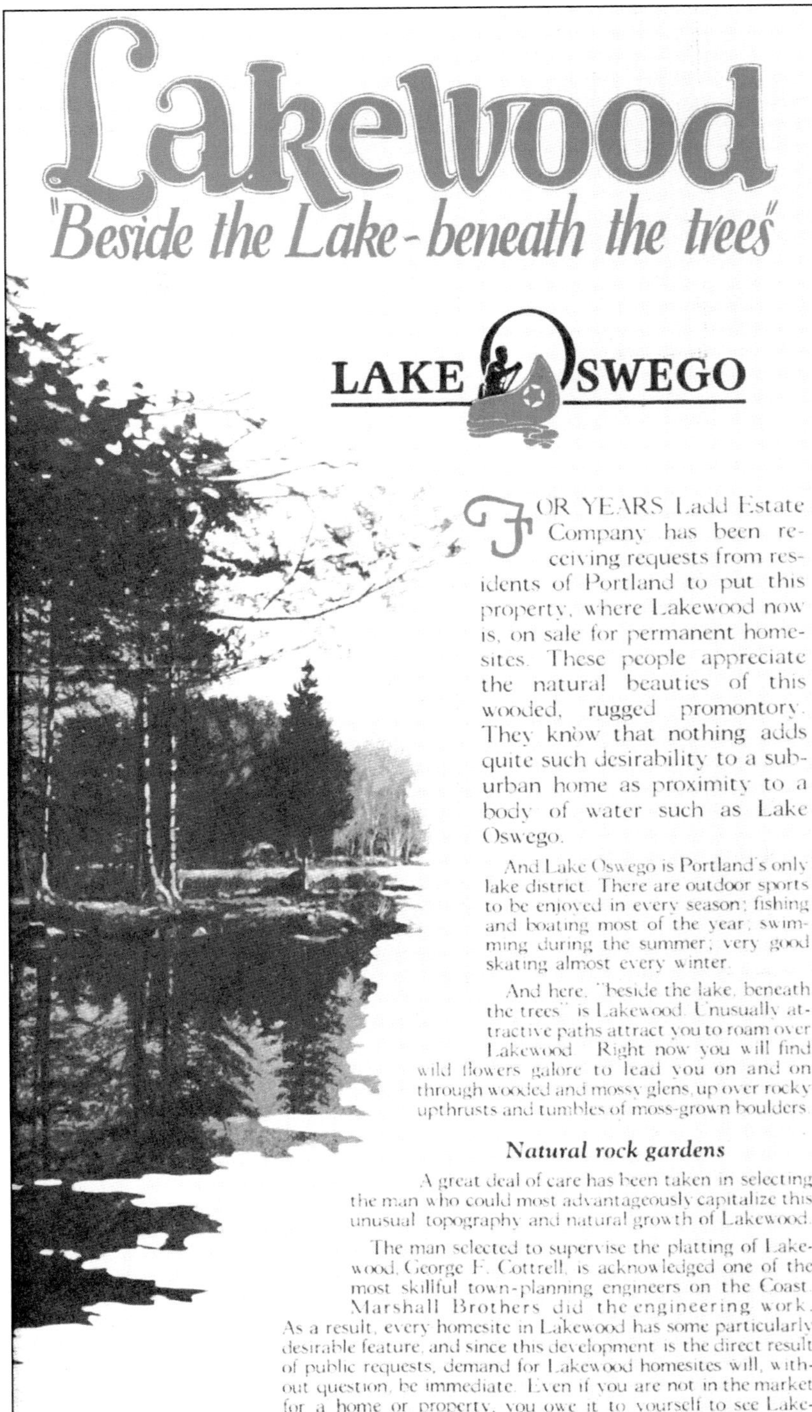

Lakewood

"Beside the Lake - beneath the trees"

LAKE OSWEGO

FOR YEARS Ladd Estate Company has been receiving requests from residents of Portland to put this property, where Lakewood now is, on sale for permanent homesites. These people appreciate the natural beauties of this wooded, rugged promontory. They know that nothing adds quite such desirability to a suburban home as proximity to a body of water such as Lake Oswego.

And Lake Oswego is Portland's only lake district. There are outdoor sports to be enjoyed in every season; fishing and boating most of the year; swimming during the summer; very good skating almost every winter.

And here, "beside the lake, beneath the trees" is Lakewood. Unusually attractive paths attract you to roam over Lakewood. Right now you will find wild flowers galore to lead you on and on through wooded and mossy glens, up over rocky upthrusts and tumbles of moss-grown boulders.

Natural rock gardens

A great deal of care has been taken in selecting the man who could most advantageously capitalize this unusual topography and natural growth of Lakewood.

The man selected to supervise the platting of Lakewood, George F. Cottrell, is acknowledged one of the most skillful town-planning engineers on the Coast. Marshall Brothers did the engineering work. As a result, every homesite in Lakewood has some particularly desirable feature, and since this development is the direct result of public requests, demand for Lakewood homesites will, without question, be immediate. Even if you are not in the market for a home or property, you owe it to yourself to see Lakewood before it is all owned privately.

LAKEWOOD BROCHURE. The casual rentals of campsites and cottages around the swimming concession at the lake's east end came to a close when Lakewood was platted out in 1924. An aerial view of it is on page 97. Today the north shore of Lakewood Bay is the "Cabana Zone," where homes can be built on pilings.

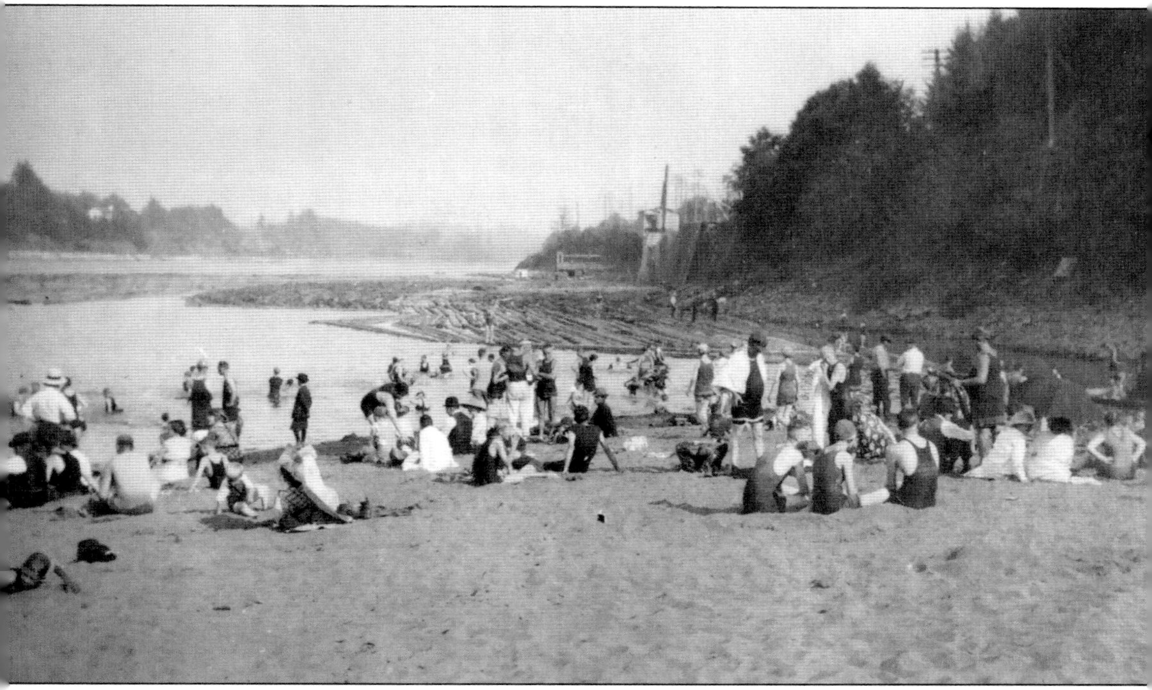

Willamette River Beachgoers. In this 1920s image, a crowd enjoys a recreational pursuit less refined than golf or polo: hanging out on a Willamette River beach at Oswego Landing. In the background are large rafts of logs waiting to be hoisted up via the log hoist on River Road. The log hoist was built around 1900 to lift logs to railcars on the line running south from Oswego. The hoist was closed in the late 1920s. At one point, a house was built atop it; it appears to be present in this picture. Parts of the hoist are still present along the Old River Road trail. On the far right in the water is an early paddleboat in which the seated boater turns a large wooden waterwheel by pedaling with his feet.

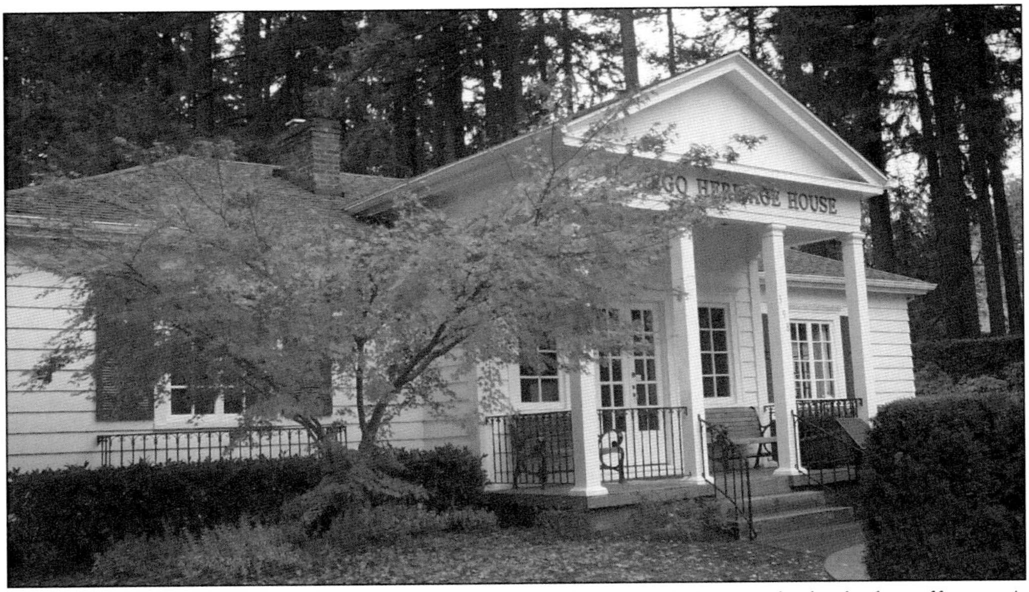

Real Estate Sales Office. In 1920, real estate developer Paul C. Murphy built this office at A Avenue and Tenth Street in a classical style interestingly unlike the less formal styles that he promoted for the Country Club District. In 1939, Dr. William Cane bought the building, enlarging it as his residence and office, and Murphy moved to the structure on State Street seen on page 108. Today the building is home to the Oswego Heritage Council. (Author's collection.)

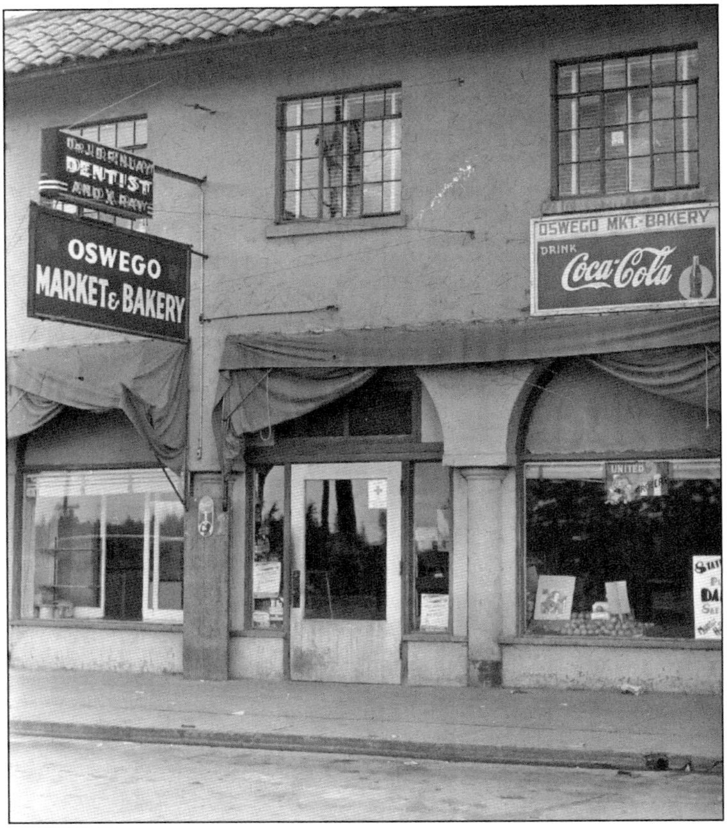

George Rogers's Second Store. George and August Rogers, longtime Oswego merchants, built this Mediterranean-style store in 1928. It is believed to have been designed by Van Evera Bailey, who also designed George Rogers's distinctive (and still standing) home on Wilbur Street in Old Town.

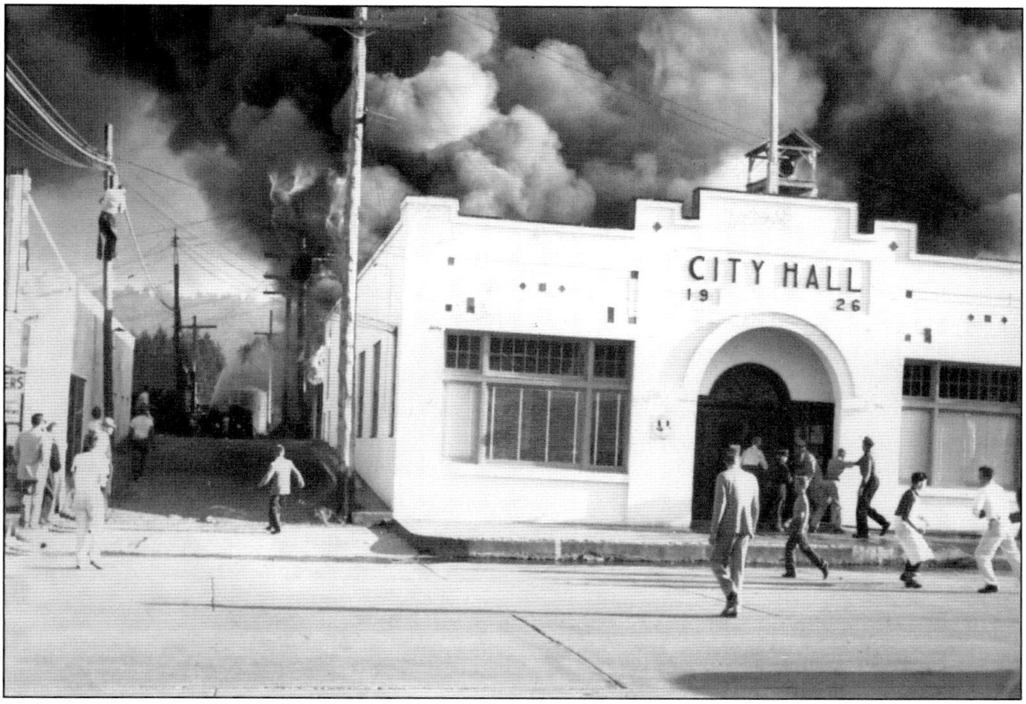

Fire behind City Hall. The Mission-style city hall is a dramatic setting for a fire raging behind it. On a telephone pole, a man perches for a better look, people run to see what is happening, electric lines spark from the heat, black smoke billows menacingly, and firefighters work hard.

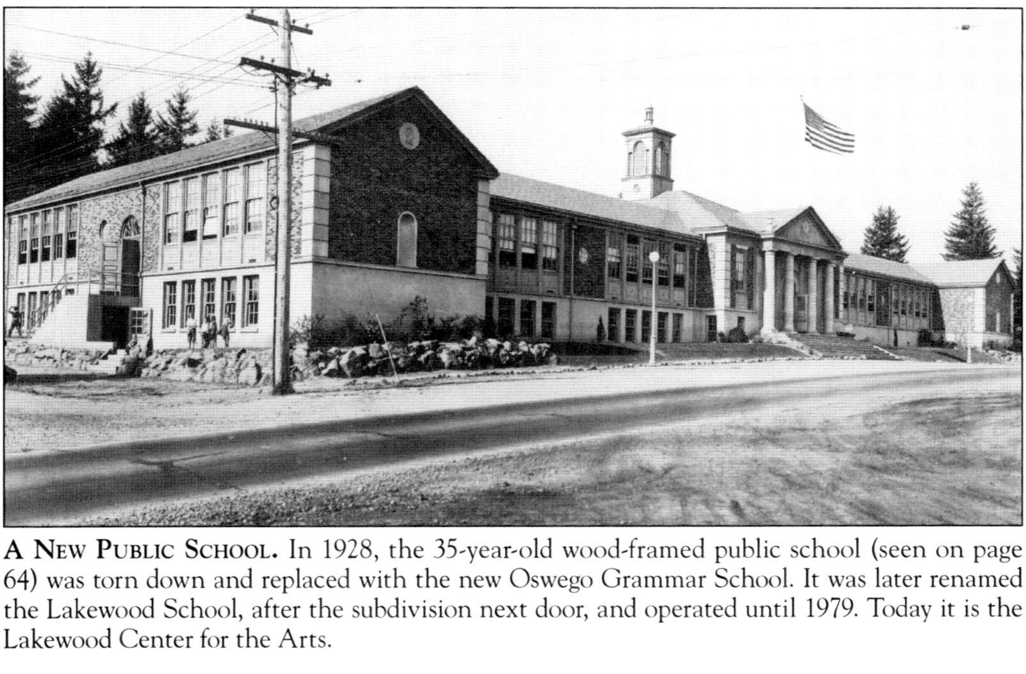

A New Public School. In 1928, the 35-year-old wood-framed public school (seen on page 64) was torn down and replaced with the new Oswego Grammar School. It was later renamed the Lakewood School, after the subdivision next door, and operated until 1979. Today it is the Lakewood Center for the Arts.

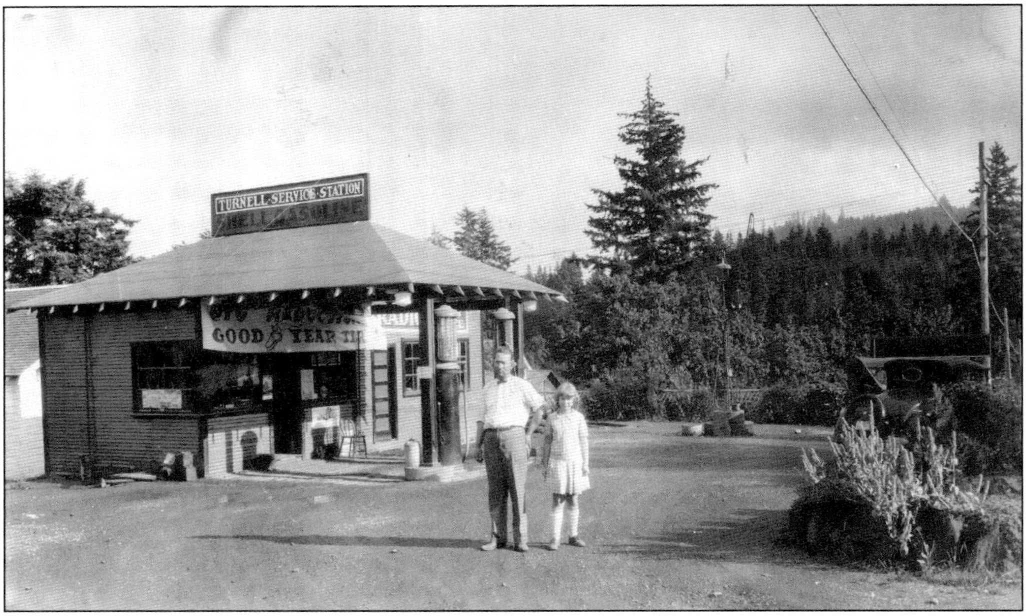

Early Filling Station. A man and young girl stand in front of the gas pumps at the Turnell Service Station around 1930. Until the 1970s, when self-service became popularized throughout the nation, station attendants generally pumped gas. In 1951, Oregon banned customers from pumping their own gas at gas stations based on concerns they would not do it properly. The ban is still in place.

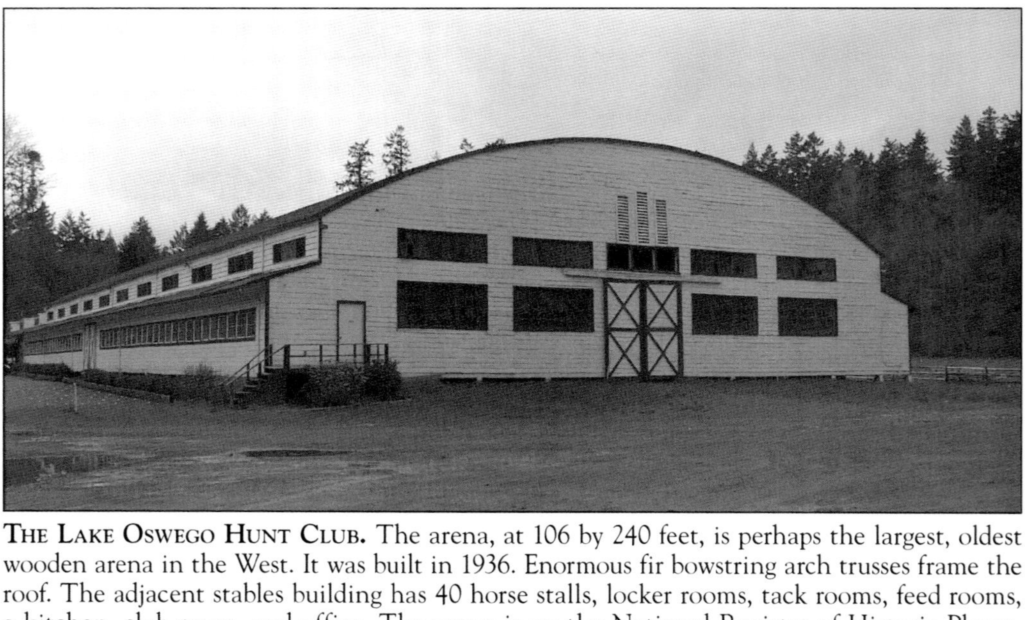

The Lake Oswego Hunt Club. The arena, at 106 by 240 feet, is perhaps the largest, oldest wooden arena in the West. It was built in 1936. Enormous fir bowstring arch trusses frame the roof. The adjacent stables building has 40 horse stalls, locker rooms, tack rooms, feed rooms, a kitchen, club room, and office. The arena is on the National Register of Historic Places. (Author's collection.)

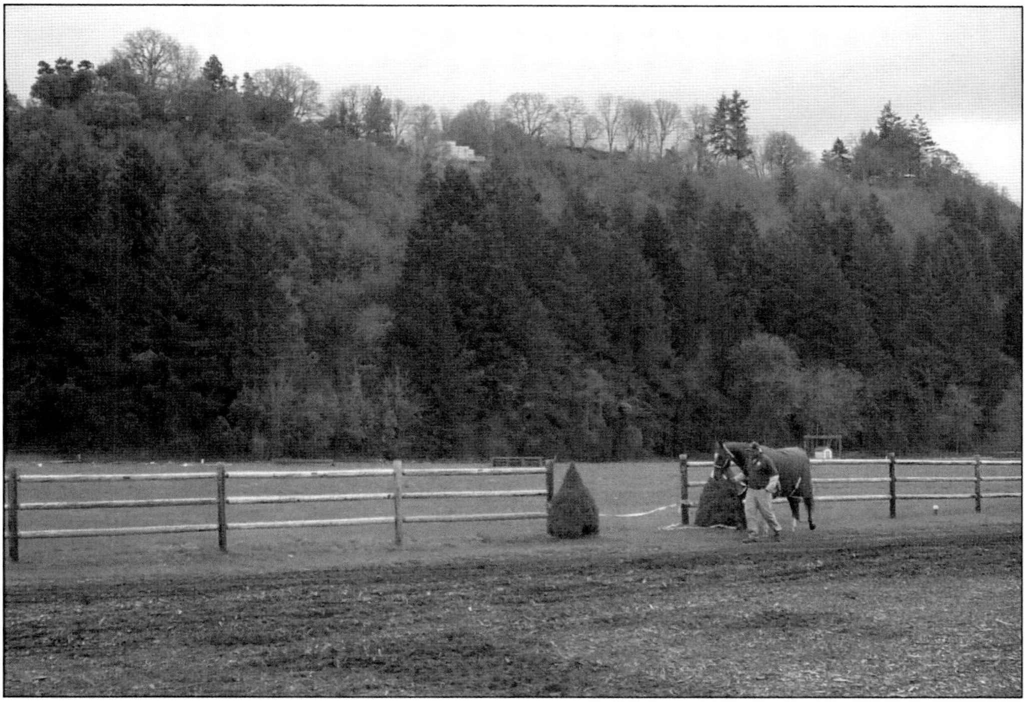

HUNT CLUB POLO FIELD AND TRACK. In 1936, when Oregon Iron and Steel proposed a riding and polo facilities to complement the Lake Oswego Country Club, it offered 19 acres and easements for riding trails to the new club, which sits at the base of Iron Mountain on Iron Mountain Boulevard. (Author's collection.)

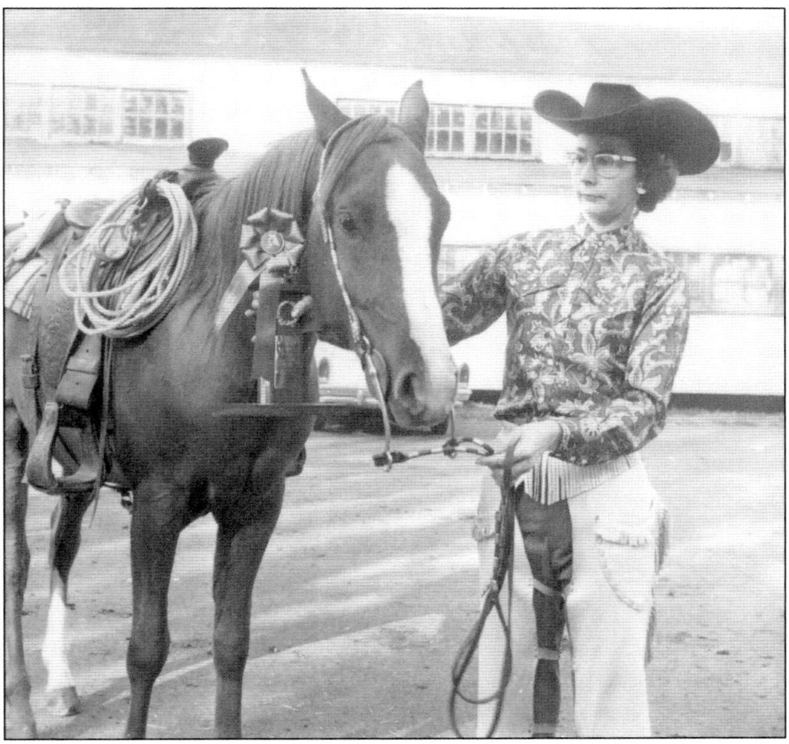

A PROUD EQUESTRIAN. This serious young woman holds her trophy and ribbon under her horse's head around 1960 during one of the many horse shows held at the hunt club in that era.

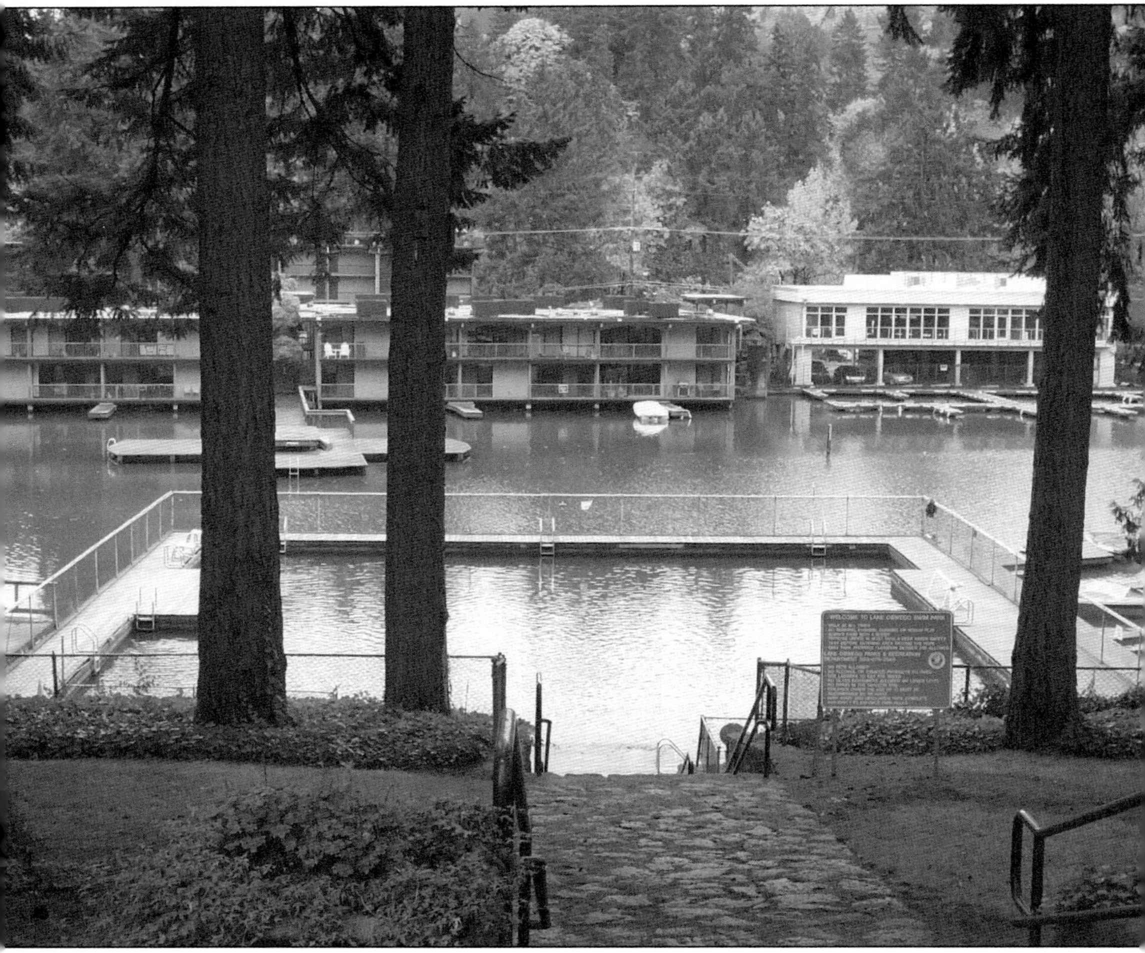

Oswego Swim Park. By the 1920s, Oregon Iron and Steel's laissez-faire policies with regard to lake access began to end. Herbert Nelson remembered, "In 1924 they built a big new boathouse and fenced off the end of the lake to charge people to go swimming. Before it was always free to anybody from anywhere to go swimming in the lake." In the 1930s, in a public works project, this swim park was built at the east end of the lake, across from the dam. In the late 1950s, the owner of Lake Oswego Public Swim, the successor to the Nelson swim and boat concession at the lake's east end, offered its property to the city. The City of Lake Oswego declined, the land was sold to a developer, and public access to the private lake ended, a situation that exists today. The Bay Roc apartments were built on the old swimming concession site. (Author's collection.)

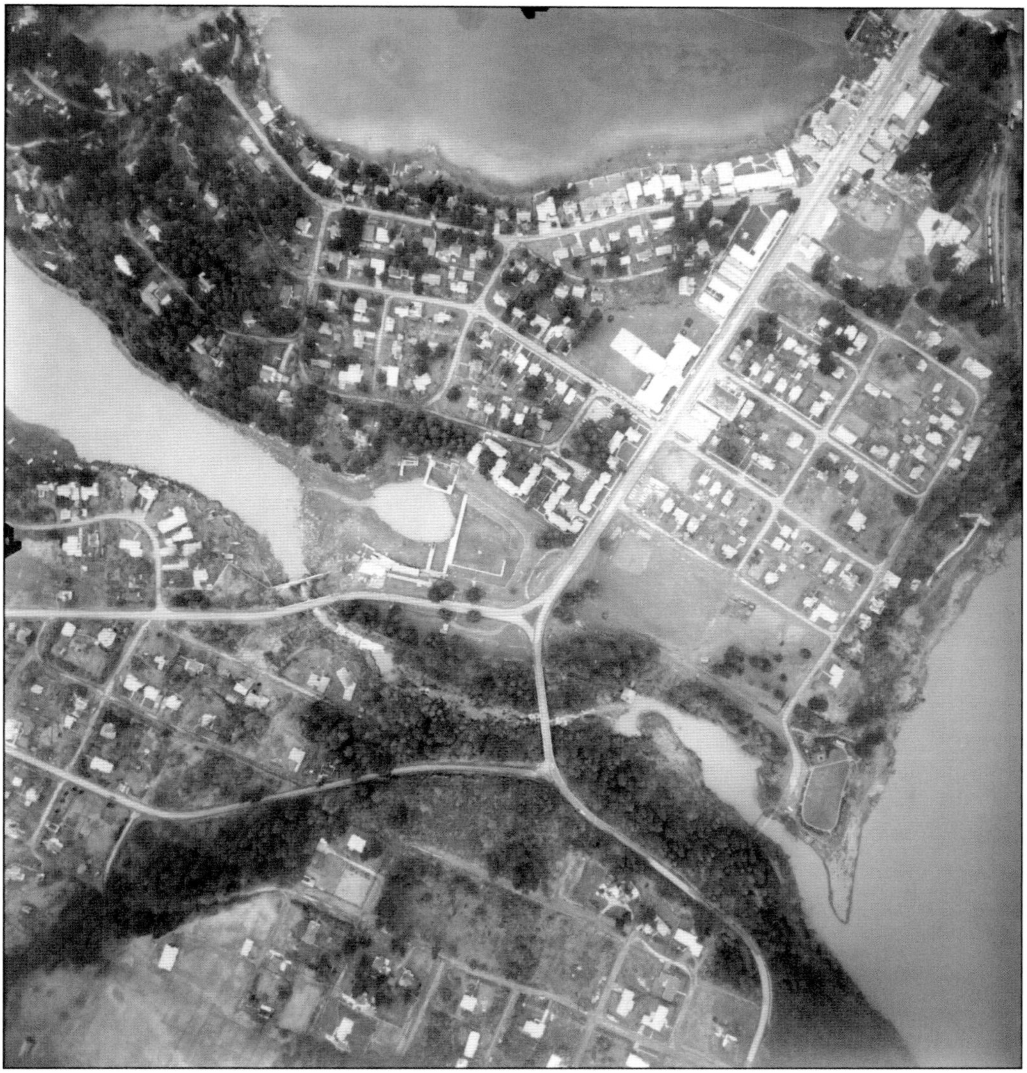

During a Lake Draw Down. Periodically, the Lake Oswego Corporation opens the dam floodgates to partially drain the lake, always during the fall or winter, when lake use is lowest. During that time, local contractors work long hours fixing the docks, boathouses, and walls of lakefront properties. Here in this 1950s image, it appears a draw down is in progress. The Oswego Swim Park is seen in the center of the photograph with what appears to be a big puddle in front of it. Lakewood Bay is at the top, and the dam, at center left, is still releasing water into Oswego Creek. The Bay Roc apartments have not yet been built; structures in the lake appear to be from the public swim park. State Street heads off to the top right corner of the photograph. After a time, the canal headgate is opened and the lake refilled using the waters of the Tualatin River. In a 2006 draw down, in an attempt to lessen the lake's algae issues, the Tualatin gate was not opened, and the lake was allowed to fill more slowly from its own watershed.

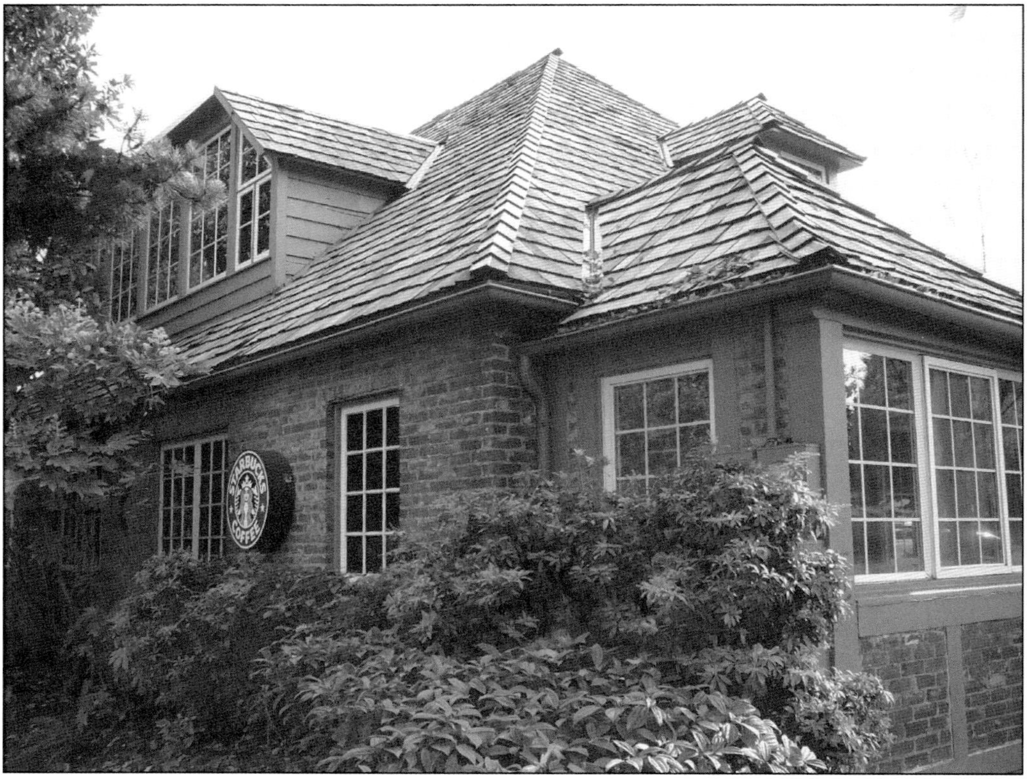

Murphy Real Estate Building. Paul Murphy moved his real estate business here in 1940 from the building seen on page 102. This building was designed by architect Richard Sundeleaf in a style to suggest an English country village, a complement to the picturesque residential styles of architecture that Murphy encouraged for the Country Club District. (Author's collection.)

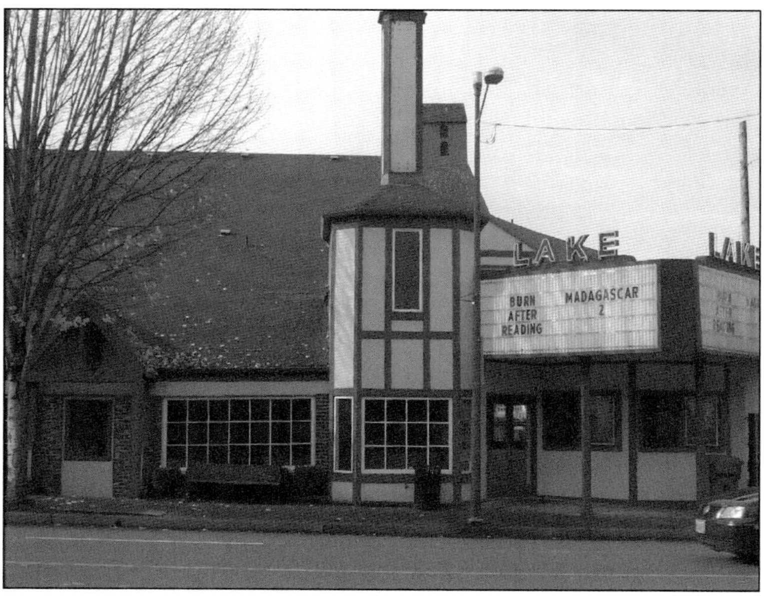

Lake Twin Cinema. Richard Sundeleaf also designed the theater in a similarly picturesque style as the Murphy Real Estate Building. It was built in 1940 in the Tudor style. Sundeleaf designed the beautiful Jantzen Apparel building in Northeast Portland and the Jantzen boathouse on Oswego Lake for the company's owner, Carl Jantzen. (Author's collection.)

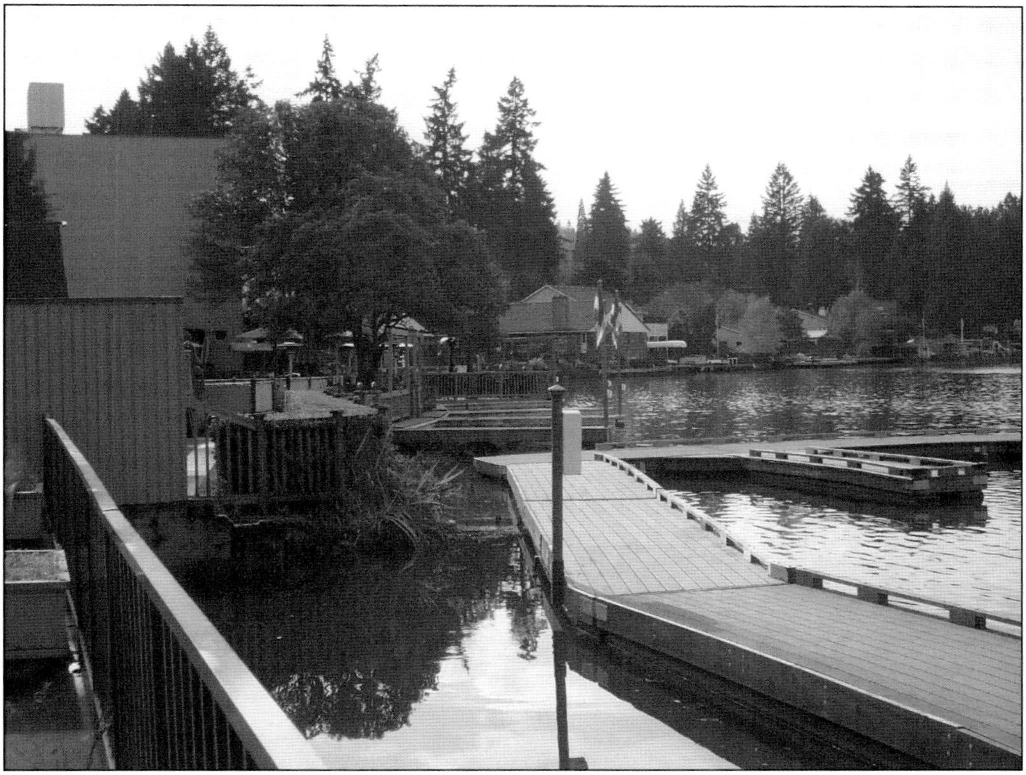

Boat Slips behind Lake Theater. One of the pleasures of living on the lake was avoiding the roads. From a private boat dock, one could motor down the lake to downtown Oswego, tie up behind the theater, and enjoy dinner and a movie before heading back home under the stars. (Author's collection.)

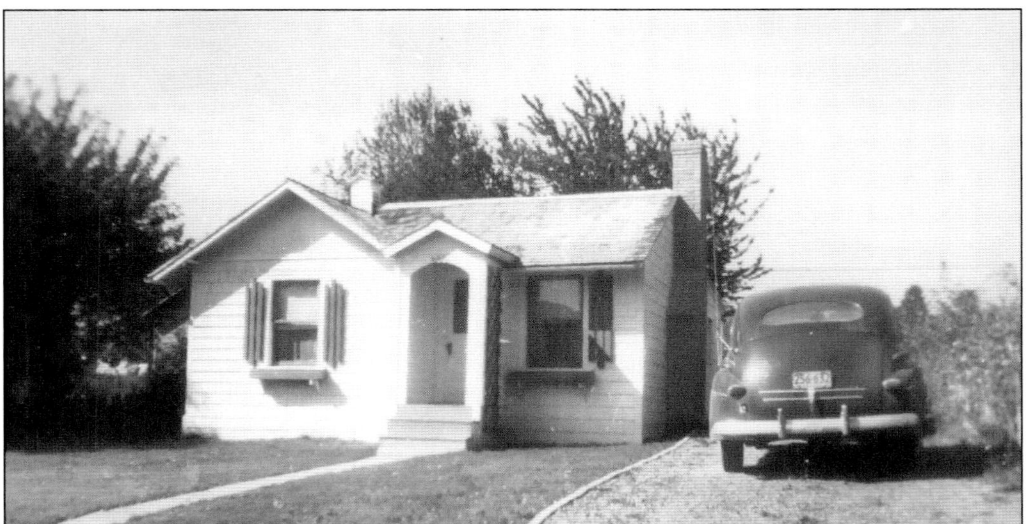

Post–World War II Home. Not all new housing was in the new developments around the lake. Infill continued in First Addition, as seen by this small home on Second Street. The enormous car seems to be about one-third the size of the home.

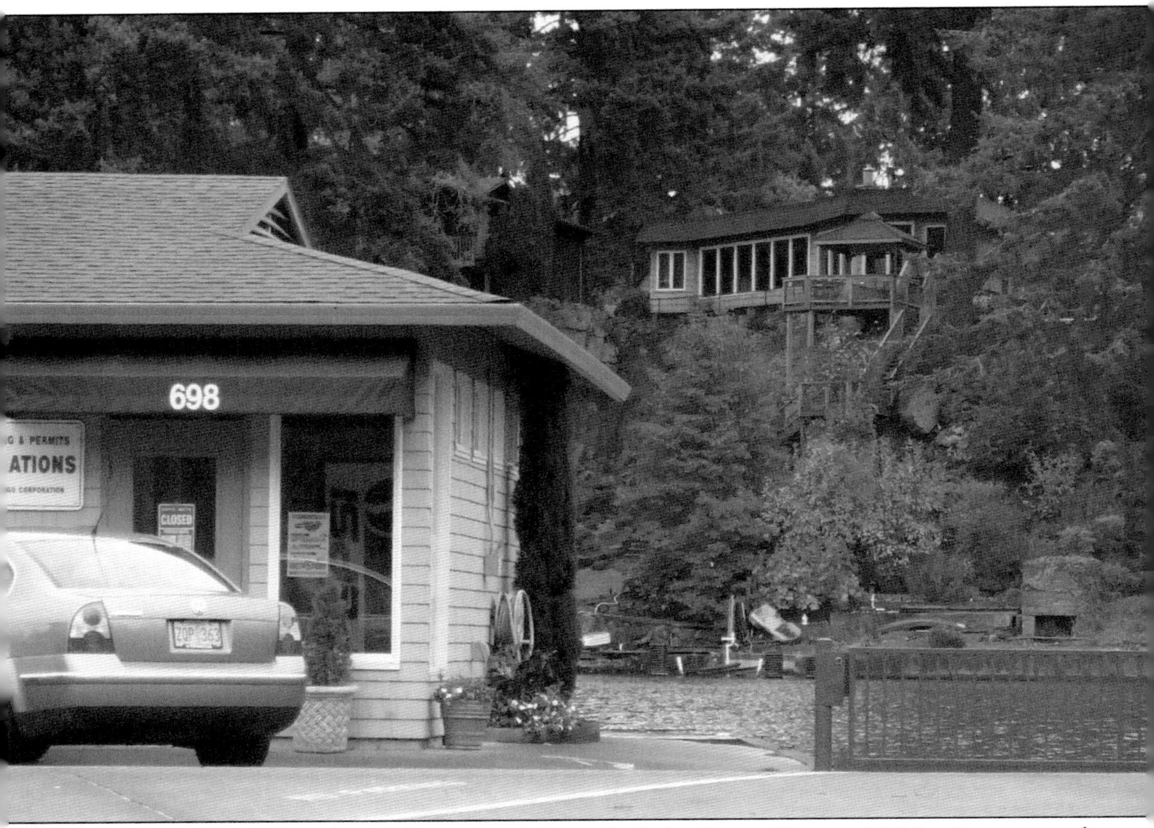

Lake Corp Office, Quarry Site. Across from the Lake Corp offices on McVey Avenue can be seen the site of the quarry from which basalt stone was cut to build the first furnace in the 1860s. A home now occupies the site. The Lake Corp owns 500 acre-feet of water at Hagg Lake (also known as the Scoggins Reservoir) in the upper Tualatin River valley and sells some of its Tualatin River water rights to the Oswego Lake Country Club for golf course irrigation. Besides managing regulatory and business issues such as boat licensing and construction permitting, the Lake Corp also deals with the lake's water quality issues, such as an overabundance of nutrients, sedimentation, and aquatic plants. Methods it has used include aeration of the lake, limiting nutrient sources, alum applications, and diver-operated suction harvests of water plants. (Author's collection.)

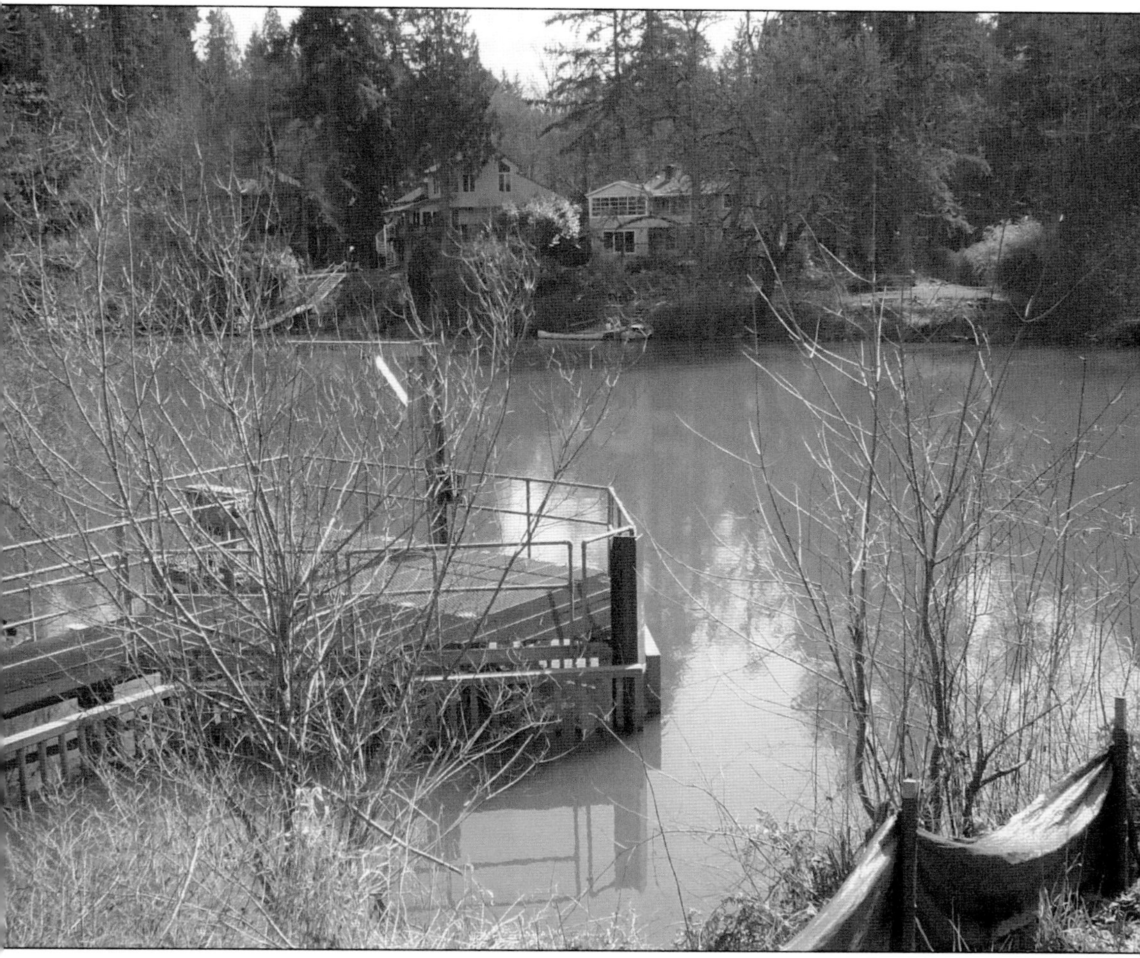

CANAL AT TUALATIN RIVER. Charlie Didzun, who was born in 1893, remembered working to keep the Tualatin Canal open as a young man: "I worked on the canal at the end of Oswego Lake for the Oregon Iron and Steel Company. We went there twice a year and cleaned out the canal and rebuilt it from the Tualatin River down to the mouth of the canal up at Lake Grove. The sides of the canal were built out of two by twelve lumber. The lumber would rot and then we would have to replace it." The lumber has since rotted away. (Author's collection.)

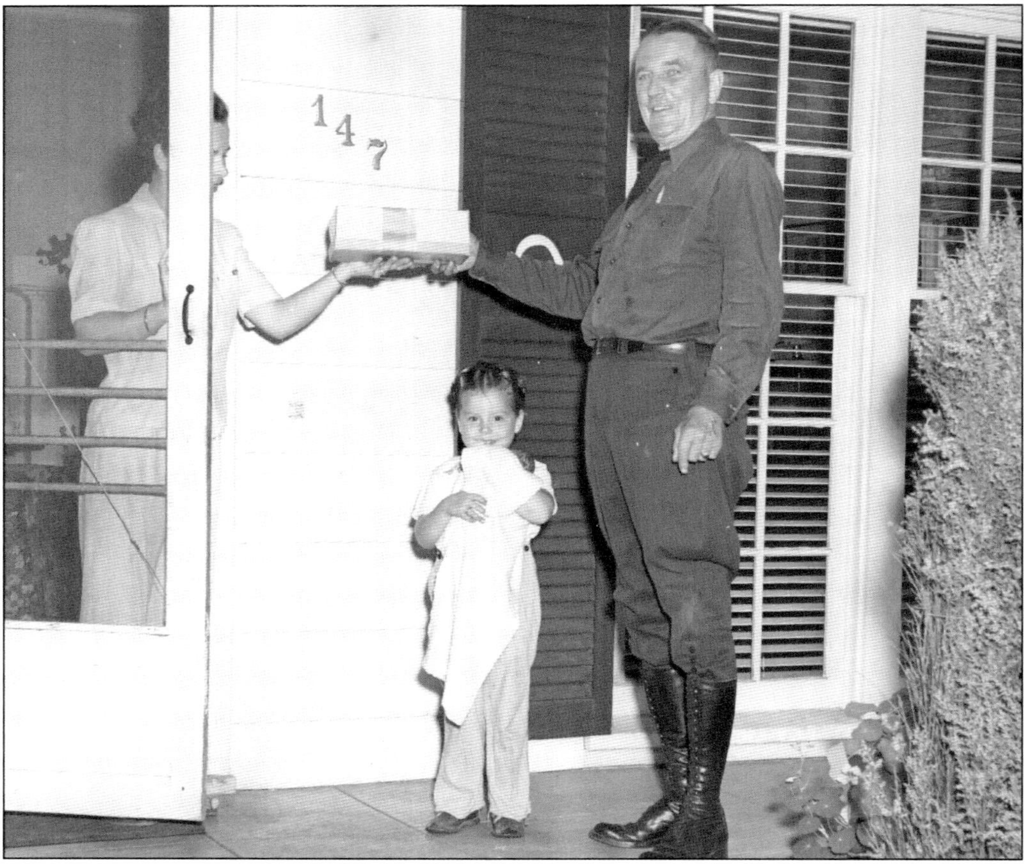

MEIER AND FRANK DELIVERYMAN. Meier and Frank was a Portland retailing icon from 1857 to 2005. It was sold in 1966 to the May Department Stores, but the name was retained until 2005 when, under control of Federated Department Stores, it became a Macy's. Here in this c. 1940 photograph, Van Twiller delivers a package to a First Addition homeowner. Her little girl clutches her doll. Twiller's posture and uniform, especially his spit-shined lace-up boots, speak of the pride he took in his work. He delivered for Meier and Frank from 1915 to 1949.

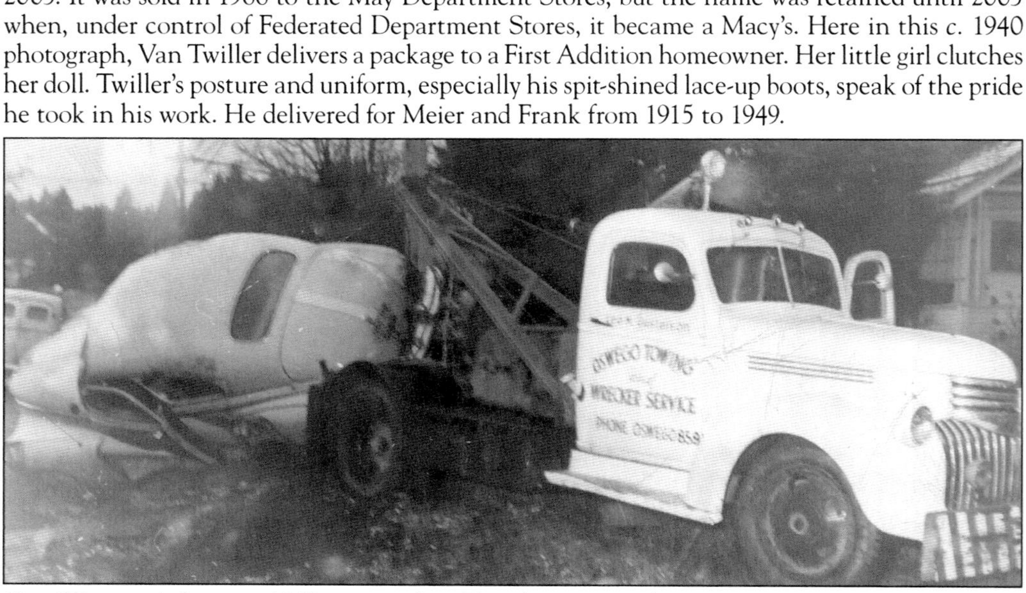

CAR WRECK. A January 1947 car wreck at Fourth Street and B Avenue provides another small glimpse into the daily life of Oswego at mid century.

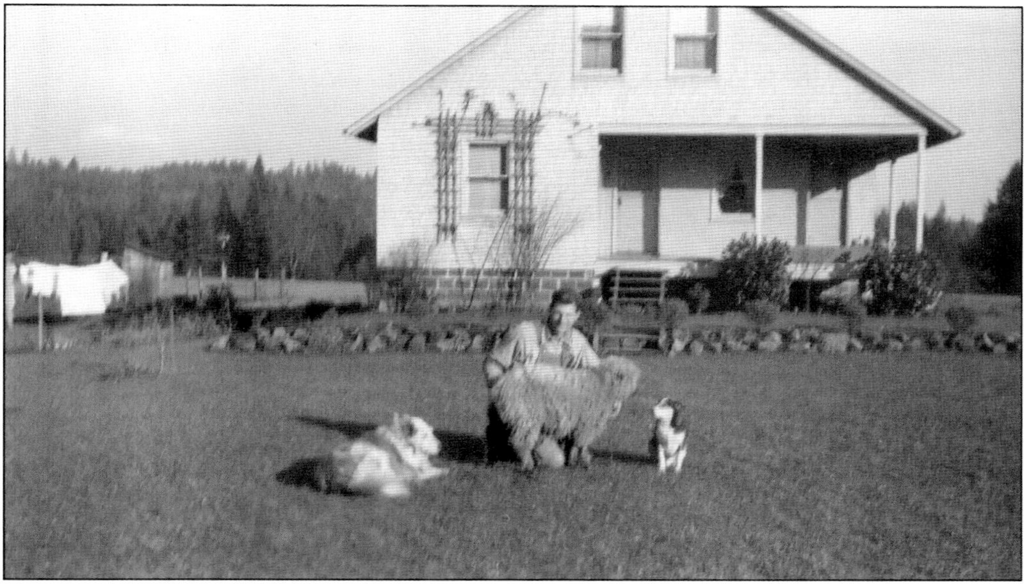

Farmer and Animals. Much of what is now incorporated into the city of Lake Oswego was still rural in the 1950s. Here at his farm on Knaus Road, north of Iron Mountain, Frans Van Twisk poses with his sheepdogs and sheep.

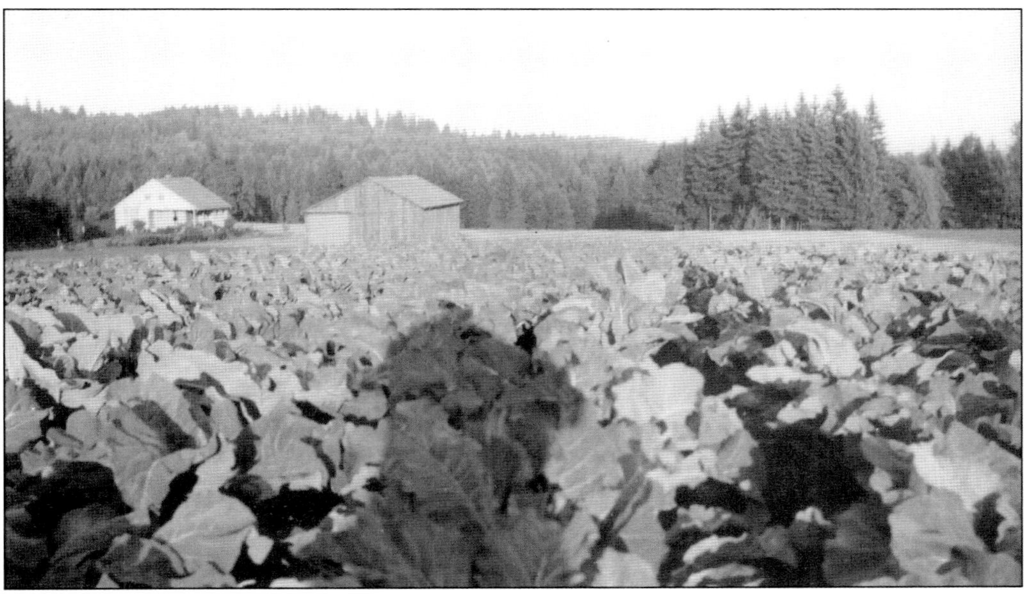

Cabbage on Knaus Road. A bucolic Oregon scene from the 1950s on the Van Twisk farm shows Knaus Road in contrast to the suburban scene there today.

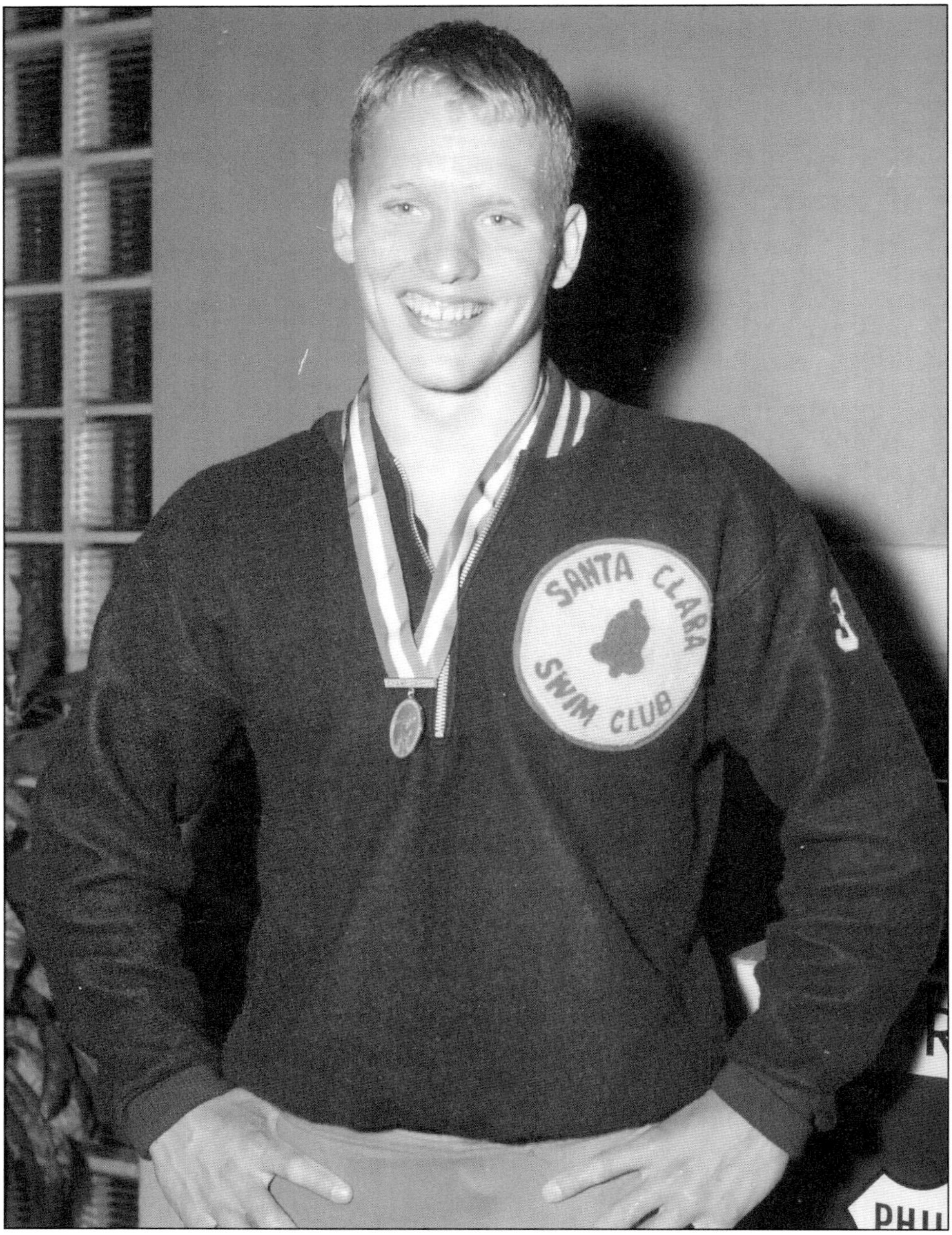

SWIMMER DON SCHOLLANDER. Seventeen-year-old Don Schollander was a member of the Santa Clara Swim Club, pictured here the year before the 1964 Tokyo Olympics. In the 1964 Olympics, he set three world records and won four gold medals, the most gold won by an American since Jesse Owens in 1936 and the most ever won by a swimmer in a single Olympic games (until Mark Spitz won seven in 1972). He had been a member of Lake Oswego High School's swim team, and as a freshman was on the team that won the Oregon state swimming championship. As a high school junior, he moved to Santa Clara, California, to train under swim coach George Haines. He later was captain of Yale's swim team and returned to the Olympics in 1968, winning gold in the 800-meter freestyle relay with teammate Mark Spitz. After the 1968 Olympics, he retired and returned to Lake Oswego.

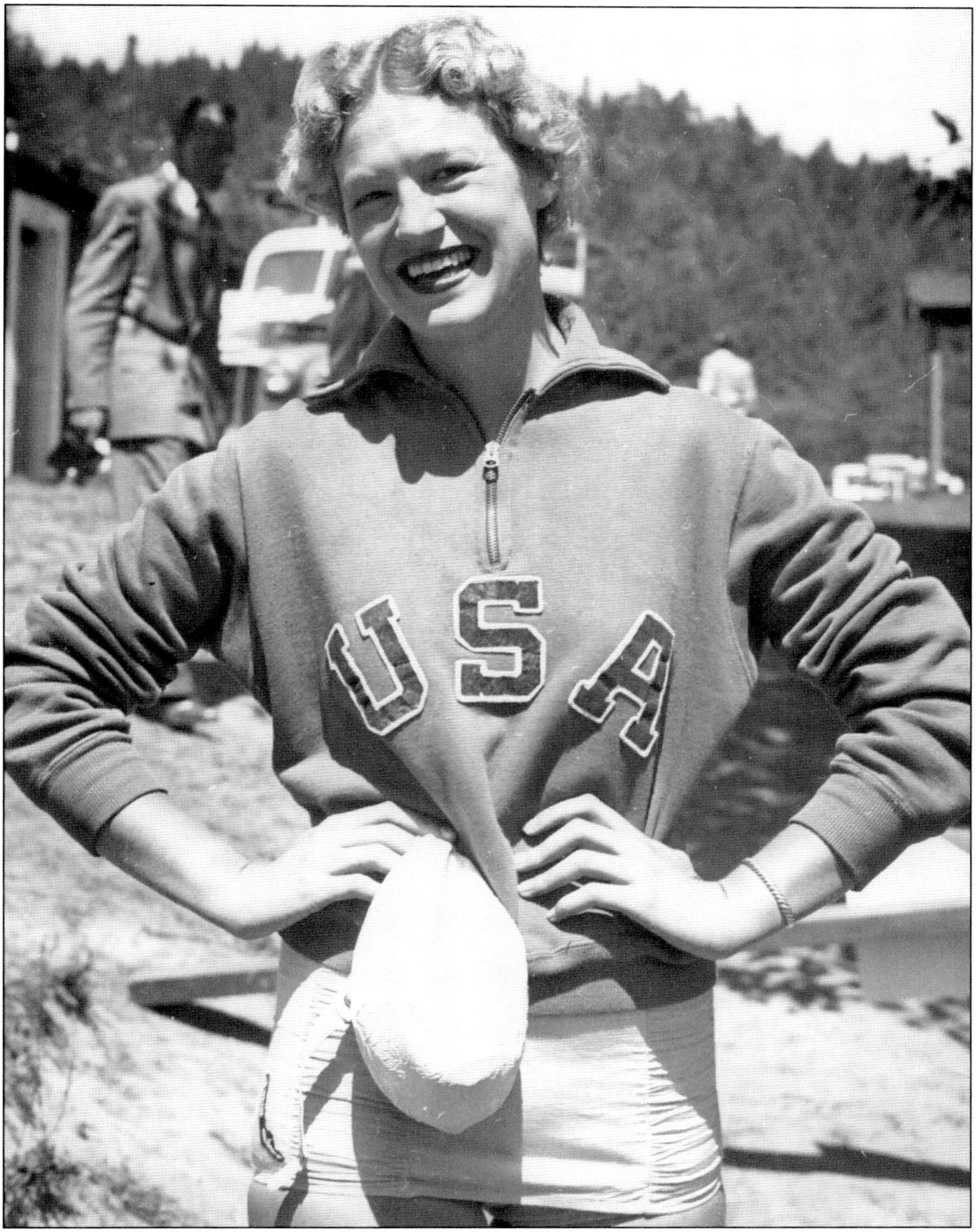

SWIMMER SUZANNE ZIMMERMAN. Twenty-three year old Suzanne Zimmerman smiles at the camera in 1948, the year she won the silver medal in the London Olympics with a time of 1:16 minutes in the 100-meter backstroke. She trained at the Multnomah Athletic Club in Portland under swim coach Jack Cody and was known as one of the "Cody Kids," swimmers who from 1939 to 1948 won 58 individual national swimming titles and three national team championships. Her mother, Edith, remembered in 1973, "I could speak about our surprise on a summer day swim meet when Sue and Nancy were about 12 years old and swam with ease the 3.5 mile lake. The starting point for the swim meets was at the Lake Grove end at Jack Bate's lawn with a good seawall for starting and ending at the Allen Morris resort in Oswego."

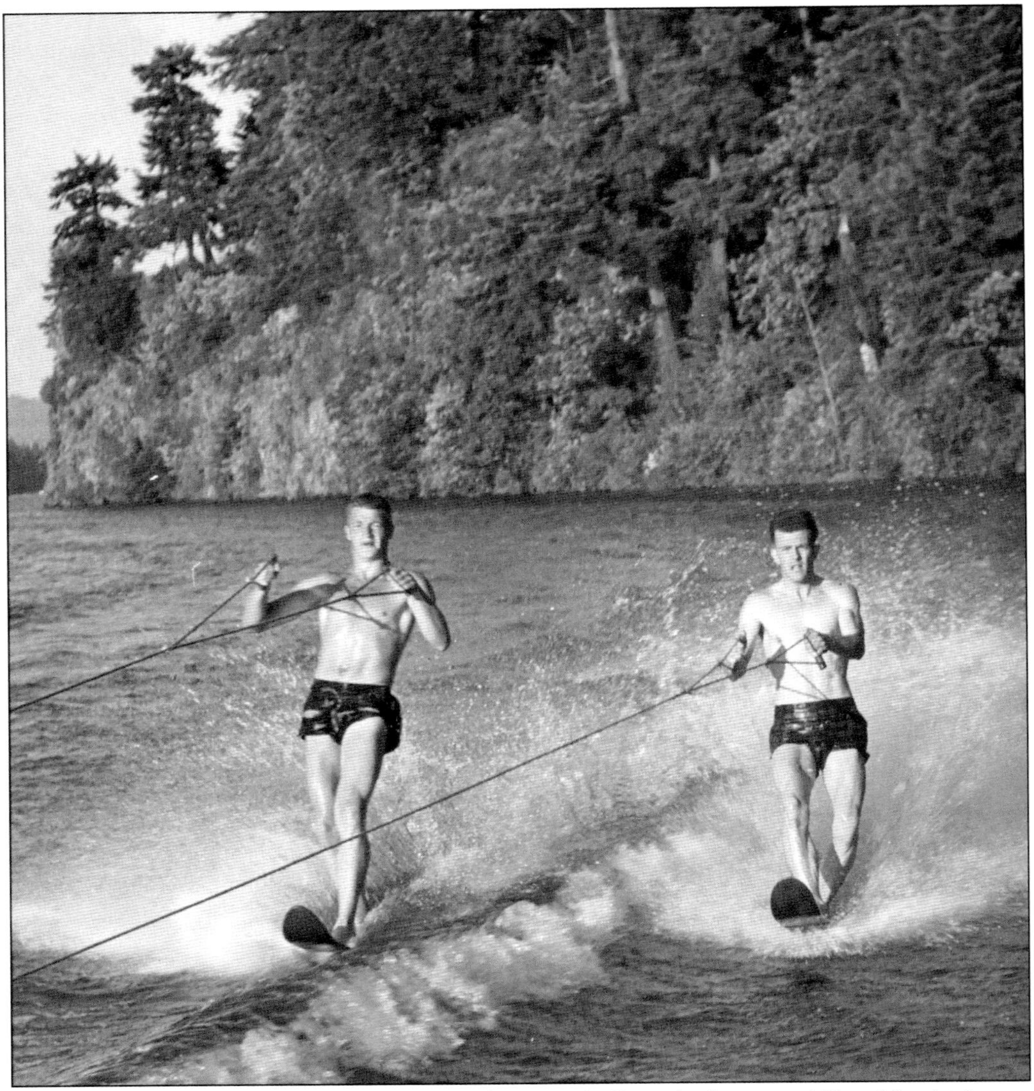

WATERSKIING ON THE LAKE. In this 1950s photograph, Don Atchison and Don Hendricks are slalom skiing, in which both feet are in one ski as opposed to two. Fred Waller of Huntington, New York, is often called "the father of water skiing" in the United States, having patented a design in 1925 for skis that he called "Dolphin Akwa-Skees." The sport reputedly was invented in Minnesota in 1922. After unsuccessful attempts to water ski using barrel staves and snow skis, an 18-year-old named Ralph Samuelson successfully skied across Lake Pepin on a pair of 9-foot homemade planks attached to his feet with leather straps. His towrope was a 100-foot-long sash cord with an iron ring on the end. After his success, he showed his sport around the country. By the late 1920s, skiing was also attracting attention on the French Riviera, promoted by Count Maximilian Pulaski. In Oregon, people like businessman Leon Bullier became one of the first to ski on Oswego Lake, in the late 1930s. Among the guests to dip into the lake, as Bullier drove the ski boat, was Yul Brynner. The American Water Ski Association was founded in 1939.

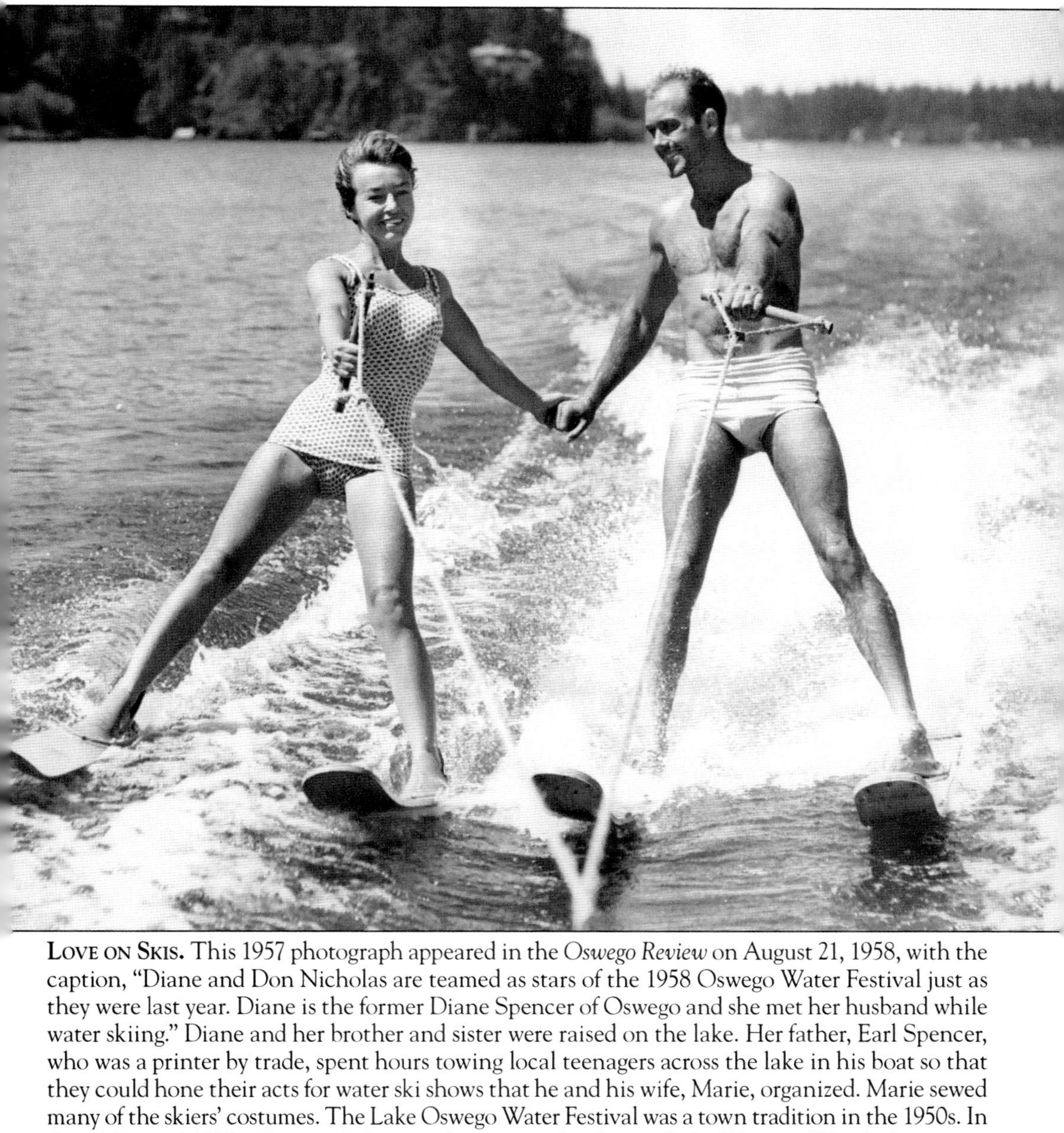

LOVE ON SKIS. This 1957 photograph appeared in the *Oswego Review* on August 21, 1958, with the caption, "Diane and Don Nicholas are teamed as stars of the 1958 Oswego Water Festival just as they were last year. Diane is the former Diane Spencer of Oswego and she met her husband while water skiing." Diane and her brother and sister were raised on the lake. Her father, Earl Spencer, who was a printer by trade, spent hours towing local teenagers across the lake in his boat so that they could hone their acts for water ski shows that he and his wife, Marie, organized. Marie sewed many of the skiers' costumes. The Lake Oswego Water Festival was a town tradition in the 1950s. In the 1960s and 1970s, Oswego Lake was the test site for skis made by Western Woods Company.

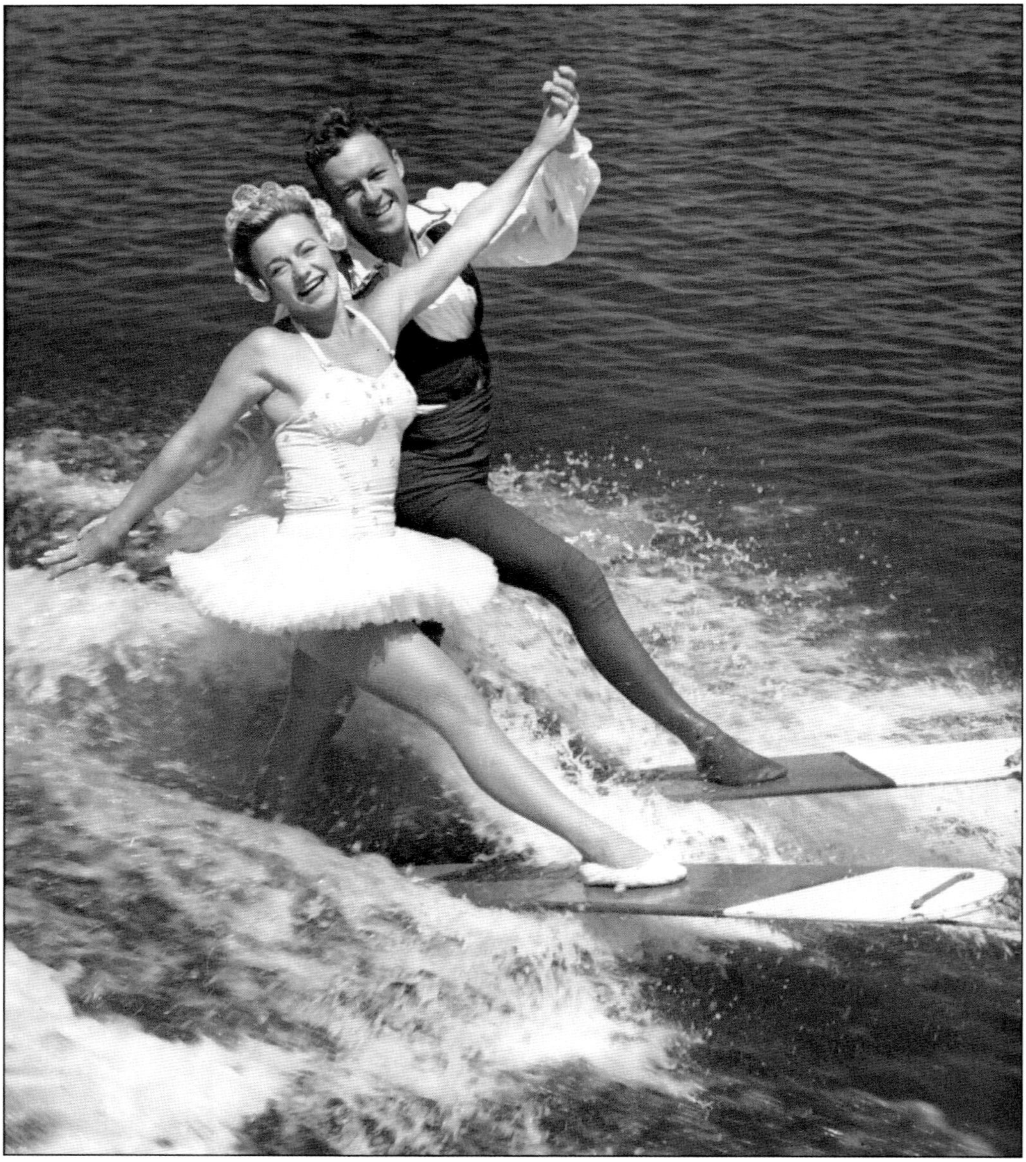

A Career on the Water. Willa Worthington and Red McGuire ski at Cypress Gardens in Florida in the 1950s. Willa's father, Wallace Worthington, owned a marina on Lakewood Bay. One summer day in 1942, he tied water skis to 14-year-old Willa's feet, put the towrope in her hand, and took off across the lake. She remembered thinking, "This is my life forever." To promote the sport, her dad founded the Lake Oswego Water Ski Club. Portland's Jantzen Swimwear provided swimsuits for its members. Owner Carl Jantzen lived on the lake, on what is still known as Jantzen Island (located off North Shore Road). Willa won three world championships and eight national titles for performances at American Water Ski Association events, and she invented several water ski tricks. She retired in 1955 from competition and went to work at Cypress Gardens, a theme park in Florida, as the prima ballerina of its water ski shows. Jantzen Swimwear of Portland designed attire specifically for Cypress Garden water skiers. In a 1999 newspaper article, Willa noted that she still skied three times each week.

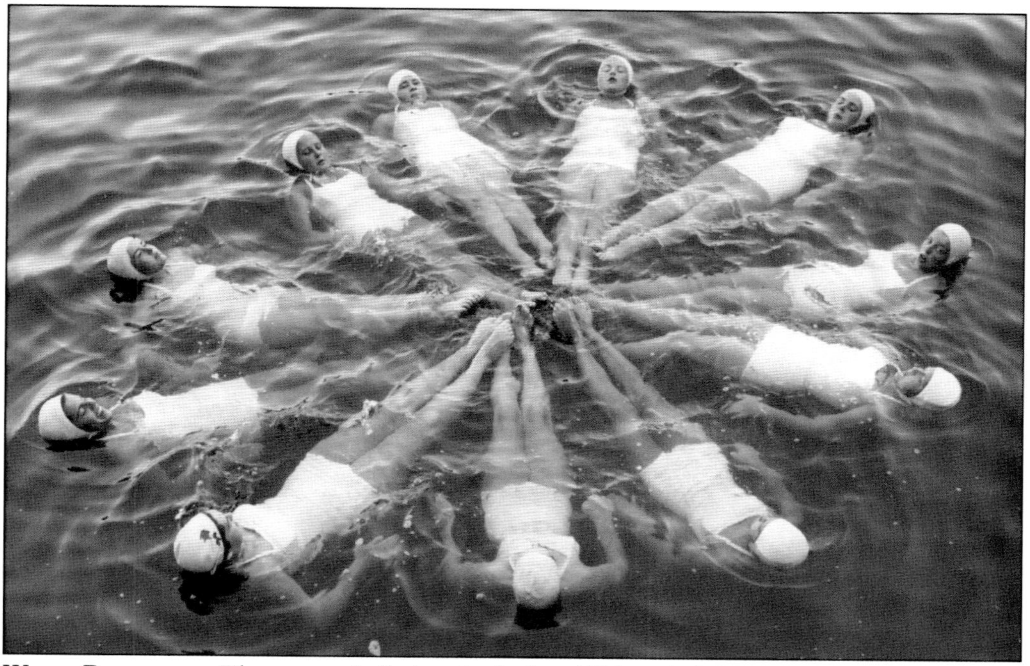

WATER BALLERINAS. These water ballerinas in the late 1950s include Marcia Gagnon, Jackie West, Marion Blew, Karen Kisky, and Sue Hoelsher. Perfection shows in the pointed toes, and the effort is revealed in the intense looks of concentration on the women's faces. Only one is smiling, but that may be because her feet are not raised quite as high in the water as her fellow ballerinas' feet!

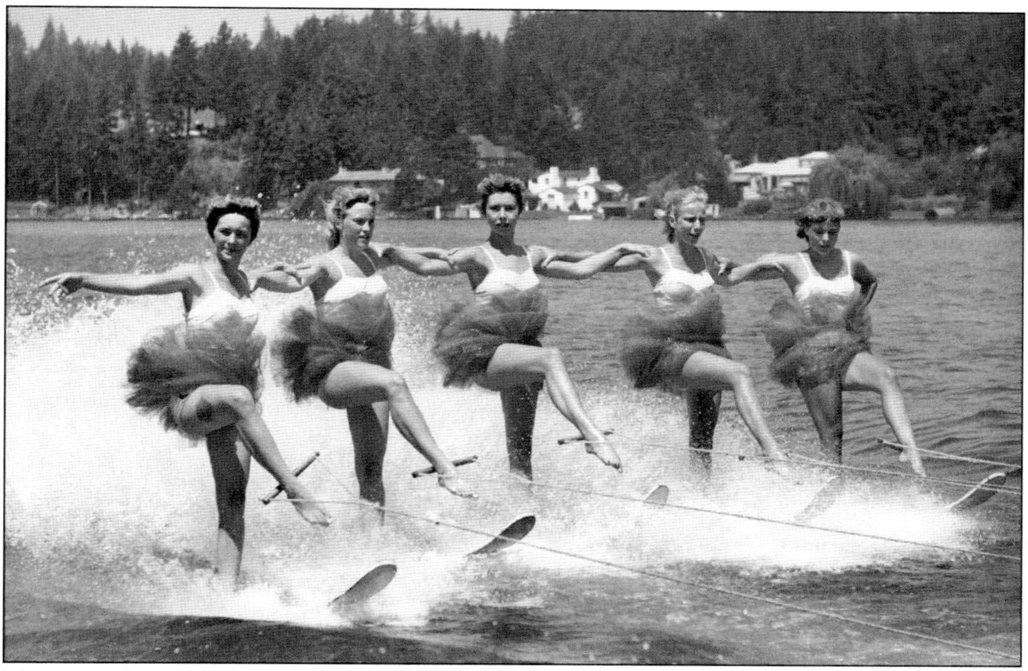

MAKING IT LOOK EASY. In 1959, on either the Willamette River or Oswego Lake, members of the Oswego Water Ballet ski in formation. They are Lita Schiel, Karen Kisky, Janet Wilson, Marion Blew, and Sandy Langoe.

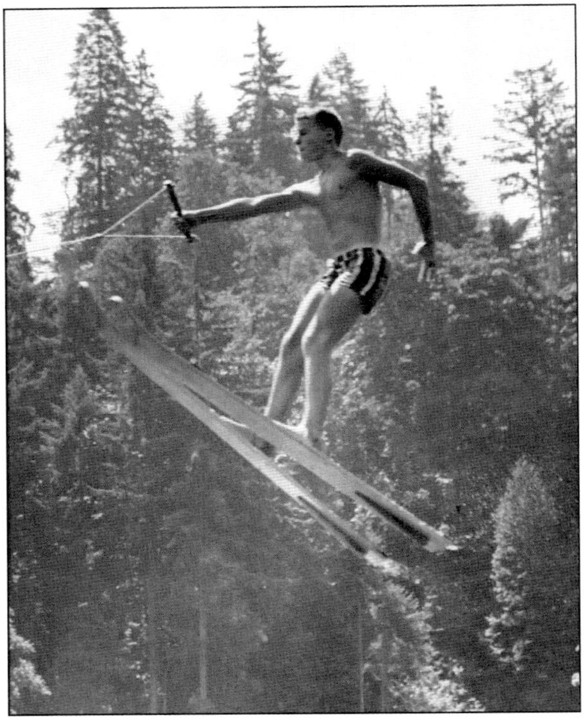

Water Festival Highlights. From the 1957 Oswego Water Festival, Stan Garside or "Bitsy" as is noted on the photograph, ski jumps on the Willamette River. In 1925, Ralph Samuelson, who had invented water skiing in Minnesota, also invented ski jumping by smearing lard on a half-sunken diving platform. He jumped from a height of 60 feet off its raised end.

Water Ski Lessons on the Willamette. Water ski fever was at high pitch in the 1950s and 1960s. This scene on the Willamette River at the mouth of Oswego Creek shows three boats and skiers at the J. C. Ski School.

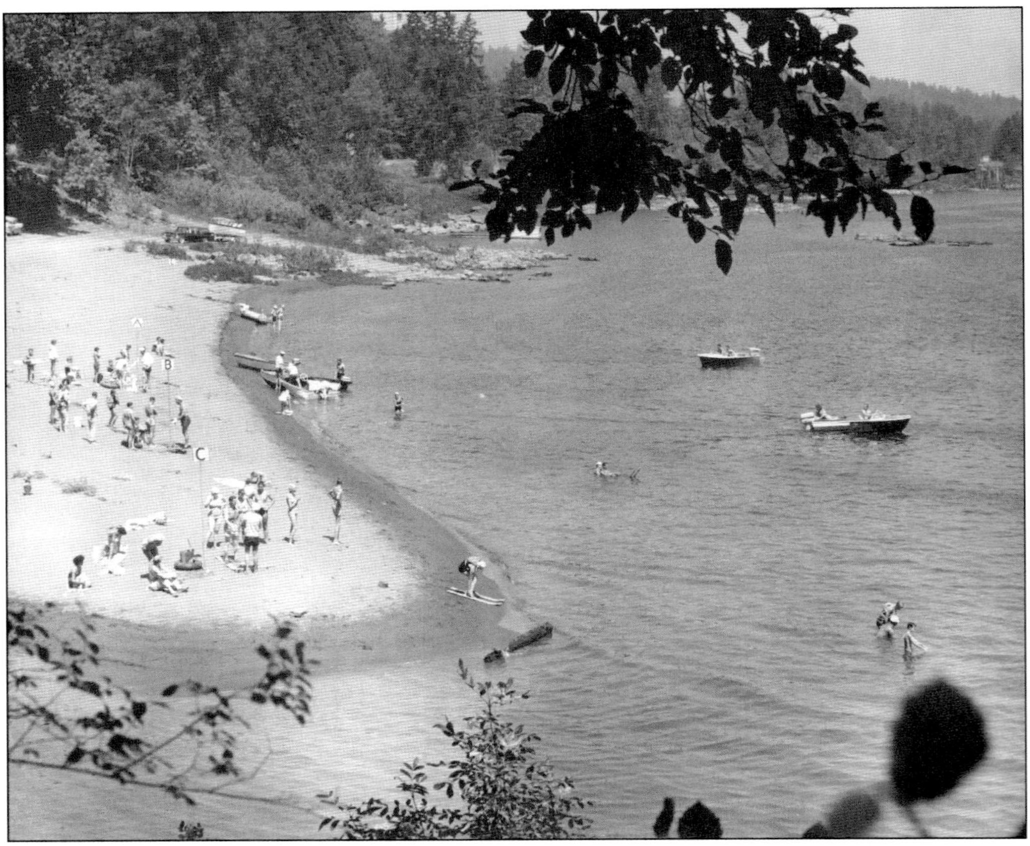

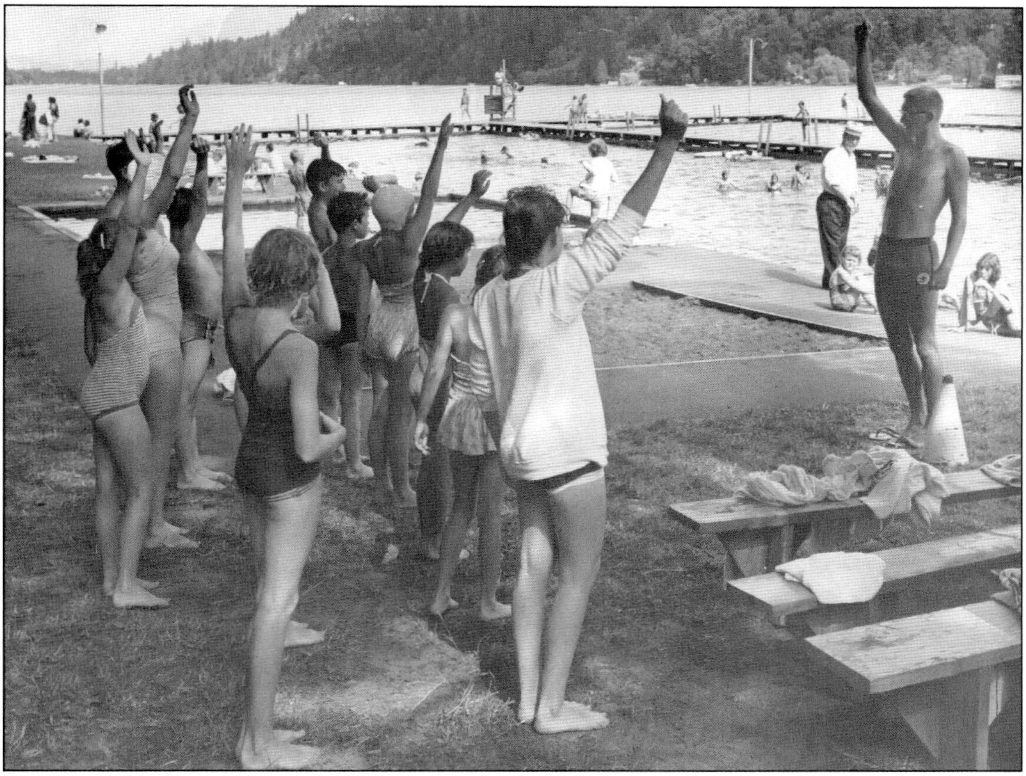

Swimming Lessons. Beginning swimmers on the lake listen to their instructor before they get wet, sometime in the 1960s.

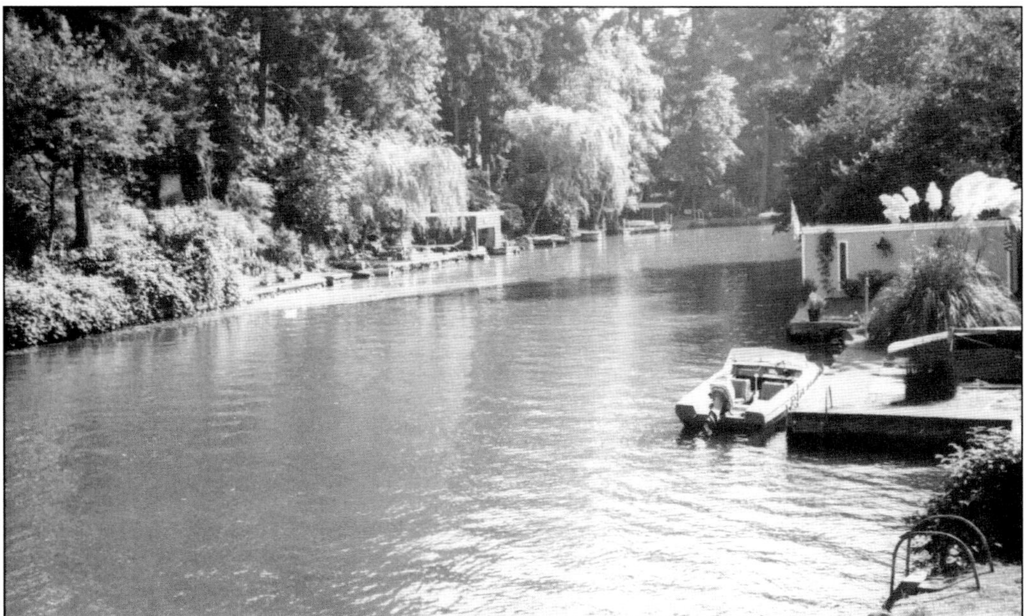

Tualatin Canal in the 1970s. Herbert Nelson recalled being a child in the 1910s: "The canal was such a beautiful brook in those days; we used to seine minnows on Saturdays. And then we would come down on Sunday morning and sell them for 25¢ a dozen for live bait."

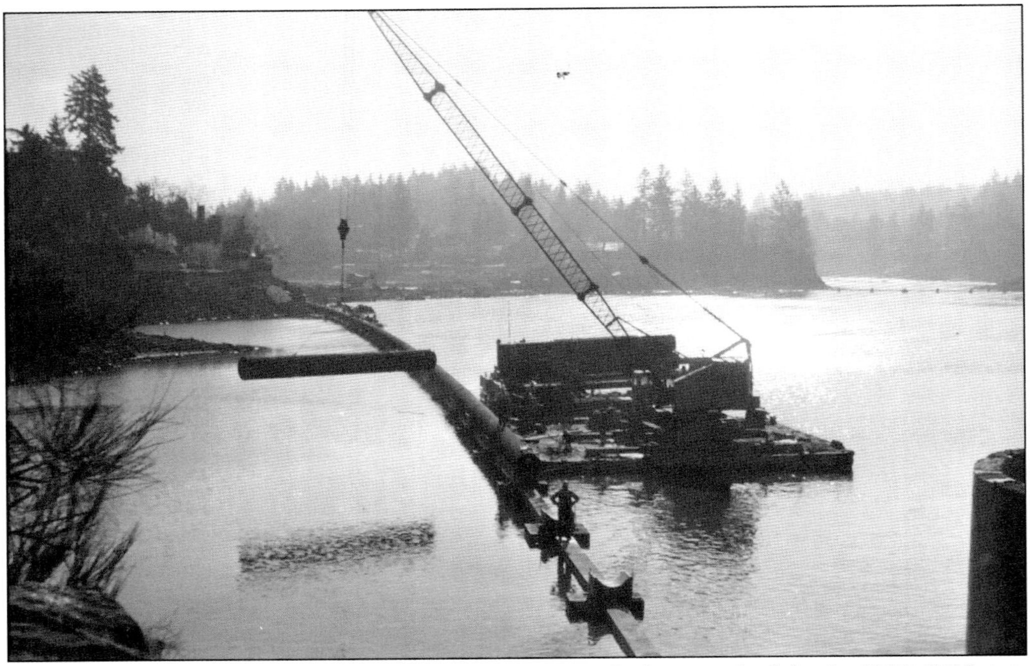

A Lakebed Exposed. In the early 1960s, sewer pipe was laid across the lake. In 2009–2010, it is to be replaced. In September 2010, the lake will be lowered 22 feet (far more than the usual draw down), so that contractors can construct a $100 million buoyant sewer line the length of the lake. The city came under orders from the state's Department of Environmental Quality to replace the 50-year-old line due to its overflows during heavy rainfall events. In the above picture, a crane on a floating dock sets a piece of sewer pipe in place. In the photograph below, an area at either the east or west end of the lake reveals its past with long-cut tree stumps seeing the light of day again as pipe is laid on the lake bottom.

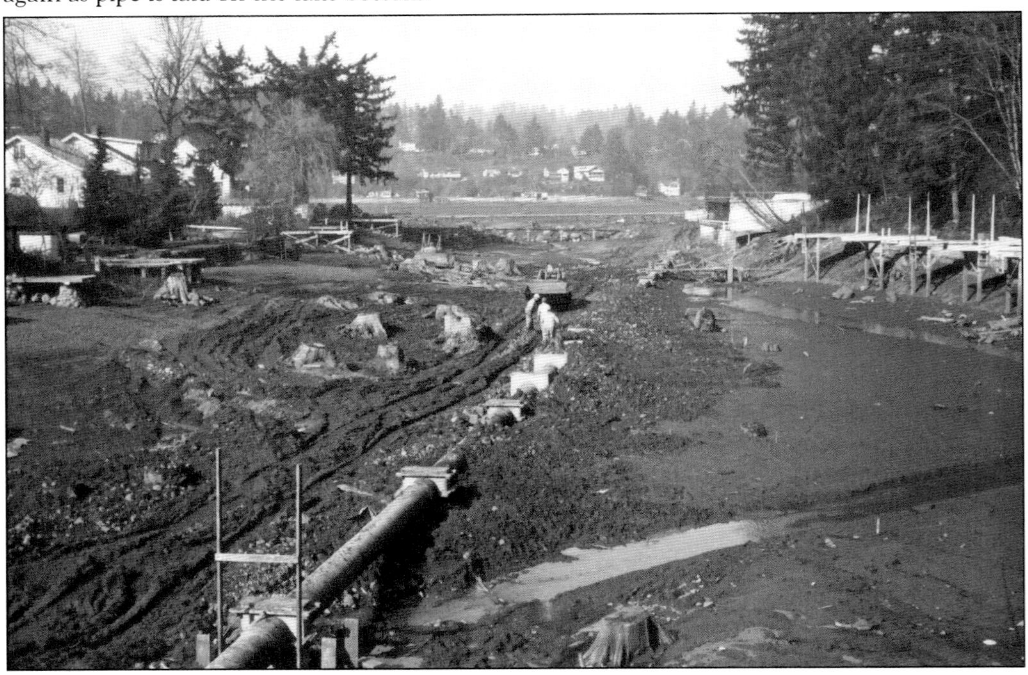

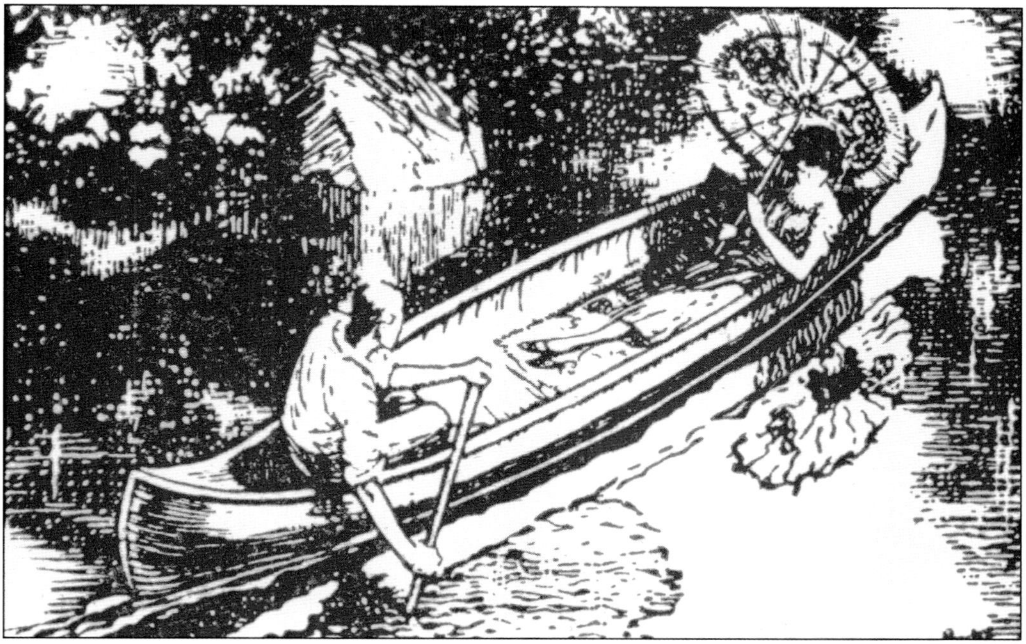

The Promise of an Idyll. A 1920s brochure for Lakewood promises, "Along Lakewood's irregular shoreline are cozy coves where you can moor your canoe in the shade of overhanging sheltering boughs."

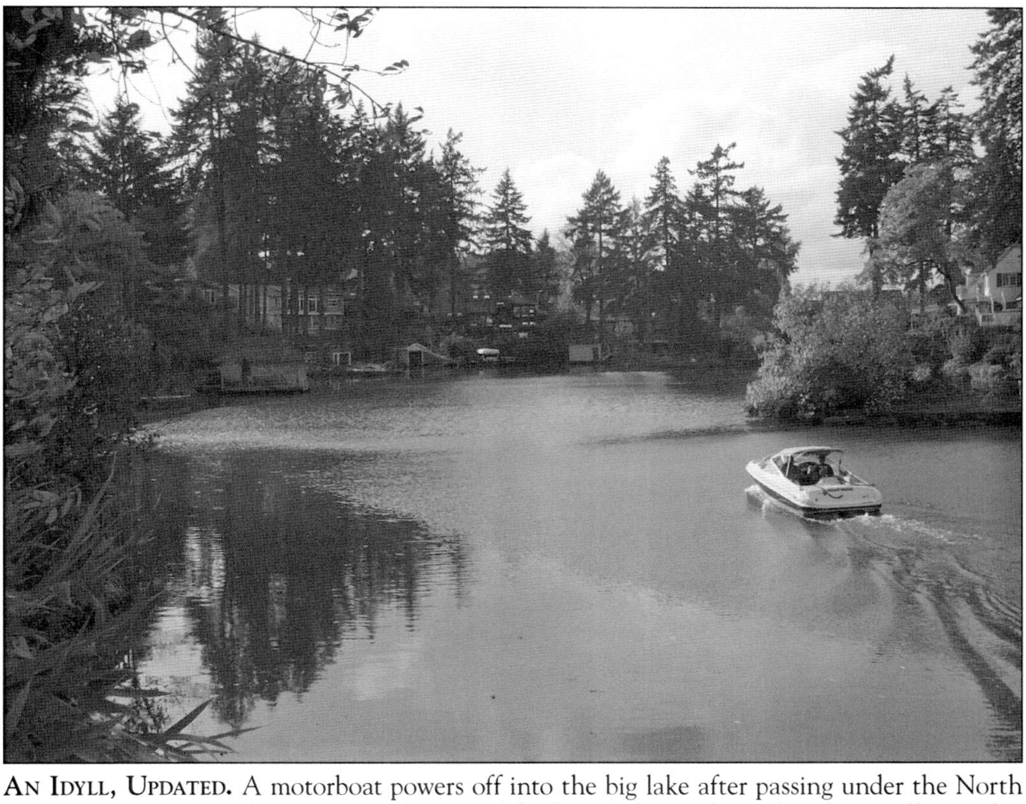

An Idyll, Updated. A motorboat powers off into the big lake after passing under the North Shore Road causeway that separates the main lake from Lakewood Bay. (Author's collection.)

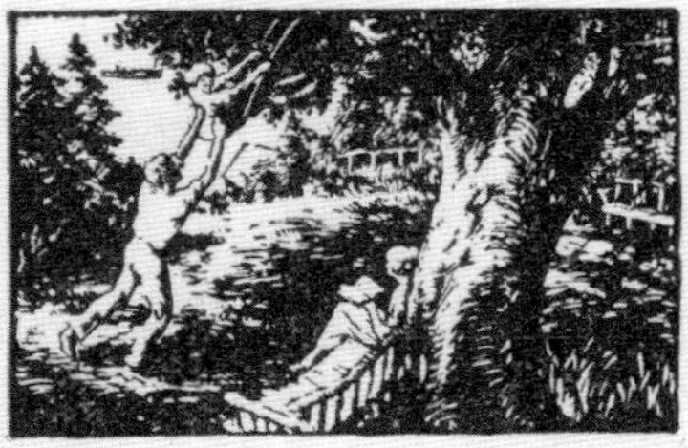

The spirit of play will reign in Lakewood—big trees with branches just meant for long rope swings—wonderful hiding places to encourage all the old-fashioned neighborhood games.

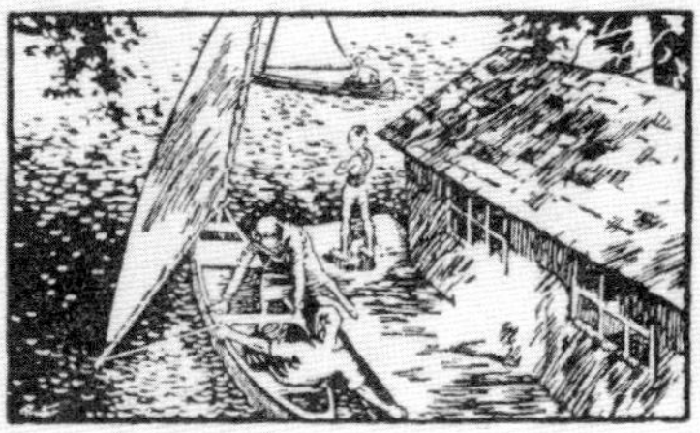

On Lake Oswego you can row, paddle, sail, troll, or just anchor and watch the cork bob. You'll catch fish, too,—perch, bass and trout.

A Bucolic Lake. From the same Lakewood brochure, a bucolic playland is promised.

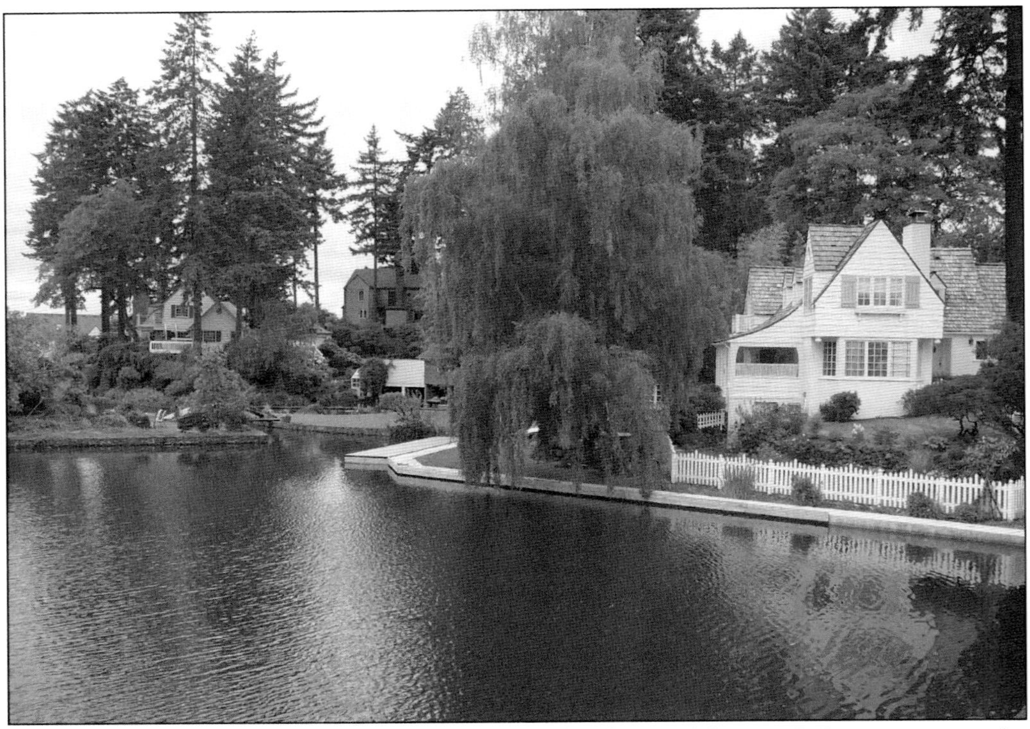

A Sophisticated Lake. While the reality along the shores of Oswego Lake is not quite the idealized romaticism of the sales brochure, it still reflects, in many places, a beautiful harmonizing of the human and natural worlds. (Author's collection.)

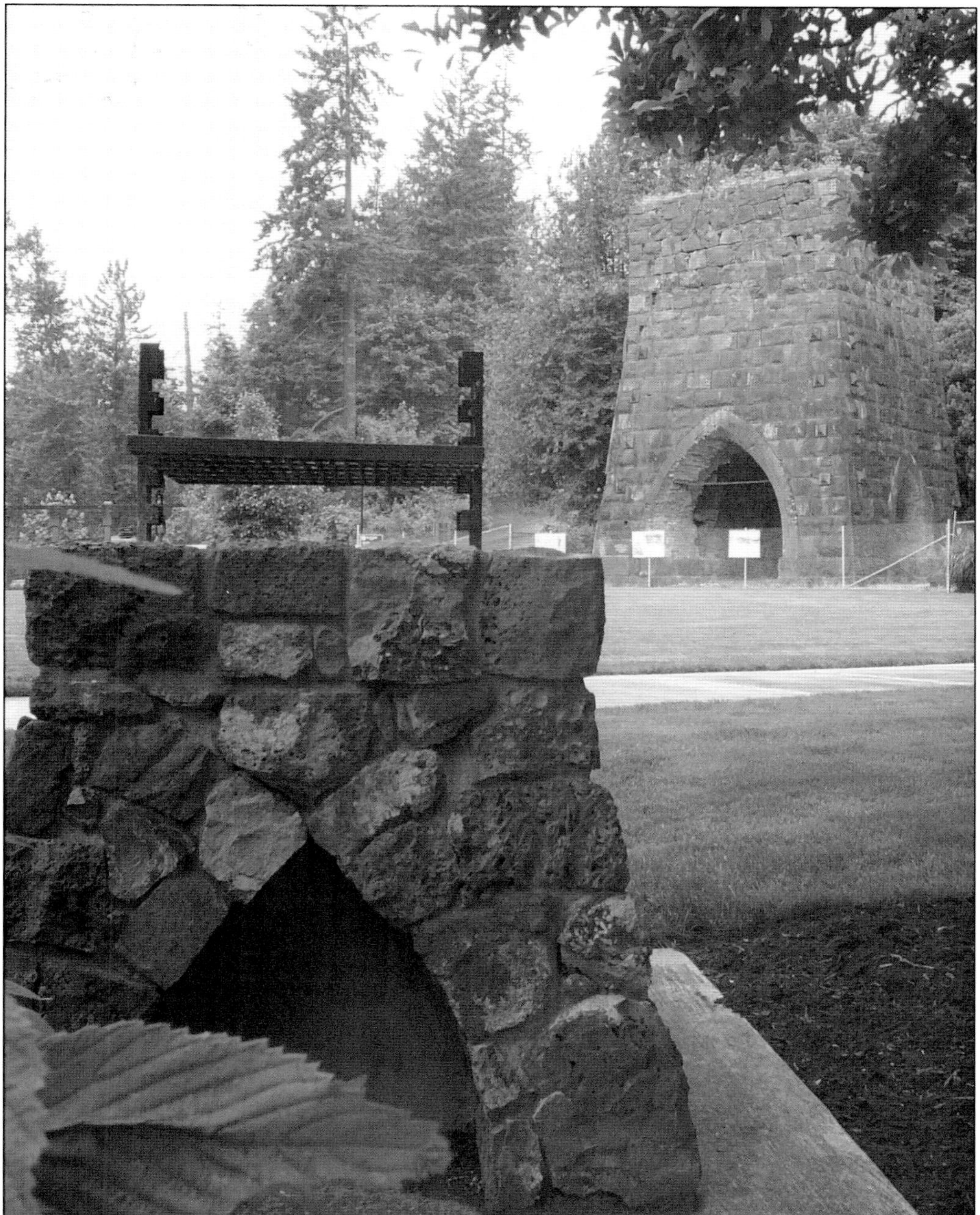

Furnace Stack Inspiration. George Rogers Park at the old Oswego Landing honors the Oswego man who worked to preserve the site of Oswego's first iron furnace. The 1867 furnace, seen in the background, is the inspiration for barbecue grills at the park, created during a renovation in the early 2000s. The grills are crafted from slag found on the site, a discarded by-product of the iron smelting that took place there 130 years earlier. The repurposing of a resource here seems an apt symbol of how Oswego has taken the raw materials of its water, its ore, and its timber, used them once, and then, through human artistry, reorganized them into a different kind of beauty. (Author's collection.)

BIBLIOGRAPHY

www.ci.oswego.or.us

Fulton, Ann. *Iron, Wood and Water: An Illustrated History of Lake Oswego.* San Antonio, Texas: Historical Publishing Network for the Oswego Heritage Council, 2002.

Goodall, Mary. *Oregon's Iron Dream: A Story of Old Oswego and the Proposed Iron Empire of the West.* Portland, OR: Binfords and Mort, 1958.

Jaquis, Nigel. "Lake O-be-gone: Green Slime and a Shareholder Revolt Poison the Waters of Lake Oswego." *Willamette Week.* April 27, 2005.

Kellogg, Claire, and Susanna Campbell Kuo, eds. *The Diary of Will Pomeroy: A Boy's Life in 1883 Oswego, Oregon.* Lake Oswego: Lake Oswego Public Library, 2009.

Kuo, Susanna Campbell. *A Brief History of the Oregon Iron Industry.* Lake Oswego: Oswego Heritage Council, 2008.

Lake Oswego Public Library. *In Their Own Words: A Collection of Reminiscences of Early Oswego, Oregon.* Lake Oswego: Lake Oswego Public Library, 1976.

www.lakecorp.com

Tims, Dana. "Long Anticipated Shoreline Pathway Soon to Beckon Along Oswego Lake." *Oregonian.* July 28, 2005: 8.

INDEX

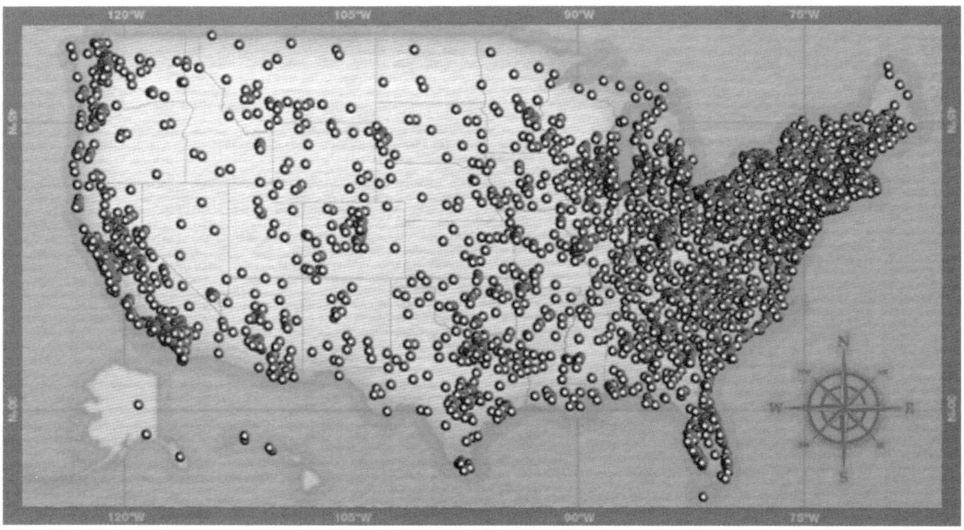